No Direct Evidence

No Direct Evidence

The Story of the Missing Sodder Children

Bob Lane Bragg

Quarrier Press
Charleston, WV

Quarrier Press
Charleston, WV

Copyright 2022, Bob Lane Bragg

Book and cover design: Rita Damous Kee

ISBN 10: 1-942294-36-0

ISBN 13: 978-1-942294-36-8

10 9 8 7 6 5 4 3 2 1

Printed in the United States of America

Distributed by:
West Virginia Book Co.
1125 Central Ave.
Charleston, WV 25302
www.wvbookco.com

Dedication

This book is dedicated to the memory of my Mother, Helen June. In my early years, it was through her urging of my father to take us to Fayetteville on some of our Sunday drives that I first saw the famous Sodder billboard. These trips sparked much discussion among us about the case and served to inspire my early interest. Helen did not live to see this book completed but I believe she would have been proud that an effort was made to discover what happened to the Sodder children.

Table of Contents

Acknowledgments:

The Fayette County Clerk's Office for their assistance in doing research.

The creators of Websleuths.com for providing a forum to discuss cases such as this.

The West Virginia State Office of Culture and History.

Carl Thompson for helping with the displays in the book.

My former Father-in-Law, Allen Workman.

Special thanks to Betsy Donahue, Caitlyn Preast, and Mitch Evans.

And many thanks to all the unnamed sources.

INTRODUCTION

As a young boy growing up in Handley, West Virginia in the 1960s and 70s, there wasn't always a lot to do. This was when it was inexpensive to take a Sunday Drive.

I always enjoyed climbing into my dad's blue 1965 Ford Mustang. It was the closest thing to a race car I had ever seen. Usually, after driving a while, the next thing I knew, we were climbing long, winding Route 60 on Gauley Mountain. This was always great fun for me because there were some unusual attractions including the foreboding Mystery Hole and the Snake Pit.

There were lots of souvenir stands along the way where I could "piss-away" my allowance, as Dad would put it. There was one place that had a lot of large ceramic statues including a gorilla that must have stood five feet tall. I wanted it dearly but the only reply I got from the front seat was, "Are you crazy? What would people think?"

We would always stop at Hawk's Nest State Park to look down at the beautiful New River Gorge. There were always places along the road to stop and get pop, candy, ice cream or maybe even Popsicles in the summer. Of course, I had to endure the constant admonishment of, "Don't get anything on the seats." I did my best.

I always remember Mom telling Dad not to go so fast because the curves upset her stomach. She would also inevitably suggest we drive up to "that sign where all those kids died in that fire." It meant doing some back-tracking and more twisty-turny roads. Fayetteville was on the other side of the Gorge but Dad almost always agreed to do it.

Mom never seemed to tire of these trips. Maybe she was thinking there was something she had missed in past visits that might provide some answers as to what happened to the children. Maybe being a mother, she could somehow relate to how Mrs. Sodder felt. Whenever I would ask Mom about it, she would say, "I think it's just awful. Those little children were so adorable."

I still remember Dad's car stopping near the Sodder sign and

Mom calling out to me to watch for cars, and her grabbing my hand before we crossed the road to get a closer look. That big sign with those little children's pictures, and the words, in large black letters saying things that to a young boy, were kind of scary like CHILDREN DIED, KIDNAPPED, BONES, BURNING FLESH, LIES.

I don't remember seeing any of the Sodder family when we stood at the sign. Maybe they were in the house looking out at us. Maybe they were thinking perhaps these people will know something. Maybe they will be the ones.

The conversation on the drive home was usually not about Hawk's Nest Overlook, the big ceramic gorilla, or even Popsicles. It was about the Sodder children and what could have happened to them. By the time we got home, all the speculation was over and my father would point out that it was none of our business. "The Italians were involved and if you stick your nose in the wrong place, you could end up in trouble," he would say.

Several years later, when I was in engineering school at West Virginia Institute of Technology in Montgomery, I met a girl and eventually married her. My father-in-law was in law enforcement in Fayette County. Sometimes, dinner conversation at my in-law's house would turn to old Fayette County cases–called cold cases today. The Sodder story came up several times.

There were times I would occasionally find an opportunity to ask my mom more about what she knew of the Sodder story. I was no longer a little boy so she told me as much as she had been told about the mystery. Mom always ended the conversations with, "It's just a shame."

In the early 1990s, and the coming of the internet, I learned how to do research for technical engineering subjects, but I also began to be interested in researching my own family's genealogy. I soon began doing it for other people as well. I learned methodology and how to plan my research with a goal in mind.

As time passed, I experienced my own divorce and the conversations and remonstrations with my ex-wife's family ended. But occasionally I still thought about the Sodder case, usually around Christmas when the local newspaper would rehash the story. At one point, I had been given a copy of a report from the West Virginia State Fire Marshal's office from around 1950 concerning the Sodder fire. I thumbed through it and found it interesting, but cannot say I read every word of it. Eventually, I put it away and forgot about it. Life marched on.

Around Christmas of 2013, the story of the Sodder children appeared once again in our local paper. This time, it was a huge article and included the photograph of the one remaining Sodder child who was now in her 70s. I thought about that old report I had been given and finally made time to read it several times.

This document is one of the few surviving official reports related to the case and is referenced extensively in this book. Using my skills as a genealogy researcher, I was able to find the Sodder children death certificates as well as other records related to the Sodder family.

A site called Webslueths.com contained nearly ten years of dialogues and discussions about the Sodder case from those who shared an interest in the case. There were also retired law enforcement officers there who offered their insight. I read all ten years of material and I became convinced that this case deserved to be explored further. It was the story of five children that seemed to be lost to history and I felt their story deserved to be told.

I attempted to communicate with some people and after a while, I had some luck–like the pot of gold type luck. Eventually, I was given a cache of files, letters, affidavits and statements related to the case from a very connected unnamed source. Some of the information I had was probably never released to the public.

I had collected a stack of paper about six inches thick. Those six inches have now become several volumes of research in addition to books on criminal investigations, evidence, and the history of the Italian people. I decided to try for the motherlode and do Freedom of Information Act requests to the State Police and the State Fire Marshal's Office. Many of the older documents I had already received concerning the case described "volumes of files" contained at each of these agencies.

My FOIA requests were answered the same way by both agencies, "no records are remaining." This is one of the most frustrating aspects of investigating this seventy-five year-old case. Many of the agencies purge their records on a regular basis. Coupled with the fact that most of the people involved have died, that makes this case even colder.

So I turned to a source that existed in vast quantities. Starting from the day after the fire, newspapers and magazines have written about the case extensively. The problem with these is often the stories are written in a way to maximize sales and accuracy is not considered nearly important.

The retelling of this story may not be a popular subject in some circles. As I discovered early on there are some people who did not want their names brought up or those of their relatives. As far as members of the Sodder family, I know there is a split among the surviving relatives about what they believe the fate of the children to be. Some want to find answers and others want to let the past stay as it is. I also know that George and Jennie Sodder wanted their surviving children to carry on looking for what happened to the missing children.

There are people named in this book who do not appear in the best light. Their descendants are not going to like the way they are represented here but what I have written has been, for the most part, taken directly from official reports, documents, and letters from the time. Please do not blame me for the actions of your ancestors.

It is not my intent to hurt anyone's feelings here but in some cases, the unanswered questions that remain can cause some people to appear questionable in their actions, or lack thereof. Occasionally, that is what history is, the telling of stories of the past that may be considered difficult to hear.

Typically, crimes not solved within the first 48 hours have a small chance of being explained. So the possibility of providing answers in this case is remote. But when you look at the pictures of those five children, to me, they deserve a good try at it. There is even a remote possibility that one of them may still be alive somewhere. That makes it even more worth it.

What do I hope to accomplish by dredging all this 75-plus years after the fact? This story has been an enduring mystery. To some of the family members that still have a desire to learn the truth, maybe in a way, this may provide a sense of closure.

I also know there are some who have stated that this is family business and outsiders should stay out of it. The fact is, there could have been a murderer who was never captured. And because five people died, this person could even be classified as a mass murderer. That is not purely family business.

I will admit that when I started this project, I had no fixed opinion of what happened to the children. There would be days when after reading letters and reports, I would set my mind in one direction. Then after reading some more, I would reverse my opinion. I hoped that I could remain neutral and unbiased. But, when you look at the faces of those children, it is hard to not feel something. I think this is what my mother was feeling when she would want to visit the billboard in Fayetteville.

One of the major limiting factors in the research for this book was the lack of physical evidence and eyewitnesses. Even the search for official reports and documents was frustrating and exhausting.

Many of my sources are magazine and newspaper articles. In some cases the information in the newspapers can conflict with that of other sources. Where this occurs, I have tried to present both sides.

It is assumed, of course, that all official documents related to the Sodder fire were kept from the public, at least until the Freedom of Information Act of 1966. But even with the "transparency of government" offered by the Act, its full implementation and acceptance in West Virginia has been slow in coming. A study performed by a West Virginia newspaper several years ago found that less than 50% of the agencies asked for information using the FOIA were willing to participate without the threat of a lawsuit.

Most of the documents used in this book were given to me by various interested parties who also want to see resolution. I did not ask where these sources obtained the documents, I was just glad to get them. There still exist letters written in the early 1940s by the WV State Police that refer to the files of the WV State Fire Marshal concerning the Sodder case as "voluminous." However, a FOIA request sent to the Fire Marshal's office in November of 2014 was answered with the reply that there are, "no files remaining related to the case." One can only assume that they were either purged, destroyed or lost.

I did hear about a suitcase full of materials that was in the hands of a Sodder family member but when questioned, they thought the suitcase had been damaged in a flood and the whole thing was thrown away. Another source close to the family once told me that a cache of documents does exist, but certain members of the family will not let anyone see it. If this is true, no one knows their motive(s) as to why it seems important to keep this information secreted.

Based on the contents of the documents I obtained, George Sodder was right about at least one thing. The investigation amounted to a very mediocre, one-dimensional inquiry. He commented in his pamphlet of 1953 that the investigation was narrow. By saying that, I'm not alluding to a huge cover-up. I'm saying that the initial investigation may not have been taken seriously by those involved. Then later, when the press became more involved, it seems the investigation became more about trying to justify the initial inept investigation.

I was also able to gain what appeared to be good information from several older detective magazines. But again, these articles were designed to sell magazines. Their accuracy is known to be historically unfavorable. One article in particular, even Mr. Sodder made clear was "about 75% wrong." Each magazine article had to be examined for accuracy and, while tempting, many had to be dismissed.

This is the story of five children who either were the victims of an intentional house fire, or an accidental one. They were either kidnapped before the fire started, or they simply died in the fire. Either someone else was involved in their murder or disappearance, or the whole thing was an accident, and all the other numerous, strange occurrences were simply a series of coincidences. Or, they were not.

These possible scenarios and the speculation may cause this book to seem complicated and I admit that may be true. As a treatment for what many have called the most mysterious case ever, there can be little doubt that a book on the subject must be complicated and require speculation.

In my defense as a writer, I have spent most of my career writing engineering reports which must be approached logically, thoroughly, and conclusively. I have used that same approach here. I'm not saying my conclusions are all correct, or are the only conclusions possible. This is an attempt to tell the story of the missing children but I will only attempt to draw conclusions where there is sufficient circumstantial evidence to make a conclusion justified.

It should be noted that some of the subject matter in part of the book is, to say the least, adult in nature. The discussion of the search for body parts of children is not for the faint of heart. There is also a part of the story that involves the possibility of grave robbing. After discussing it through several chapters, to the writer, the seriousness and tragedy of the whole thing can become lost in a matter-of-fact approach. It should be noted that the gravity and solemnity of the plight of these children was never lost to me, but details such as this must be examined to attempt understanding.

Why write a book about this case now? Mainly, this story has existed my whole life and where I grew up; and has remained a mystery. I felt that with the proper research, I could do this story justice after 75 years. The mystery may or may not be solved here but what can be promised is an interesting look into the past, at a baffling case, and an unbiased analysis of the information that still exists.

Bob Lane Bragg, 2022

Chapter 1

The Beginning

As long as we live we will dig into it - to come out with an explanation on what really happened...

George Sodder, 1968

George Sodder (born Georgieo Soddu) was an Italian immigrant who came to the United States in 1911 at the age of thirteen from Tula on the island of Sardinia, which at the time was part of the Italian Kingdom[1]. He was accompanied on the voyage by a brother, possibly named Leo, who did not stay in America very long supposedly because he missed a woman back in Sardinia.[2]

Little about George's early life, both in Sardinia and in America is known. Even his surviving descendants know little about his time in Italy or why he came to America. But it is known that George had two brothers in Tula, one named Sini Ignazai Soddu, and the other Giau Gavins Soddu.

One rumor was that George was sent away by his family so that he would not later be held responsible for the debts of his father. No known records could be found to verify this.[3]

Georgio landed in New York, and there are later records of him working in Pennsylvania and Michigan. One source states he worked on the railroads carrying water and tools to laborers. In 1917, when George was 22, he registered for the selective service for the First World War, listing Michigan as his home. This record shows him working as a plumber's helper in Detroit. His draft registration card also documented the fact that Sodder sent money back to Italy to support his parents.

By the early 1920s he had settled in West Virginia. There, he began a life in the coal mines where the work was long and hard. To supplement his income, George also drove a taxi cab at night.[4]

1

Jennie Laurlessa Cipriani was born in 1902 in Foggia, Italy, the second oldest child of Joseph (Giuseppe) and Martha (Martenea) Cipriani. The family migrated to the United States and arrived in New York in 1904. They later spent time in Pennsylvania before ending up in the coal fields of West Virginia. A 1920 United States Census Record lists the Cipriani Family (labeled incorrectly as "Cipron") as being comprised of:

Joseph	*Father*
Martena	*Mother*
Jennie	*(born 1902)*
Mary	*(born 1909)*
James (Jimmy)	*(born 1914)*
Emma	*(born 1916)*
Edna	*(born 1919)*

Also, according to the same census record, next door was the oldest brother, Frank Cipriani and his wife Louisa.[5]

George and Jennie Sodder (Photo Source unknown)

Jennie first met George when he came into her father's store for supplies in Smithers.[6] They were married on November 4, 1922 in Charleston and lived in Smithers, along with many other

Italian immigrants.[7] There were stories that Jennie was supposed to have married someone else as part of a deal among Italian families, but the details of this story are lost to time.[8]

Naturalization

In 1923 at the age of 25, George Sodder applied to become a naturalized citizen. From the application that still exists in the Fayette County Courthouse, many things can be discovered. The name on the application is for George Sodder but it is signed George Soddu, his given Italian surname. George was listed as being five feet-seven inches tall and 147 pounds. The application states his birthday was November 24, 1897 and that he arrived in the United States on April 1, 1911 at the Port of New York. He was from Tula, Italy and he left there aboard the ship, *The Urona*.

At the time of this naturalization application, George and Jennie were living in Scarbro, about 25 miles south of Smithers. As part of his application, George had to swear he was not an anarchist, a polygamist, a believer in polygamy, and that it was his intention in good faith to become a citizen of the United States of America. The document was filed at the courthouse on February 10, 1923.[9]

There is, however, no record of George ever following through and completing the naturalization process. In fact, Mr. Sodder is quoted in a newspaper article in the late 1940s that he felt that as long as he obeyed the laws of the United States, and held no allegiance to his former country, he did not consider naturalization necessary. He either considered the conditions in America so good, or conditions in his old country so bad, that he was happy to make America his home. But the real story of the Italian migration that eventually led to Giorgio's and Jennie's arrival in America begins many years earlier.

Italian immigration

It is estimated that between 1880 and 1915, nearly 13 million Italians left the Italian Kingdom. Around four million ended up in the United States.[10] The economy of northern Italy was industrialized while the south was agriculturally based. The south was referred to as the *mezzogiorno* which was the former independent and sovereign state of southern Italy, the Kingdom of the two Sicilies.[11]

Approximately 84% of Italian migration was from southern Italy.[12] Many were craftsmen, masons, and miners. But there were more who had no skills and were willing to do virtually any labor for a chance at a better life.

Once the immigrants were processed through Ellis Island, they were dispersed throughout America, wherever there was a need for cheap labor. In West Virginia, they mainly mined coal and worked on the railroads. The Italian migration peaked in 1913 with nearly 284,000 Italian coming to America that year alone.[13]

Poverty

Perhaps the two most prevalent reasons Italians were willing to leave their homes and families was the impoverished conditions at the time and the availability of jobs in other countries. At the time of the great Italian migration in the late 1800s, many Italians were near death from starvation and sickness. It was common for women to scrape plaster off the walls to mix in with dough to make the bread go a little farther.

One of the root causes for the poverty was that the feudal system still dominated southern Italy. This system dictated that a small number of landowners controlled a large amount of land and that it was passed down from generation to generation. So, the average worker or laborer[14] had no chance to ever improve their station in life, no matter how hard they may have worked. In return for protection and being allowed to live on their lord's land and farm it, they were obliged to share their crops with him and be loyal. Many of the younger workers felt their only answer was to leave Italy.[15]

Birds of Passage

One interesting phenomenon was that nearly half of those who migrated to America eventually returned to Italy after they had saved enough money. These immigrants usually came to the larger cities where wages were better than those in rural areas. They were referred to as "Birds of Passage."

For many of the other 50% who did stay in America, they still sent part of their earnings back to their family to provide badly needed support. There were some Italian immigrants who were known to have made the trip to America and back to Italy several times. The wives who were left in Italy to await the return of the husband were known as "white widows." Some men saved enough money to send for other relatives to make their home in America as well.[16]

Padrone System

The immigrant labor pool became so essential to American business that they were willing to pay a brokerage fee to get workers on the assembly lines and in the coal mines quickly. As with many other instances, when an opportunity to make money appeared, there was always someone to take advantage of it. This was the case for the contract labor brokerage service, or what was later termed, the padrone system.[17] This system of supplying immigrant labor to American industries became very popular in the late 1800s and was profitable to all concerned, with the exception of the immigrants themselves.

The role of the padrone in the life of the immigrant could start with the padrone coming to a town in Italy and announcing the opportunity for jobs in America and signing up individuals who may fit a particular job. Once a deal was made, the padrone took care of everything. They were an intermediary between the employer and the employee. They provided a bridge between the language barrier and the culture barrier, a place to live and food to eat. If there was trouble, the padrone was the emissary between the immigrant and the police or the legal system. They even helped the immigrant with letters and sending money back home.

And, for those Italians who wished to return home after they had made enough money to break the cycle of poverty, the padrone could arrange that too. All this for a price, of course. Ironically, it was in the best interests of the padrone for the immigrant to do as well as possible because he was paid by both the immigrant and his employer. The better the job, the higher the padrone's percentage.

Considering the role of the padrone, this could be one possible explanation as to how the young George Sodder was able to survive alone in the United States after his brother returned to Sardinia. The padrone took care of virtually every need of the immigrant, which could include supplying young George with a place to sleep, food to eat, and some money in his pocket. A padrone could also have been contacted by George's parents to help facilitate their son's adjustment to the United States.

Political Oppression by the North

The Kingdom of the Two Sicilies was occupied in 1860 by the northern Piedmontese Kingdom or the Kingdom of Sardinia. A ten-year civil war followed because of ill-treatment of the people in the south by the northern occupiers. This war resulted in the death of nearly a million people, mostly Neapolitans and Sicilians.

It is important to note here the resentment felt by the southern part of Italy towards the wealthy, industrialized North. There was an unbalanced system of taxation on the South as well as unfair tariffs on goods coming from the *mezzogiorno*.[18] Politics played an even more important role when the workers began to develop anarchy and socialism that would benefit the common man. But, in the 1870s the government took steps to stifle these leftist leanings and to continue the landlord system.[19] Later, when Mussolini and his fascists took control of Italy, this all changed.

Natural disasters

During the early part of the 1900s, several natural disasters brought the southern part of Italy to its knees. In 1906, Mount Vesuvius erupted and destroyed Naples and surrounding towns.[20] Two years later, an earthquake and subsequent tidal wave swept through the Strait of Messina taking over 100,000 people in that town alone.[21] During this same time, the Italian wine industry was destroyed by disease.[22] This blight put thousands of people out of work.

Sardinian Emigration

Generally, the reasons for Sardinian emigration are typically thought to be the same as those for the rest of Italy. They began their migration later than those from the Italian mainland and there were only around 100 Sardinians leaving a year.[23] The immigrants who came to America from Sardinia were mainly artisans, miners, and farmers.

Another possible reason to leave Sardinia was the subculture of criminal activity. From the times of ancient Rome through the late 19th century, there is evidence of crimes and lawlessness that was what today is termed "banditry." These crimes consisted of cattle rustling, smuggling, and roadside robbing the rich land barons, and kidnapping wealthy landowners.[24] These bandits appear to invoke the same methodology as that of what would later be called The Black Hand or Mafia.

Italians Immigrants in West Virginia

In the late 1800s, the workforce in West Virginia was made up of nearly all western Europeans. Early immigrants had arrived from England, Ireland, and Scotland mainly. This migration made up nearly 90% of the state's overall workforce.[25] The need for immigrant labor in West Virginia was due, in part, to the early stages of union organization efforts which caused labor costs to skyrocket. As Italian immigrants poured in (with the help of the padrone), they ended up in areas where they could find jobs readily, easily, and without too many questions being asked. The isolated areas of West Virginia's coal fields were very suited for this.[26]

There soon came to be so many Italian immigrants in West Virginia that eventually, the Italian government opened a liaison office in Fairmont to look after the interests of their nationals. Guiseppe Caldori, the Italian government's consular agent in Fairmont, was called in during several labor strikes in Fayette County to try and help mediate and to protect the interests of his countrymen.

Fayette County

While large numbers of Italians who came to West Virginia settled in Clarksburg, many also came to southern West Virginia. Montgomery, Smithers, Boomer, and Alloy were all Fayette County towns that saw their populations swell with Italian immigrants.

The new arrivals brought their culture, food, and their religion. They brought their language too, but that usually disappeared by the second generation in America. The Sons of Italy in America (SOIA) became an important part of the lives of Italian Americans and supporting its founding principles became a big part of their lives.

The SOIA was founded on several basic principles: 1) the support of the Italian government, including the policies of Mussolini and 2) the establishment of life insurance policies for families in order to protect them financially if the father or breadwinner died.[27]

Another concept the immigrants brought with them was the cultural idea of mutualism. Basically this is, "I'll do this for you, if you do that for me." In other words, if one person owns a general store, then the second person agrees to buy all their supplies from your store if you agree to buy all your lumber from the second person's lumber yard.

Social security is a form of mutualism. Everybody pays into the system and over time, you are secure in your later years (theoretically). The idea of mutualism allows for each participant to emerge from any transaction with a win-win situation. This idea became so successful and lucrative with the Italian American immigrants that a separate level of leadership developed that became the guiding force of the concept. This leadership soon became more of an enforcement group of mutualism among the Italians, specifically for those who did not wish to participate. Over the years, this leadership has been known by many different names, Le Cosa Nostra, Black Hand, Camorra, Mafia.

Fayetteville

Originally known as Vandalia, Fayetteville was established around 1825 by a settler named Abraham Vandalia. The development of the town centered around the selling of goods and supplies (or mercantiles as they were called then) related to the timber industry. But since the town was also the geographical center of the county, it became the location of the county's first courthouse around 1837.

As Fayetteville continued to develop, several newspapers sprang up, giving rise to the town's second most abundant business, printing. The town was also home to several local banks conveniently located near the new courthouse. Some of these buildings still stand today and were built by local Italian stone masons which give them a beautiful exterior finish.

George and Jennie had five children while still living in Smithers. They moved around frequently, as did most people who followed the coal mining jobs then. By 1935, they had moved to Fayetteville. Perhaps tired of the continual relocation his growing family had to endure, George eventually left the coal mines. He went to work for Janutolo and Company, a Fayetteville hauling and transfer company which also had an engineering company, a construction company, a lumber yard, and a general store.

In the early 1940s, the Sodders bought an eight-room house located just outside of Fayetteville along what was then Route 21 but today is State Route 16. Coincidentally, it is also known as the Robert K. Holiday Highway.[28] The property was registered in Jennie's name only, perhaps due to George Sodder not being a naturalized citizen, or to protect the house from being seized by creditors later.

One of the partners in the Janutolo Company agreed to co-sign the loan for Mr. Sodder and in return, Mr. Sodder agreed to make this man the beneficiary of a homeowner's insurance policy on the house in case something happened to it. That way he would be reimbursed immediately for his loan to Mr. Sodder.[29]

John, George, Joe, and Mary Ann Sodder as young children.

Sylvia Sodder Source: Sodder family.

10

Within a few more years, their family had grown to ten children.[30] Mr. Sodder, an independent thinker, found little value in clinging to many of the cultural traditions he had left behind in Italy. Perhaps because he left there at such an early age or because what he found in the United States was to him, a whole new world, George Sodder became an American, through and through and had no use for the past. It was said that he did not even allow his children to speak Italian around the house, only the Inglese.

George Sodder, American Businessman, Source – Sodder Family Member

While little is known about George Sodder's upbringing in Sardinia or America, somewhere along the way, he learned a very strong work ethic. The people of Sardinia have always been known for being hard workers. Mr. Sodder's desire to be self-reliant would later become admired in Fayette County. Generally, it can be said that what usually accompanies a strong work ethic is an equally strong idea of honesty and integrity. In other words, Mr. Sodder was known as a man of his word but also a man of strong beliefs and opinions who was not afraid to stand up for them if necessary, even if it made him unpopular with some.[31]

It is unknown why, but in 1943 Mr. Sodder left the Janutolo Company and went out on his own. Perhaps it was an expression of his confidence in his own abilities and desire for self-sufficiency. Some stories claim there were disagreements with the owners of the company, perhaps over Italian politics.

In any case, George and Jennie bought the Dempsey Transfer Company that was said to be failing at the time. With the help of his two oldest sons and with Jennie handling the books, George began operations as an independent businessman. Mr. Sodder applied for a commercial truck driver's license in 1942.[32] They eventually began to use the basement of the house as a repair shop for their trucks. By 1945, the Sodder Trucking Company had six trucks.[33] Early on, they primarily transported goods and supplies from Fayette Station where the railroad station was located, to Fayetteville, and back again, a trip of about five miles each way.

The same thing that made George a success in business, could be considered to have made him unpopular with some of the local Italians. His dedication to becoming self-sufficient required a firm resolve. He carried this through also to his personal beliefs. As with most Americans, George Sodder felt that the fascist dictator Benito Mussolini was a threat to freedom.

Other Italians living in Fayetteville felt that Mussolini had made Italy into a great country that was on the brink of becoming a world power. They resented George Sodder expressing his opinion about Mussolini and they told him as much. Mr. Sodder's family claimed that he endured many threats from his fellow Italians, including receiving an actual Black Hand letter.[34]

Many of these pro-Mussolini Italians were possibly members of the Sons-of-Italy in America (SOIA). Before World War II, the SOIA was heavily involved in promoting Mussolini's fascist policies in the United States.[35]

Enemy Alien Laws

Just as with many Japanese and Germans who were living in the United States during the war, many Italians were the target of suspicion and investigations, mostly because they were allies with Germany. An enemy alien is an alien, living in the United States, who is designated as an enemy during wartime due to permanent or temporary allegiance to a hostile power.

By 1942, representatives of the Order of the Sons of Italy in America had petitioned the American government to change the status of non-citizen Italians from "enemy-aliens" to "loyal aliens" if they had a soldier fighting in the war against the Axis powers in Europe. In October of 1942, a bill was introduced to Congress to change the status of these aliens which would have helped to expedite their naturalization process.[36]

On October 12, Attorney General Francis Biddle announced that Italian aliens would no longer be classified as enemy aliens and would be allowed to participate in the nation's war effort unencumbered. Biddle announced that the Office of the Attorney General had "thoroughly investigated all 600,000 Italians living in the United States and had found it necessary to only intern 228 Italians." [37]

Fascists in West Virginia

This re-classification of enemy-aliens did not apply to Italians who still held a strong loyalty to Mussolini. And not surprisingly, some of them lied about this fascist loyalty on their naturalization applications. It seemed that in West Virginia, there had been a large group of Italians that had escaped investigation by Attorney General Biddle and remained loyal to Mussolini.

At around the same time of this new Italian-alien legislation, the FBI was in the process of one of the largest round ups of Italian aliens and active fascist groups in West Virginia history. The first of various raids on suspected Italian fascists was in mid-October, 1942. A small army of FBI agents, West Virginia State Police, and members of the Beckley Police Department, totaling some 30 law enforcement officials, conducted an eight-hour raid in Beckley and surrounding Raleigh County rounding up 23 illegal Italian aliens.

Confiscated were nearly 400 rounds of ammunition, eight revolvers, four rifles, three shotguns, 200 dynamite caps, 75 feet of dynamite fuse, eight cameras, 15 signaling devices, three short-wave radios (found to be tuned to stations in Italy), various maps showing the advances of the Axis armies, newspaper clippings detailing the sinking of American ships and other Allied losses, a supply of Italian literature, documents, and letters. The 23 Italians from the raid were released on their own recognizance until they could be formally charged.[38]

The day after this raid, a similar raid was conducted in Smithers and Boomer, nabbing an additional 38 illegal Italian aliens with many of the same type of items found. This raid also collected a motion picture projector and documents, literature, and letters that were said to have "definite fascist sympathies."[39] Another raid was conducted two days later in Weirton, arresting 43 Italians.[40]

By 1945, Mr. Sodder had been in the United States for over 30 years but for one reason or another he had never become a naturalized citizen. However, his loyalty to the U.S. had never been questioned. Those who knew him found him to be a man who was grateful to the country that allowed him the freedom to become an independent businessman.

Chapter 2

The Fire

"You are going to be paid back for the dirty remarks you have made about Mussolini."

F. G. Janutolo to George Sodder, 1945

Christmas 1945

On a cold and icy Christmas Eve night in 1945, the Sodder family were making final preparations for a large Italian Christmas celebration. The younger children were home from school and the older members of the family had finished their day's work. The Sodder's modest home, located about two miles north of Fayetteville, had been decorated with Christmas lights.

The family was disappointed because the second oldest son, Joe, was still in North Carolina where he was awaiting discharge from the Army. For this reason, the family was not putting up a Christmas tree. The Sodders were a close-knit family who missed Joe greatly but were still grateful that he (and older brother John) had made it through World War II unscathed.

The parents, George and Jennie, were the first to go to bed with their youngest child, Sylvia, who was only three. It was around 9 p.m. Just a little later, two of the older boys, John and George, also known as Ted, who both had been helping their father with his business for most of the day, drifted off to bed while five of the younger children received their mother's permission to stay up and continue to play with their new toys. They were Maurice, Betty, Jennie, Louis, and Martha.

Mary Ann, the oldest daughter, had fallen asleep on the couch in the living room where the children were playing. Eventually, the house became quiet, and all was in readiness for the huge Italian Christmas the following morning. But as fate would have it, when morning arrived, their home of ten years would be a pile of ashes and five of the children would be gone.[41]

While the Second World War had officially ended just four months earlier, a war of a different kind was about to begin for George Sodder. He would spend the remaining 24 years of his life battling the powers-that-be on all levels--from the Fayetteville Fire Department, law enforcement agencies, prosecuting attorneys, governors, all the way to the head of the Federal Bureau of Investigation, J. Edgar Hoover. The family even sent letters to each U. S. President who held office in the 1950s and 60s asking for help to find the children.

Local weather reports state that light snow was falling, and a chilly wind was blowing hard. The next twenty-four hours would become one of the strangest set of events they, or anyone could ever experience.

The story of the Sodder fire actually began about three months earlier. One of the first strange incidents possibly related to the fire was a visit to their home by a local insurance agent, Rosser Long. Mr. Long had been referred to the Sodders by Fiorenzo Janutolo for whom Mr. Sodder used to work. Mr. Janutolo had also co-signed the bank loan that Mr. Sodder used to purchase his house about ten years before. On this particular visit, around September, Mr. Long suggested the idea of Mr. Sodder purchasing life insurance on himself and his family.

Slightly taken aback, Mr. Sodder made it clear he was not interested in purchasing any life insurance. Continuing with the tenacity that makes an insurance agent either a success or a failure, the agent then suggested that Mr. Sodder should increase the amount of insurance he carried on his house from $1,500 to $1,750. He related that this had been suggested by Mr. Janutolo since he was the co-signer of the mortgage. (Mr. Janutolo was also the beneficiary of the Sodder's homeowner's insurance policy should something happen to the house). Again, Mr. Sodder declined. The agent went away without making a sale that day.[42]

Several weeks later, a seemingly normal event that had occurred several times before took a strange turn when a stranger showed up at the Sodder's house. During the course of the conversation, the stranger, apparently on his own volition, walked around to the back of the Sodder house with Mr. Sodder accompanying him. Later, Mr. Sodder would find this, in and of itself, unusual.

When they reached the rear of the house where the power came from the line to the fuse box, the stranger remarked, "that's gonna cause a fire someday. It's faulty." Mr. Sodder explained that they had recently had an electric stove installed that required a new, separate power line to come into the house and that it had all been installed by a licensed electrician and checked by the local power company. The stranger eventually left and never returned.[43]

According to the West Virginia State Fire Marshal's investigation and subsequent report, after the conversation about insurance with Mr. Long, and still around sixty days before the fire occurred, Fiorenzo Janutolo is alleged to have had a conversation with the Sodders regarding the insurance. According to the report, Mr. Janutolo is said to have told the Sodders:

"I see you have refused to take out insurance and refused to sign the papers to settle Mrs. Sodder's father's estate. Your goddam house is going to go up in smoke and your children are going to be destroyed. Also, you are going to be paid back for the dirty remarks you have made about Mussolini."[44]

Is it prophetic that within sixty days this is exactly what would occur? Mr. Janutolo was never questioned about the remarks he was alleged to have made. Consider the irony of this statement. Someone who accurately predicts what is going to happen to the Sodder's house and their children, and this person has a financial interest in what happens to the Sodder's house, as well as a revenge motive in relation to the Mussolini comments, and the police do not question him.

One other occurrence the Sodders later found to be strange was the fact that they had noticed a man in a black car parked along the road near the entrance to their property.[45] The man seemed intent on observing the children as they got off their school bus in the afternoon. Since the man was not breaking the law and did not approach the children, nothing was said or done. The Sodders noticed the man parked along the road several different times.[46]

These curious occurrences had been long forgotten by the time Christmas had rolled around. George Sodder and his sons John and George Jr. had spent the afternoon making food and freight deliveries to local businesses and were tired when they arrived home in the early evening.

John, the oldest son, had just recently returned from military duty in World War II. He had served as a staff sergeant in the South Pacific campaign where he received many medals.[47]

By 6 p.m. on Christmas Eve, the eldest daughter, Mary Ann had arrived home from her job at a department store in Fayette-ville, where, at the request of her parents, she had also purchased gifts for the children. As is a local Christmas custom, they were allowed to open a few of their gifts that night.

The exhausted parents decided to go to bed about 10 p.m. Their bedroom was on the first floor. They took their youngest daughter, Sylvia with them for whom they kept a crib in their bed-room.

John told a newspaper reporter the next morning that the two boys decided to go to bed around 11 or 11:30 p.m.[48] and retired to their upstairs bedroom.[49] The upstairs consisted of two bedrooms, one for the girls, and one for the boys. Both John and George later said that they did not remember if the other boys came to bed while they were still awake or not.

Before she retired, five of the children asked Mrs. Sodder if they could stay up to play with their new toys and listen to the radio. Mrs. Sodder told them they could as long as they finished their chores before going upstairs to bed. These chores normally consisted of closing the curtains, pulling the shades, and locking the doors. The two boys, Louis and Maurice, also had the job of going outside and feeding the cows and closing the chicken coop. The chores were set up so that even the youngest child had a job to do.

The children who asked to stay up were Jennie, Louis, Mau-rice, Martha Lee, and Betty. Mary Ann had decided to stay up as well, reading some magazines while the children played. She eventually fell asleep on the sofa in the living room. She usual-ly slept in the upstairs bedroom with the other girls. One of her chores was to get all the small children upstairs to bed. In all, nine of the children normally slept upstairs in the two bedrooms. So Mary Ann probably stayed up since the five children had asked to stay up.

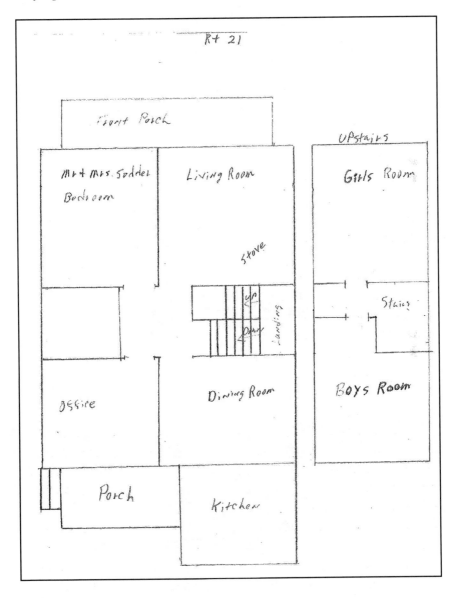

Floorplan of the Sodder house that burned in 1945, (unnamed source) Not to Scale.

Mary Ann Sodder. In some stories, she is called Marion. Source – Sodder family member

John Sodder, Source – Sodder Family Member

C. A. Raper, WV Assistant Fire Marshal Source- Charleston Gazette

At the time, listening to the radio, or "radioing" was popular with all ages. One account says the children were listening to Christmas carols and reports of sightings of Santa Claus.

Late Night Phone Call

At around 12:30 a.m. Mrs. Sodder was awakened by the telephone in the home office. Accounts of this call vary but it is generally accepted that the caller was a woman asking for someone who the Sodders did not know. Another account said the woman asked for someone who had no reason to be there, implying that the Sodders may have known this person. Either way, Mrs. Sodder told the caller the person they were looking for was not there.

Other accounts say she told them they had the wrong number. The woman who was calling apologized for disturbing them. Mrs. Sodder accepted her apology and hung up. Just before Mrs. Sodder hung up, she said that a man in the background let out a peculiar laugh or sound. Other accounts say it was the woman caller who let out the strange laugh, still others say, "There was raucous laughter and glasses clinking in the background as if there was a party going on." Still other accounts say that Mrs. Sodder got the impression that someone was trying to make her the butt of some kind of joke and she was slightly aggravated when she hung up the receiver.

After Mrs. Sodder hung up, she noticed Mary Ann still asleep on the sofa. Mrs. Sodder must have assumed the children went to bed by themselves and decided not to awaken Mary Ann. She then checked the fire in the coal stoves. Usually, by this time of night, the fire in the kitchen and office stoves had gone out completely and there was only some noticeable hot ashes left in the stove in the living room.

She also noticed that the children had not performed any of the chores but decided to not make them come back downstairs and do the chores. She, instead, did them herself. A decision she regretted for the rest of her life because it would have settled the question as to whether or not the children were still in the house then.

Since nothing is mentioned in any of the reports to the contrary, it is also assumed that Mrs. Sodder did not go and check on the outside chores assigned to Maurice and Louis. She later reported that she did leave the light on in the living room before returning to bed, probably in case Mary Ann woke up and decided to go upstairs to bed.

About half of an hour later after returning to bed, Mrs. Sodder heard what sounded to her like a rock or hard ball striking the highest pitch of the roof and rolling off to the gutter. George and Jennie's bedroom was located on the part of the house that was just a single story and the roof would have been directly above their ceiling. Also, that part of the roof was made of tin which if the object was being rolled on, would make a distinct sound. Since the sound did not seem to repeat itself, Mrs. Sodder thought nothing more about it and began to drift back to sleep.

In Alloy, located along the Kanawha River, there still exists a large metals plant that employed many workers at the time. These workers were so spread out that the company would dispatch a bus each night, for each shift that picked up the workers and took them to the plant and then later returned them home. One of the routes of this bus was into Fayetteville and it happened to be passing by the Sodder house the night of the fire. There was a man either riding or driving the bus who became an important witness. It is unknown if the man came forward right away or if he was eventually located by one of the private detectives later hired by George Sodder. The most interesting part of his statement was that he said as he was driving past the Sodder house, he saw what appeared to him as "fireballs being rolled onto the roof of the house."[50]

Within a short time, Jennie was awakened, yet again. At first, she was not sure why but then she smelled smoke. She woke George and got up to investigate. Opening their bedroom door, she saw heavy smoke in the hallway. She ran down the hall towards the office and saw what she described as, "a virtual sheet of flames descending from one corner of the ceiling with flames and smoke in the corner of the office near a desk and around the telephone."

She later described the fire as being so hot, she couldn't touch the phone. She then ran back towards her bedroom, screaming to everyone "the house was on fire, wake up and get out." She later remembered that upon first discovering the fire, the light in the living room was still on, or "burning", as it was still colloquially referred to at the time. George Sodder later said in his statement to the WV State Police that these "still burning" lights had helped the family members who did survive to escape the burning house.

Mary Ann had been awakened by her mother's screams. She went straight to her parent's bedroom, got Sylvia out of her crib and took her out of the house. In order to keep her safe, Sylvia was placed in the cab of one of her father's trucks. Another account says that Mary Ann gave the baby to an on-looker, but this source was considered unreliable. And, since this happened quickly, it is likely the spectators had not yet arrived.

Meanwhile, Mrs. Sodder returned to her bedroom and got George out of bed. He had not responded at first. This time she got him up. At this point in the chaos, she realized that she had not seen any of the other children come downstairs but assumed they had awakened.

The first thought that went through George's mind was that the fire might still be small in nature and that he could put it out. Without even bothering to put his shoes on, he hurried out the kitchen door toward the rain barrels that sat at the bottom of each gutter of the house. But on this bitter cold night, the barrels were all frozen solid.

After waking George, Jennie ran back to the bottom of the stairs. There, she saw the two oldest boys appear at the top of the stairs, still groggy. The fire was spreading very quickly. The houses in the area had been built long before the requirements of fire proofing. So, perhaps they knew the house was going to burn fast. The two oldest boys, who had been sleeping in the same bed, said they had called the other children on their way down the sec- ond-floor hallway. Here begins one of the most controversial parts of the tragic story.

In the initial statements regarding the fire taken by the West Virginia State Police the following morning, John Sodder was quoted as saying that when he was calling to the other children, he thought they were still asleep, but he was sure he heard a reply from one of the younger boys. Another account said that John actually shook his brothers to get them up. Still other accounts state that he said he heard nothing from his brothers. Later, when questioned further, John said that he was mistaken, or he said that he had been misquoted about Maurice and Louis.

The two older boys made it down the stairs and out the front door but not before scorching their hair and the tops of their ears. John also said that initially they went downstairs without attempting to carry their other brothers because they did not realize initially that they would go downstairs and help put the fire out. But once they got to the steps and were about halfway down, they realized there was no returning to the second floor.[51]

In a conversation with the author, a Sodder family member said that he had seen the scars of the fire on the hands of Ted.[52] The fire had literally been on top of them as they fled the house and there had been no chance of going back into the house once they were out. The fire spread that quickly.

As the family gathered outside in the cold, some still in their bare feet, they quickly realized that five of the children were not with them. In desperation, Mr. and Mrs. Sodder attempted to get back into the house but they were blocked by the flames. Mr. Sodder then tried to re-enter the house by breaking a window but again the flames stopped him. Somewhere in the process of breaking the window, he slashed his arm on the broken glass.

Believing the five missing children were still trapped upstairs, George looked for the ladder that was normally kept beside the house, all the time literally screaming for the children. He hoped they would appear at the windows and he could get them to jump.

Realizing that the ladder was nowhere to be found, and probably out of sheer desperation, George, still bleeding profusely, tried to literally climb the outside of the house.

Mr. Sodder and John thought of using their trucks as a way to possibly access the second floor. There were apparently two trucks there since both Mr. Sodder and John tried to start one of them. But neither truck would start either because of the cold weather, or perhaps in their panic, the men flooded them.[53]

While all this was unfolding, Mary Ann ran next door to the

home of Mr. and Mrs. Garlfield "Gar" Davis. Mrs. Davis attempted to call the Fayetteville Fire Department, but she could not get the switchboard operator to respond. It is unknown how long she continued to try or if she ever did reach the fire department.

At about 1 a.m., Thomas E. Smith of Beckwith was on his way home from Beckley and drove past the Sodder house while it was burning. The *1940 United States Federal Census* listed Mr. Smith at 55 years old and his occupation as a farmer.[54] Smith drove by near the same time Mrs. Sodder first reported that she smelled smoke.

Smith drove on past, searching for a phone to call the fire department. He stopped at a nearby night spot called Crass's Park and attempted to use the phone but was told it was out of order. Lonnie Johnson and Jeff Akins, the proprietors or managers, were said to not be there. It is known from police reports that some of the patrons--Peggy Price, Virginia Beasley Bucklin, Everett Bucklin, and Lester Cook decided to leave the bar to go and watch the fire.

Lonnie Johnson later gave a statement to the West Virginia State police regarding his actions. Johnson said he and several other people were having a party in his apartment over the Moonlight Inn about a quarter mile south of the Sodder home. In Johnson's statement, he said that one of the people at the party was a taxicab driver from Bluefield whose name he was unable to remember. Two of the boys at the party had left and were returning home to Beckwith. However, they returned to Johnson's apartment shortly after they left and wanted to use the phone to call the fire department because George Sodder's house was on fire. But, they were unable to reach the operator. In his statement, Johnson states that:

"We immediately started for the fire in the taxicab, my wife, and I, Grover Adkins, Fanny Ackers, and Allen Janney and the cab driver."[55]

The presence of a taxicab would be a source of confusion for many years. While Johnson claimed that one of the attendees of his party was a taxicab driver, Marion Sodder claimed in her statement of 1968 that Johnson intended to use the taxi to haul away the chain blocks he had stolen in the Sodder barn while the fire was burning.[56]

Meanwhile, Thomas Smith turned around and traveled the two miles back to Fayetteville and was finally able to contact the Fayetteville fire chief by phone. Chief Morris told Smith, "We know about it." When Smith asked Mr. Morris if they were going to respond to the fire, Morris replied, "I don't know." Becoming agitated, Smith informed the fire chief that there were children trapped and burning in the fire. Smith reported later that Morris "did not make a reply." Disgusted, Smith was said to have hung up and begun the drive back to the Sodder house.

By Smith making the statement that children were trapped in the house, it can be assumed that he must have stopped and spoken to someone. Another reason that it can be assumed that the two women named above arrived early on in the fire was that at one point, one or more of them claimed that they saw one of the children in an upstairs window. She later changed her story and denied saying this, another common theme in this story. But, regardless, at the point these people arrived at the fire, the second story of the house must have still been standing.

At some point during the burning of the house, Mr. Sodder or another member of the family noticed Lonnie Johnson in their garage, which was separate from the house. He was found to be stealing a set of chain hoists from the ceiling of the building. It was determined later that Johnson, possibly with the assistance of his partner Dave Adkins, did take one or two sets of chain hoists from the garage. Johnson later admitted taking the hoists and tossing them over an embankment so he could return and pick them up later.

Several days after the fire, Mr. Sodder obtained warrants for these two men accusing them of larceny. Johnson failed to appear for his hearing and was later arrested. Eventually, he pled guilty to the charges and paid a $25 dollar fine. Adkins fled the area and shortly thereafter joined the Army to avoid criminal prosecution in the matter. He spent two years in the Army, apparently to avoid paying a $25 fine.

At some point during the night, it is assumed that Fire Chief Morris initiated Fayetteville's version of a fire alarm: a phone tree system whereby one firefighter phoned another, who phoned another. The department had no loud fire alarm or bell. No one knew if Morris had any better luck in reaching the telephone operator or if he simply drove around to as many members of the department as he could locate. By morning, he arrived at the scene of the fire with just three other firemen.

After reporting the fire, Thomas Smith returned to the scene and joined a growing number of spectators. By the time he arrived, the house had been consumed due in large part to wind blowing the fire. Since most reports say the house was completely destroyed in between 30 to 45 minutes, this must set the time that Smith returned at about 1:45 to 2 a.m. Mr. Smith then left the scene to go home but then returned at about daybreak. No record exists to describe if Smith had words with the firemen about how late they were.

By the time all these attempts had been made, the house was a raging inferno and nothing more could be done. The family stood helpless in the cold winter night watching their home collapse into the basement. And with it, they believed at the time, the five children who were not standing with them.

It is impossible to imagine the pain and emotions going through the minds of the family. While spectators and other local officials kept arriving on the scene, the Sodder's took refuge in a small roadside shed that had been used as a vegetable stand the previous summer. Later that morning, Mrs. Sodder, Mary Ann, and Sylvia were eventually taken to the house of Mrs. Sodder's parents who lived in Smithers, about 24 miles away.[57]

Reports from the time record at least four different vehicles that went past the house. There were probably more. This is a fact that becomes more important later in the story. Some of the on-lookers claimed they tried to help by pushing some of the Sodder vehicles out of the fires range. Others simply stood in shock and watched the tragedy unwind as they found out there were children still in the house.

Many of Fayetteville's volunteer firemen were still away at war. Still others were out of town because of the holiday. The firemen who were still in town, were, of course, asleep and many people still did not have telephones and had to be contacted in person. Once they were finally reached, the fire department took nearly eight hours to reach the Sodder residence which was only two and a half miles from town. Reports of the time state that the fire department hooked up a pump to a nearby creek and extinguished the remaining parts of the embers in the basement until the fire was completely out.[58]

The Sodder family remained in the shelter that morning. Mr. Sodder was taken to the local hospital to treat the large cut on his arm and for shock. Mary Ann Sodder's personal account written in 1968 stated that the fire had "completely burned-out hours before."[59] Some accounts state the firemen did not arrive until 9 a.m.[60] The members were Chief Forrest Judson Morris, Arnold Dempsey, and James Roles. Another person who was alleged to have been there from the fire department was named Arnold Jacobs.[61] The Assistant Chief, Cortez Davis and Captain John Dooly were not present that night.[62]

Chief Morris's excuses as to why it took them eight hours to travel the two and a half miles vary according to the different sources available. First, he said that since it was Christmas and he had trouble waking enough men to answer the call. He also said the snowstorm from the previous night was too severe to take the truck out. (But apparently, it was not too bad for Mr. Smith, the people who came from Lonnie Johnson's party, the taxicab driver, the bus driver, and others who were traveling on Route 21 that night.) He also claimed that the Sodder house was out of the jurisdiction of his department and that he could not come until he could find someone who knew how to drive the large fire truck because he could not.

The Sodder children missing after the fire were Maurice Antonio Sodder, age 15,[63] Martha Lee Sodder, age 12[64], Louis Erico Sodder, age 9, Jennie Irene Sodder, age 8, and Betty Dolly, age 6. These were the same five children who had earlier asked if they could stay up and play with their new toys. The iconic pictures that have usually accompanied any story about the Sodder children were school pictures taken within months of the fire.

The five Sodder children missing after the 1945 fire, left to right, Maurice, Martha, Louis, Jennie, and Betty Sodder. Source: Sodder Family

The first officials to reach the site after the department were two West Virginia State Troopers from the Fayetteville detachment named R.W. Rule and F.E. Springer. The original report prepared by Trooper Rule states:

> *At about 9:00 a.m. December 25, 1945, information was received by Trooper F. E. Springer that Mr. George Sodder's house had burned. Trooper Springer and the undersigned (Trooper Rule) went to the scene of the fire. When we arrived at about 9:15 a.m., we learned that the fire had occurred at about 1:30 a.m. and that five members of the family had burned to death. The remaining members of the family were found in a small, two-room building near the scene of the fire where they were interviewed.*

The two troopers began an investigation of the premises and shortly had come to the initial conclusion that the cause of the fire was probably faulty wiring. Along with smoking in bed, this was a common cause of house fires then.

After the troopers arrived, the fire department continued to spray the remains of the fire. Any stream had to be small since this area was essentially sitting on top of the New River Gorge. This meant that the flow of water to extinguish the flames was no doubt small and slow, perhaps no more than a regular garden hose.

As soon as the debris was cool enough, a search was initiated to try and locate the remains of the five children, and possibly discover a cause of the fire. The State Fire Marshal's Office, who would usually take charge of situations such as this, had been called but at this point had not arrived. Representatives were in transit from Charleston, nearly 60 miles away.

The only known photograph of the remains of the Sodder house, Christmas morning, 1945[65] . Courtesy of Beckley Register-Herald

By this time, the crowd had grown considerably. Neighbors, as well as some of Mr. Sodder's employees had arrived to offer any help they could. How could they have known the nature of the task in front of them when they were asked to help dig for the remains of Mr. and Mrs. Sodder's five small children? The searchers were: Fire Chief F. J. Morris, Joe Sodder (This had to be a mistake in the Fire Marshal Report because Joe was still in North Carolina waiting to be discharged from the Army. Most likely, this was John Sodder), Emanuel Moles, Bill Bickford, Jimmy Arthur (a next-door neighbor), George (Ted) Sodder Jr., Arthur Moles, Carl Bragg, and Garnet Arthur. There were possibly others in the search party but these names are the ones listed in the police reports.[66]

It is specifically stated in the Fire Marshal Report that several members of the volunteer search party "quit in disgust" because of the way they were being "ordered around" by Chief Morris and were tired of his attitude. The report also states that the search ceased at 10 a.m. Knowing that the fire department arrived at around 8 a.m. and allowing time to cool the smoldering ashes with water, the search could not have lasted for more than an hour and a half.

It was at this point the Chief Morris went to the food stand where Mr. Sodder and his family were still taking refuge and informed them that he and the searchers "had made a thorough search of the debris and no trace of the remains of the children were found." Mrs. Sodder's first response was, "that's impossible, there has to be something." According to Mary Ann Sodder's statement, Morris is said to have added that they had searched the remains with a fine-tooth comb and had found nothing.[67]

As upset as the Sodders already were, their exasperation was further compounded by this announcement. A magazine article from 1967 quoted Chief Morris as saying, "This is the most completely burned-up place I have ever seen in the course of my sixteen years with the department."[68] Assistant Fire Marshal Raper later stated that from the looks of the remains, "there must have been a tremendous fire"[69]

James Roles of the Fire Department who was at the fire that morning, was interviewed by the *Charleston Gazette* in 1995. 85-year-old Roles stated, "we looked through the ashes all day. I don't think they (the children) burned in there." He added that they never smelled flesh burning as they normally would in a fire of this nature.[70]

F. J. Morris had been the Fayetteville Fire Chief for about eight years. He was appointed to replace J. R. Caldwell in November of 1937.[71] He had already been a member of the local fire department for many years.

In order to illustrate the extent of the controversy surrounding the Fire Chief's initial and subsequent comments regarding the remains of the children, all available reports and articles will be disclosed here. These, varying accounts will show the breadth of what was reported at the time, what was disclosed to the public, and what was not. This includes all the different law enforcement and regulatory agency's reports, as well as newspaper and magazine stories. It should be kept in mind that in any official report, mistakes can be made and hopefully, later corrected.

A second Fire Marshal report from 1952 states that, "Chief Morris located Mr. and Mrs. Sodder at about 10:00 a.m. and informed them that they had made a thorough search and that no trace of the remains of the five children were found." The "fine-tooth-comb" was again referenced. In contrast to his initial comments to the Sodders that morning, in a 1968 article from *Inside Detective* magazine, 23 years after the fire, Morris is quoted as saying:

> *"I didn't completely search the ruins. I looked thoroughly where the beds should have been and over the majority of the whole site. I didn't finish the job to my satisfaction because I heard you (Mr. Sodder) were going to cover the place with dirt."[72]*

If this is true, this could be one of the reasons that the other searchers felt they were being unreasonably directed as to where to search and not allowed to search the whole area. Most official accounts also say it was actually Chief Morris who first suggested filling in the basement as a cemetery. But this statement, even though it is directly the opposite of what he said the morning of the fire, is minor compared to other reports.

In another part of the same report from 1950 it states:

> *Fire Chief Morris and all persons who assisted in searching the debris state that if there had been any remains of the children present in the debris, it would have been found by them. Numerous burned and undamaged coins were recovered from the debris.*

The searchers of the debris named in this report were questioned carefully in regard to the thoroughness of the search, conduct of the searchers, and spectators, etc. Some of the searchers became disgusted at the attitude of Fire Chief Morris and abandoned the search. It appeared that Mr. Morris was continually nagging at them and ordering them around.

The source of the chief's "bad attitude" could be attributed to several factors. It is likely that the Chief was greatly chastised when he finally arrived. At the time, it was believed that five children had died, and the parents were extremely upset.

Morris again stated his position in a story from the *Charleston Gazette* on November 14, 1948, that he did not search the site to his total satisfaction. He stated that he did look thoroughly where he thought the children's beds should have been and over that majority of the site. He further implied that he had planned to return to the site and search further but claimed that did not happen because four days after the fire, Mr. Sodder filled in the site with dirt, without consulting him.[73]

In a letter written by Mary Ann Sodder in 1968:

That same morning the Fire Chief and eight other men searched the ashes remaining. The fire had burned out completely hours before. We asked the Fire Chief if there were any traces left of the bodies of the children presumably still in the remains of the burned house. He said, "We searched as if with a fine-tooth comb and we could not find a thing." However, a few days later he produced a piece of flesh saying that it was a part of a human body. We could not understand how this soft piece of flesh could have survived the fire, yet there was no trace of bones or teeth.

A story in the December 26, 1945 *Charleston Gazette* states that, "The bodies of the youngsters were burned beyond recognition." This same story quotes John Sodder as saying that, "he made an unsuccessful attempt to reach his trapped brothers and sisters, but flames blocked his path."[74] However, there is no other account of the day that refers to the bodies of the children.

In the original State Police report of January 21, 1946, John Sodder gave the following statement:

I heard my mother yelling, I awakened my brother George and we went in the other room and shook the other kids, and then we ran downstairs and was going to try and put the fire out. The fire was too big by then and I started to go back upstairs and bring the kids down but I could not get back upstairs because the fire was all around the stairs by then and I could not get through it.

In another story of the time, John Sodder was quoted as saying he only yelled at the other two boys in his room, Louis and

Maurice. John also said that he thought he heard one of the boys say "all right" when he told them to get up. John was later re-interviewed by a detective hired by George Sodder and John told him that, "he wasn't sure he had heard his kid brother's voice, that he thought he had heard it but, in the confusion, it might have been his brother, George's voice."

But this change in story does not account for what John said in the State Police report about going into the other room (assumedly the girl's room) and shaking the kids. In December 2005, Jonathan Bandy, a grandson of John Sodder, in an effort to further clarify his grandfather's statement, made the following declaration on Websleuths.com:

To clear a few things up....the idea that my grandfather (John) woke up the children is incorrect. He only yelled at George (Ted) to get up. The other children were in a different room. That is something that he said was incorrect in the Unsolved Mysteries book. Nonetheless, the book is the closest depiction to what really happened. There are a few more side stories that I have knowledge of...and will share when the time is right.

We already know that part of this is incorrect. There were only two bedrooms upstairs. Ted Sodder also stated several times over the years that he thought he heard one of the boys respond but he was not sure. And, to date, Jonathan Bandy has not publicly disclosed any additional stories.

In a December 26, 1945 story in the *Fayette Tribune*, it states that "part of one body was found." Two days later in the *Beckley Post Herald*, it states that "a few bones were found."[75] This is also incorrect.

In the second contradictory Fire Marshal report of 1952, Fayette County Prosecutor Carl Vickers was quoted as saying that, "a piece of a backbone and a human liver was found." (Although this was later said to actually be an animal liver with no bones attached). Again, in the same story, acting coroner for the Sodder inquest and Justice of the Peace, W.H. Level of Oak Hill was quoted as saying, "As I remember it, nothing was found."[76]

In the 1950 Fire Marshal report it states the following:

The searchers of the debris named in this report were

questioned carefully in regard to the thoroughness of the search, conduct of the searchers, and spectators, etc.

No member of the searching party, or anyone else contacted, with the exception of Jimmy Cipriani, Mrs. Sodders brother, ever saw any bones, mass of flesh, or tissue comparable to the mass alleged to have been buried in the debris by Mr. Morris. No person present ever saw the box buried by Morris.[77]

The old police rule-of-thumb that eyewitness testimony is the most unreliable type is alive and well in this case. The contrasts and contradictions are numerous. To give an example of this phenomenon, it was estimated that nearly 1,500 people witnessed the assassination of Abraham Lincoln and there were nearly as many different accounts of the shooting given to the police.

After telling Mr. Sodder that no remains of the children had been found, the Fire Chief recommended that he put some ashes in a box and bury them in the debris of the fire as a sort of memorial to the children.[78] Mr. Sodder refused saying he would not bury ashes. And again, in telling this to Mr. Sodder, he does not mention the mass he supposedly found.

On the morning of the fire, at around 9 a.m. the West Virginia State Fire Marshal's Office received a phone call from the Fayette County Assistant Prosecuting Attorney Carson notifying them of the fire and the loss of life. Assistant Prosecutor Carson requested that even though it was Christmas Day someone from the West Virginia State Fire Marshal's office come to Fayetteville and investigate.

At around Noon, Chief Assistant State Fire Marshal, C. A. Raper arrived accompanied by Howard M. Welcher, from the Arson Department of the National Board of Fire Underwriters Charleston office. They immediately went to the office of the County Prosecutor, whom, they were informed, was still at the scene of the fire, conducting a coroner's inquest. Traveling to the Sodder's property, they were informed that a coroner's inquest had been conducted.

When details of how the debris of the fire had been searched earlier in the morning were told to Raper, he was not pleased.

While the volunteer searchers most likely had the best of intentions, they were obviously not trained in investigating a potential arson scene.

Carl Raper joined the Fire Marshal's office in 1930 and later made chief field assistant in charge of arson investigations and inspections in 1945. In 1948 Raper was appointed acting Fire Marshal and the next year appointed Fire Marshal and would remain in the post for nearly fifteen years. At the time of the Sodder fire, Raper had been investigating fires for nearly fifteen years.

With all the amateur searchers going through the debris, it is impossible to know accurately what was removed from the scene, or what may have been placed there. Some accounts describe how pieces of tin roofing, truck engines, appliances and other objects that did not burn were removed. No one associated with the case at that time, with the possible exception of Raper, could have conceived of how important the preservation of the scene would be later on. The mystery that evolved in a relatively short period of time possibly could have been stopped on that first day if proper procedures had been followed.

Steps that should have been taken include roping off the area and limiting access of sightseer's who flock to these kinds of events. And even though it was Christmas Day and the temperature was supposedly near zero, the investigation should have taken place right away, beginning to end.

Coroner's Inquest(s)

After being informed by the Fire Chief that there were no human remains in the debris, the Fayette County Prosecuting Attorney, Carl Vickers decided to hold a coroner's inquest at the site. The author spoke with a former Fayette County official who said in those days, it was common practice to hold a coroner's inquest at the scene of a crime or a death, especially if the conclusions seemed to be obvious.[79]

A coroner's inquest is basically a judicial inquiry held to determine the cause of a person's death. They are usually conducted by a judge or other government official and the results, or verdict, are determined by that official or, in many cases, by an impaneled jury. Sometimes, depending on the circumstances of the death, an inquest may require an autopsy.

Fayette County had a coroner, but the only medical examiner's office was in Charleston. Possibly because the verdict seemed obvious, the local Justice of the Peace H. C. Level acted as the coroner and the Fayette County Prosecutor assisted or oversaw the inquest. Generally, inquests are only conducted when deaths are sudden or unexplained, such as the Sodder case. Usually, an inquest may be called at the order of a coroner, a judge, a prosecutor, or sometimes based on a request from a family member.

Another requirement of a coroner's inquest is the taking of statements, interviewing potential witnesses and possibly the calling of witnesses. If the morning after the fire, the Sodder's were claiming that the fire "had been set" as the newspapers of the day claimed, it would seem this should have been enough to have compelled the investigators to conduct interviews before rendering a verdict.[80]

By holding an inquest on the site less than twelve hours after the fire, it is obvious that Vickers had no intent to investigate further, interview witnesses, or hear testimony of any kind. He had reached a conclusion, even though Mrs. Sodder declared that she believed the fire had been set intentionally. Even the State Police and Fire Marshal had intended to return to the scene to speak to the Sodders after the family had time to compose themselves. However, even this was impeded by Mr. Sodder filling in the foundation of the basement with dirt four days later.

The first coroner's jury was made up of local citizens who were at the Sodder residence the morning of the fire.[81]

1. Cleante G. Janutolo, Jury Foreman – Prominent Fayetteville businessman. He either owned or partially owned many local businesses including Fayetteville Savings and Loan, an engineering company, construction contracting company, coal company, lumber yard, building material supply company. Mr. Sodder had worked for one of the Janutolo companies up until about 1942 when he bought the Dempsey Transfer Company. Janutolo was also

responsible for the construction of many of the beautiful cut stone buildings and walls that still stand in Fayetteville today. A small park still exists in Fayetteville that bears his family's name.

2. Floyd C. Shuck was a bank bookkeeper at Fayetteville Savings and Loan, owned by the Janutolos.

3. John Duval Shultz, President of the Fayetteville Federal Savings and Loan Assn. Was also a member of the local Rotary Club, along with local insurance agent, Rosser Long, Businessman F. G. Janutolo, and Cleante Janutolo.

4. Forest Judson Morris, Fayetteville Fire Department Chief. Also worked as a bookkeeper or clerk for Janutolo and Company.

5. Lacy Neely was the county clerk for Fayette County. Any official documents that were associated with the County, would have his stamp or signature.

6. Jackson Theodore Jennings, a local coal miner who lived in Fayetteville with his wife Gertrude in the 1940s. Possibly an employee of Mr. Sodder's or a neighbor.

Fayetteville Savings and Loan was well represented on the jury with the President, one of the owners, and the bookkeeper. The empaneled jury quickly returned a verdict that the five children had all died from smoke suffocation and the fire had been accidental.[82]

On December 26th, a second inquest was held before Judge H. C. Level. At that inquest, Mr. Janutolo reported, "no parts of the five missing children were found in the debris of the fire."[83] It should also be pointed out here that there are no reports of the Fayetteville Fire Chief offering any information about anything related to the case.

Other newspaper accounts of the time state that an inquest was also held on Friday, December 28th. This was perhaps a more formal hearing which would have provided a written transcript. If this is correct, (i.e. not the inquest from December 26th), this makes a third inquest related to this case. But, regardless of which inquest is considered, the verdict was the same for all. The children had died as a result of suffocation and/or the fire.

In the minds of this jury, led by Cleante Janutolo, there was no direct evidence of any other possible conclusion. Vickers was quoted in the local newspaper as saying, "There was nothing left to investigate. It was complete destruction and the jury rendered, I think, the only possible verdict under the circumstances."[84] This was even though the fire had only occurred two days before. Not much time for investigation or consulting the Fire Marshal and their trained investigators.

Acting Coroner Level, on the other hand, was quoted in 1948 as saying that there was "something peculiar about it at the time." He was also critical of the members of the jury stating they (the jury) did not seem to realize the importance of having more evidence on which to base their verdict.[85] This shows that there was at least one official associated with the early investigation who felt there was possibly more to it than was brought out at the time.

It was also stated that Vickers consulted with Judge Thrift about the possibility of the fire being the result of arson, but Thrift agreed with Vickers that at the time, there was no evidence of being intentionally set. Accounts also show that attorney, C. E. Mahan questioned witnesses at the preliminary hearing, which was probably another name for the coroner's inquest. The answers to his questions convinced him that the children probably did die in the fire.

Unconvinced, Sodder employed two additional attorneys, former judge J. W. Early and M. R. Renick, both from Fayetteville.[86] Further, and as odd as this sounds, it was implied at this hearing that the reason it was assumed that the children had died in the fire was that they had not been seen after the fire.

Knowing that Mahan was able to question the coroner's witnesses at the inquest leads to the conclusion that Sodder's attorney could have called his own witnesses at the time, if he had any at this early stage of the investigation. This would have been a good opportunity to bring out the claims of various witnesses who saw a man in a car several times watching the children getting off of the school bus, the incident with the man who claimed the fuse box was going to cause a fire, or even the threat the house was going to go up in smoke and his children would be destroyed. But there is no record that this line of circumstantial evidence was questioned.

There is some evidence showing that Lonnie Johnson was a witness at the inquest and described how he had cut the phone lines to the house, thinking it was the power line. His associate from that night who helped him steal the two chain hoists from the garage, Jeff Adkins, had already fled the area and joined the Army, and would not return to Fayette County for two years.[87]

After the verdict was announced, it was later brought up by the officials that if at a future time some new evidence was found, it could be reopened, and the evidence considered. In the mind of Mr. Sodder, when he later became convinced that the children did not die in the fire, this meant that he must be responsible for any future investigation. In addition, the burden would then be on Mr. Sodder to convince authorities that the evidence was sufficient to justify reopening the case. Over the next 24 years, this task would prove to be insurmountable.

On December 30th, as a result of the verdict, five death certificates were issued listing "fire and suffocation" as the cause of death. For each of the certificates, C. G. Janutolo is listed as the person giving the information probably because he was the Foreman of the Coroner's Jury. C.I. Dodd, a local mortician, is listed as the funeral director, even though there were no bodies. Dodd would later play a larger role in the mystery surrounding the case.[88]

An interesting note in looking at all five of the death certificates is that they all not only appear to have been filled out by the same hand, but all the different signatures contained in the certificates appear to be by the same hand as well. This could indicate that it was considered a formality to produce these certificates and get the case closed.

Investigative Report

On the morning after the fire, after surveying the scene, Assistant State Fire Marshal Raper had a conference with State Troopers Rule and Springer and the other officials gathered at the site. It was decided that they would not subject the Sodders to any additional questioning at that time. They agreed to return at a later date to obtain statements. However, before the two men from the Fire Marshal's office left, they firmly instructed Mr. Sodder to do nothing further to the site and that if anything else pertinent to the fire or the death of his children was discovered, he should notify the department immediately.[89]

In the meantime, Trooper Rule and the Fayetteville detachment of the State Police would continue his investigation for the Department of Public Safety (State Police) and he would later contact the Fire Marshal's Office when he thought it would be a better time to talk to the Sodders. As a result of this agreement, the Fire Marshal did not prepare their typical report of the fire. Since the Office of Public Safety was already investigating, Raper decided to leave it to them.[90]

By the time Raper and Welcher were leaving the scene of the fire, the State Police made a preliminary determination as to the cause of the fire. Trooper Springer was quoted in a story in the *Montgomery News* from December 26, 1945 as saying, "the fire apparently started in the basement and was due to defective wiring. It spread rapidly to all sections of the structure."

In order for this determination to be quoted in a newspaper the next morning after the fire, the reporter would have had to speak to the trooper the morning of the fire. This means the trooper had made his assessment of the scene and had made a determination as to the cause of the fire that same morning. The trooper had to have made this determination before speaking to the Sodders or interviewing anyone to any significant extent. He also must have known that there had been no remains of the children found in the debris of the house. Why this raised no suspicions in regard to a possible cause of the fire is unclear.

In the final report issued by the WV State Police on January 21, 1946, the cause of the fire is listed as follows:

Undetermined, but it is believed that the fire started either from defective wiring at the place where the electric wire entered the house or from spontaneous igniting of combustibles in the basement. The latter is based on the fact that the

41

basement had been used as a workshop for dismantling and repairing truck motors.[91]

Trooper Springer said that the conclusion of the cause of the fire was based on the fact that the electrical switch box was located near the estimated point of origin of the fire, as told by Mrs. Sodder in her statement. Mr. Sodder would later dispute this claim saying the house had just recently had the wiring upgraded for the installation of an electric stove by a licensed electrician.

The state police would also later change their determination of the start of the fire and said it probably started on the roof of the house.[92] Mr. Sodder also refuted the claims made that he had large quantities of drip gas and truck tires stored in his basement, both of which would be highly flammable.

Chapter 3

The First Investigation

"I think somebody set the fire."

Jennie Sodder, 1945

Most everyone received their news either from newspapers or movie newsreels. Stories of the fire were published the next day in the *Beckley Post Herald*, and the *Charleston Gazette* and later in the *Fayetteville Tribune* and *Montgomery News*, (both weekly papers). Later the story was picked up on the wire and by the next day, it appeared in at least twenty different newspapers throughout the United States and in at least two languages.

In the December 26 issue of the *Beckley Post-Herald*:

Mrs. Sodder and other survivors believe the fire was set, and an investigation will be held. The mother said she couldn't find the ladder to the upstairs loft when she noticed the fire, and reported other circumstances which she considered suspicious. Officers discount her theory, and believe faulty wiring was responsible.[93]

The casual observer might think that considering the differences, it would seem the State Police came to their initial conclusion as to the cause of the fire rather quickly. While it is unknown to what extent they did conduct further investigations, it is known that they did not interview the Sodders any further. Their report did not become final until January 21st, nearly three weeks after the fire, and the final conclusions did not change from what the police assumed that first morning.

Mr. Sodder had refused to leave the scene of the fire until the debris had been searched and word of the fate of his children had been given. After being told there were no remains of his children present in the debris, Mr. Sodder was taken to a hospital in Fayetteville to treat the laceration to his arm and significant blood loss. He was later sent for bed rest because it was determined he was suffering from shock.

Mrs. Sodder, Mary Ann, and baby Sylvia were taken to Mrs. Sodder's parents in Smithers to rest.[94] It is reported they stayed there overnight but soon returned to Fayetteville to be together again as a family in the hour of tragedy they were having to endure.[95]

In one newspaper story, Mr. Sodder was quoted as saying, "that he knew of no enemies which he or any member of his family might have, thus leaving no reason to suspect that arson was involved."[96] While saying this, it does not mean that Mr. Sodder did not share the feelings of his wife about the fire being set. It just means that he did not have knowledge of who his potential enemies could be. Or, he was very wisely not willing to admit it at the time. More will be discussed later on this.

Fire Chief Claim of Finding a Mass

At around 10 a.m., Mrs. Sodder's brother, Jimmy Cipriani arrived at the scene of the fire. He stated that he had been called by Mr. Janutolo (which one, Cleante or Fiorenzo, is not clear) at his home in Montgomery.[97] It is also unclear if Mr. Cipriani arrived alone or not, but newspaper accounts state that John Sodder was being comforted, or was in the company of his cousin Joseph Cipriani, a son of Jimmy Cipriani. So it can be accurately assumed that Jimmy Cipriani brought along his son.

The following is a direct excerpt from the 1950 Fire Marshal report regarding Mr. Cipriani's arrival at the site:

Some Italian unknown to him (Cipriani) showed him something in a tub on paper which appeared to him to be several joints of a backbone approximately 16-inches long and possibly a portion of liver. The liver or mass of flesh appeared to have been attached to the bones, He does not know what he saw and where it came from. The person who showed him made no comment or explanation.

Reverend James Frame, minister of the Fayetteville Baptist Church arrived at the scene early in the morning and tried to give comfort to the family. It is unknown if the Sodders were members of Reverend Frame's church. It is reported that he led the family in a prayer trying to give them solace in a time of unfathomable sorrow.[98]

In the 1952 Supplemental Report by the State Fire Marshal's Office, Assistant Fire Marshals C.R. Cobb and M.M. Arthur state the following:

Mrs. Sodder stated on a previous date her suspicions were first aroused when the Reverand (sic) James F. Frame, pastor of the Fayetteville Baptist Church is alleged to have made the statement that the human heart would not burn.

Mrs. Sodder states further that she received information through T.C. Simmons that Reverand (sic) Frame had called the home of Mrs. Gar Davis and instructed them to put ice on the liver or what remains were found in the debris (at which time the weather was near zero)[99]

Reverand (sic) James F. Frame was interviewed in his home at Fayetteville (1-25-52). He states that: He went to the scene of the fire on the morning of December 25, 1945 where he met the Sodder family. He held prayer with them and did his utmost to console them in their time of grief.

While at the scene of the fire one of the persons searching the debris handed him a part of an internal organ about the size of his fist. It appeared to him to be a part of a lung and was water logged. He placed the mass on a piece of stove pipe near the scene and left it there. He did not remain at the scene for any length of time due to the extreme cold weather.

He states that he never made any telephone calls to the home of Mrs. Davis as alleged by the private investigators.

Reverand (sic) Frame is, and always has been, of the opinion that the children perished in the fire, however, he may have stated while at the scene of the fire that other parts of the bodies should have been found. He states further that when he arrived at the scene of the fire that the basement of the home was a blazing inferno.

Reverand (sic) Frame is a prominent minister, having been a pastor of the Emmanuel Baptist Church in Charleston, West Virginia for a number of years and pastor of other good churches throughout West Virginia. His conduct and veracity is above reproach.

Mrs. Gar Davis states that to her personal knowledge, Reverand (sic) Frame never made any calls to her house and if he talked to anyone at her home they made no mention of it to her.

Towards the end of the same report, it states the following:

To date (1952), it has been established that four people saw some remains of the bodies, namely; Jimmie Cipirani (sic), Carl B. Vickers, F.J. Morris, and Reverand (sic) James F. Frame.[100]

The account of the morning after the fire given in C. R. Cobb's 1952 report directly conflicts with a report he wrote just eighteen months before and sent to Fire Marshal Raper, where he stated that no remains has been found until 1947.[101] Again, we see here the Fire Chief's idea of putting ashes or remains in a box and burying them. This will be discussed more in a later chapter.

Let's carry this a little further. Back to the 1950 report on Page 13, it states the following:

An inquest was held on December 26, 1950 before W. H. Level, Justice of the Peace for Fayette County, W. Va. Mr. Janutolo was foreman of this coroner's jury.[102] Mr. Janutolo reported to the Squire that no parts of the five missing children were found in the debris.[103]

There is an obvious typographical error in regard to this listing of the date, December 26, 1950. This date would be six months after the date of this report (June 30, 1950), itself. The writer of the report, Mr. C. R. Cobb, most likely meant December

26, 1945, the day after the fire.

As far as the paragraph goes, again, we are back to no parts of the children being found. And, it can be easily assumed that Mr. Janutolo was at the site that morning since he was called upon by Prosecuting Attorney Vickers to serve on the hastily empaneled coroner's jury. So, he saw what happened, what was found and what was not found.

It would be assumed that any competent jury would usually spend several hours investigating all angles of the situation before rendering a verdict. Especially considering that the Sodders claimed they believed the fire was arson. At least no less than several days of investigation were called for to cover all bases and interview witnesses or search for witnesses to explain the lack of remains. At the bare minimum, wait until the State Police and/or Fire Marshal finish their reports.

While it would be another three weeks before this report was submitted and the conclusion was virtually the same, it would have still given the impaneled jury something to base their verdict on. But it was Christmas and everybody wanted to get back home and out of the cold. And the answers seemed obvious.

Going a little further, on Pages 14 and 15 of the 1950 report it states:

> *No member of the searching party, or anyone else contacted, with the exception of Jimmy Cipriani, Mrs. Sodder's brother, ever saw any bones, mass of flesh, or tissue comparable to the mass alleged to have been buried in the ruins by Chief Morris. No person present ever saw the box buried by Morris.[104]*

Someone here is either mistaken, in error, or simply lying. The differences in the 1950 and 1952 reports are not small, simple, typographical, or irrelevant details that could be easily dismissed. These differences are significant facts directly associated with key events and actions of individuals connected with this case. The difference in the reports is one of the most important issues that lends itself to the mystery of the case.

The specific differences are in one report, someone says, "no, I saw nothing." Then eighteen months later, they say, "yes, I did."

47

And these responses are not concerning, "where were you on this date" or "What did you have for breakfast," or some other minor detail. The questions were, "did you see some possible human remains of a child?" I would hazard a guess that if they had seen partial human remains, especially those of a child, it would be something they would never forget and it would have been recorded properly.

Another person who claimed to have seen what was termed as "remains" the morning after the fire was C. I. Dodd, a local mortician who arrived with his son who happened to be visiting his father. Dodd would come back to the scene later in the day after most everyone had left and searched the ashes himself. His full statement is below:

Statement of C. I. Dodd, made November 11, 1951, at Dodd Funeral Home, Fayetteville, West Virginia.

I was called to the scene of the Sodder fire some 12 hours after the fire by Dr. James F. Frame. He phoned me about noon on December 25, 1945 saying he thought they had found something that perhaps I should take care of. I immediately drove down there in my car. I believe my son C. R. Dodd of Webster Springs, West Virginia went with me. When we arrived (at the scene of the fire) I don't believe anyone else was there. I picked up a garden rake, and in my opinion, I raked the ashes in the basement very thoroughly and found nothing. I did however notice what I believe was a # 2 wash tub (zinc) in the front yard. It was partially filled with ashes. On top of the ashes was an object that was covered with a coating of ash dust. I touched it with the rake and it was very soft. I believe it was liver, but I'm sure it had never been exposed to extreme heat, else it would have been cooked or a solid form. This was very soft. I would estimate the weight, just from looking at it, at 2 or 3 pounds. I didn't pick it up nor did I remove it from the scene. I left it because I was sure it was not the remains of a human body that had been in the fire.

I raked the ashes for about an hour and didn't even find a bone of any kind. In view of this fact and considering the short length of time the house burned, it is my opinion the Sodder children did not perish in the fire.

C. I. Dodd[105]

Here, the liver in a tub is mentioned, similar to the statement of Jimmy Cipriani, but nothing about bones. And are so-called human remains left at the site in a wash tub? Some reports claim that Dodd was called because something had been found that he needed to take charge of (meaning as a mortician) but when he got there, he was told there was nothing. Was the liver left there on purpose by the man that Jimmy Cipriani described as "the unknown Italian" for others to see in order to convince them that someone had perished in the fire?

C. R. Dodd of Webster Springs was visiting his father on Christmas Day. A part of the statement given by Dodd's son, states:

Statement of C. R. Dodd, at Dodd and Rort Funeral Home at Webster Springs, West Virginia taken on Nov.28, 1951, about 1:00 P. M. relative to the Sodder fire on Dec. 25, 1945.

It is my opinion that, if the Sodder house did not burn more than an hour, it would have been an impossibility for all the five bodies to have been completely consumed by fire. The torso of each body should have been intact, the outer surfaces burned of course, and the arm and leg bones should have been found.

I have been told by Mr. Sodder that someone allegedly found what turned out to be raw liver in the debris. It is my opinion from past experience with burned bodies that if the body from which the liver came was exposed to sufficient heat to burn the rib bones, then the liver would have at least been in a cooked state and therefore solidified like ordinary beef liver.

I have also been informed that there were four lumbar vertebrae found when the basement was excavated in 1948, but no other bones were found. If these bones were found in good

49

condition, then in my opinion the whole vertebrae column should have been found.

C. R. Dodd[106]

We need to pause for a moment and examine the statements of this father and son. There are several fundamental differences here.

Point of Difference	Father's Statement	Son's Statement
Time of the trip	Around 12 p.m.	10:30 or 11:00 a.m.
Trip prompted by a phone call	The trip was prompted by call from Dr. James Frame	No phone call prompted trip to son's knowledge
Who went on the trip to the fire	Father says he believed his son was with him.	Son says "I'm not positive it was my father I went with"
Anyone at the site when the Dodds arrived	No one else there	6 to 8 others there including F. J. Morris
Was a search of the ruins conducted while the Dodds were there	Father says he raked the ashes for about an hour but found nothing	Did not search nor saw anyone else searching. Said the ruins did not appear to have been searched by that time.

These differences are quite substantial. It is like two completely different accounts of the situation. The first thing to keep in mind is that the statements were taken nearly six years after the fire and memories of what actually happened can fade with time. Second, this is also a good case to show the shortcomings of eyewitness testimony. A hundred people can witness an event and tell a hundred different stories. Third, the morning after the Sodder fire the entire community was in chaos. People were scrambling to make sense of what had happened, to help the survivors, and to get back to their families for Christmas.

The conclusion that seems obvious here is that the father and son did not take the trip together and were possibly there at different times. The son even states that he drove past the scene of the fire earlier on his way to Fayetteville to visit his father. He could have stopped then. That would be closer to the time he claimed he was there. Both men make it clear they were not sure if the other was with them.

By the time the father went there at around noon, everyone had gone. The liver had been found, or delivered to the site. The father could have been there at the time when Morris had already left but was planning to return and bury the liver in a box he found at the Sodder barn.

The key point here is that both men agree that because of the short duration of the fire itself, that there was no way that the bones of the children could have been destroyed. It is likely this is why private investigator Simmons and his assistant O. D. Fisher decided to take their statements, along with that of Harold Gay. They all had seen the liver in question at one time or another.

As the number of spectators multiplied, it is impossible to speculate how many people may have gone through the debris of the fire trying to help. What could have been taken from the site, or what may have been added?

Accounts say that hundreds of people came to offer condolences or just to see for themselves if what they had heard was true. Witnesses claimed to have had to park several hundred yards away from the house.

People were already beginning to organize assistance and show support for the Sodder family. Local representatives of the Red Cross began almost immediately gathering food, clothing, dishes, and other supplies for the family. The Fayette County Board of Education provided a stove for cooking meals.

Clente Janutolo, the foreman of the hastily assembled county coroner's jury was quoted in a local newspaper as saying that he was going to erect a small house that would provide temporary shelter until a more permanent structure could be built.[107] On December 29th, a letter was sent out to hundreds of residents in Fayetteville from the local Catastrophe Committee of the Fayetteville Community Citizens, which was an anonymous group of citizens that took the lead in organizing help whenever a situation such as the fire took place. A letter requesting support read in part:

Help is needed, definitely needed. Everything they had was burned. The father, a hard-working, self-respecting citizen who gloried in fending for his large family without assistance until this calamity engulfed him, himself was injured in the fire. And in the words of one who knows, he was left "less than nothing."

This letter is NOT a solicitation of charity. It is not a solicitation of anything. It is only to let you know how you can help, if that is what you want to do. A dollar, or a few dollars, from each of us whose children are snug and cozy..... and ... alive...from those of us who have enough and WANT to help, can ease the terrible burden of these, or neighbors.

So, if you are one of those who want to help, here's the way to do it. Simply mail or hand this letter to Nick Crouse at the bank, together with your contribution, and he will see that it reaches its destination. No one but you and Nick...and God... will know whence it came. To the stricken family the help will come, not from individual charity, but from the great heart of the community of which they are a part, a community that believes such a calamity should not be borne alone.

The Mayor, the President of the Business Men's Association, and its President-elect, and other citizens whom you trust, know of the writing of this letter and approve of it. PLEASE DON'T contribute unless you really want to. Nobody but you will know whether you do or not. This letter simply tells you how you may do it gracefully, in the time of greatest need, and in the traditional sprit of our good little community... if that is what you want to do.[108]

Within a week of this letter being circulated, several hundred dollars had already been raised. Nick Crouse, president of the local bank organized the effort and soon, it was reported that a check for $1,430 was presented to the Sodders by then Fayetteville Mayor T. A. Myles. Later, as more money was collected, a second check was presented to the family for a smaller amount.[109] As time passed, help in other forms continued to pour in from the local community to assist the family in the recovery process.

Newspapers also reported at the time that John Sodder, had received a check for $500.00 from the Army after his discharge a few weeks before and that the check had been destroyed in the fire. Several representatives of the Red Cross assisted him in getting a replacement check.[110]

Even with the loss of five children, the Sodders still had others to take care of as well as a business to run. It is unclear if any of the trucks Mr. Sodder used in his business were damaged or destroyed on the night of the fire. There were reports that some of the Sodder's business equipment was moved away from the fire.

Mysterious Visitors

Three days after the fire, an incident occurred that, to the Sodders, seemed very strange. While they had been receiving condolences from the entire community, four strangers came to their house expressing a desire to "see their babies." It was assumed at the time that this meant they wanted to see where the five children had died. The overall demeanor of these strangers aroused the suspicions of the Sodders. From the questions they asked, the strangers gave the impression they seemed to be more interested in seeing if the Sodders suspected anything instead of expressing sadness about the children's death. The strangers eventually left and were never seen again.[111] Other accounts of this same incident suggest that the four people were intoxicated and their motives were born more out of inebriation rather than maliciousness.[112] Referring to someone else's children as "their babies" could be another West Virginia common way of speaking with no malicious intent attached to it.

The Sodders' new house was located about 150 feet from the

one that burned. It is difficult to comprehend the trauma of having to look out of a window and see the black hole that used to be your house.

How do you explain to your children or answer their questions about what happened to their siblings without breaking into tears? These parents had to remain strong and determined to keep their family together and their business running. In the days following the fire it was reported that hundreds of people came to see the site. As happens in tragedies such as this, it attracts the morbidly curious along with the sincere, and eventually the site becomes more of a spectacle or tourist attraction, rather than the place where five children had died and a family's life had been torn apart.

With the endless passing of sight-seers, the tragedy became intrusive to the family because all they really wanted was the chance to grieve in private. To a proud man like George Sodder, too many visitors, no matter how well meaning, probably became annoying very quickly.

By Saturday, December 30th, Mr. Sodder had resigned himself that neither the Fire Marshal nor the West Virginia State Police were returning, as promised, to conduct a more thorough investigation. He therefore decided to go ahead with the family's original plans to turn the site into a burial place for the five children. He commissioned Jimmy Cipriani to fill in the hole that used to be their home, all the while, having no idea of the problems this would create later when questions arose about whether or not the children had actually died in the fire.[113]

In one account, Mr. Sodder was quoted as saying, "I have been called idiotic for covering up the ruins but I believed at the time that the children were dead and I didn't want their remains, even if they were invisible, to be trampled on."[114] Later that same day, after the foundation of the house was filled with dirt, five wreaths were placed at the site with each of the children's names on them.[115]

The Fire Marshal later stated in the 1950 report that he had driven by the site of the fire several times and noticed the site had been filled in with dirt. Therefore, he felt that no further investigation would be possible.

The Funeral

A service for the five children was held on Sunday, December 31st, at 4 p.m. at the Sodder home with hundreds of people attending. A police officer was used to direct traffic as people were slowing down to see what was happening.

It was considered an unusual service at the time since it was for all five children. Mr. and Mrs. Sodder were too overcome with grief to attend. The five remaining Sodder children attended the funeral service including Joe Sodder who had finally arrived home from his Army post. It was noted at the time that the five remaining children were visibly affected. The baby, Sylvia, was held in the arms of her oldest brother, John. The three other children stood beside him during the service.

Reverends W. H. Foglesong and James F. Frame and Charles W. McNutt of the local Methodist, Baptist, and Presbyterian churches, respectively, spoke at the service trying to offer words of comfort and consolation and encouragement for the future.

Wreaths of flowers were arranged and the five wreaths placed at the site the day before with the name of each child were turned, facing the audience. An account states that the site, "made a beautiful cemetery located on a knoll overlooking the highway and that eventually nature will overtake and obliterate all traces of the fire and it will be as other cemeteries."

There was a choir singing "Lead Kindly Light" after which Dr. Frame told the attendees to try and "look up and beyond the trials and troubles of the present to a future which can be made brighter by love, sacrifice, and better living." Dr. Foglesong read the commitment service consisting of "ashes to ashes, dust to dust" using flower petals for the symbols. Reverend McNutt then gave the benediction which concluded the service.[116]

The burial place for the five children on the Sodder property. Markers for the children can be seen in the middle of the photograph. Source: Sodder Family.

When the time came to restore phone service to the temporary Sodder home, the phone company service man surprised the Sodders by telling them that the phone line coming from the utility pole to the old Sodder house had been cut, not burned through. More investigation, mainly by private investigators, located the man who did this in a supposed attempt to stop the fire, believing it was electrical in nature. The man's name was Lonnie Johnson. He was an owner or operator of a local beer joint known as Crass's Park.

The Ladder

On the night of the fire, when George Sodder was attempting to get his children out of their upstairs bedrooms, he found that his ladder was missing from the location where it was normally kept, right beside the Sodder house. Several months after the fire, Mr. Sodder told his wife the ladder had been found about seventy-five feet from the house, "over an embankment."[117]

The area, on the Sodder property, where it was found would have had no reason for the use of a ladder and nobody knew how it could have ended up there. While the initial investigators made little of its disappearance, calling it a minor detail, the Sodder family felt very differently. George Sodder tried to explain many times that the ladder was always in the same spot next to the house.

On the night of the fire, Lonnie Johnson admitted to cutting the phone line. He claimed he did it thinking it was the power line, and that by cutting the power, it would then stop the fire.[118] The phone lines that were cut were nearly 14 feet above the ground and could not have been cut without the aid of a ladder.[119] The ladder was found to be missing when Mr. Sodder tried to use it that night at around 1:30 a.m.

Another incident the night of the fire involving Johnson was the stealing of a set of chain hoists from Mr. Sodders barn. This was no simple task that could have been done quickly or surreptitiously. In Mary Ann Sodder's 1968 statement she stated that the chain hoists had been securely attached to the ceiling since they were used to pull engines out of cars or trucks. It was from here that the hoists would have had to be disconnected that night and this would obviously have taken some time, planning, and possibly some assistance.[120] Add to this, it was the middle of the night, near zero degrees, and a house fire was either raging, or about to be.

Removing the chain blocks was not as simple as may have been previously described in other accounts. The task would have taken time to disconnect them from the garage ceiling, then to "take them down the road," as Johnson described to the State Police in 1952, and "throw them over the embankment," presumably to come back and get them later.[121]

Johnson was well known as a notorious liar, had been arrested several times, and had even lied in his statement to the police. It is known that he lied in another part of the statement about the presence of the deputy sheriff when he was interviewed by a private detective in 1949.[122] And, he lied by omission by not including in his statement that he had cut the phone lines. He also did not admit that he failed to appear for his hearing twice, concerning his arrest for stealing the chain blocks and had to be re-arrested. He did admit to it in a separate hearing.

But again, at one point, he claimed to have cut them with a

pair of pliers and later changed his story and claimed to have done it with a knife.[123] Who carries a pair of pliers with them on Christmas Eve at 1 a.m., coming from a Christmas party and just happens to find the occasion to use them at a house fire?

It is not known if Johnson was asked about using the ladder but there is nothing in his statement indicating that he used it. Perhaps if he did admit to using the ladder, he would then have had to explain how the ladder was found "75 feet away, over the embankment," like he did the chain blocks.

It just seems strange that the phrase "over an embankment" was used by two different people to describe some of the happenings that night. From that, it may be possible to connect the two occurrences with speculation. He did seem to have an opportunity to steal both items that night, but to also steal or move the ladder, he would have had to have lied even more in his statement because he claimed to be with several other people that night. Nothing exists today to confirm if any of the other people at Johnson's midnight Christmas party were questioned.

It would have been normal investigative procedure to try and substantiate someone's story who was as closely associated with the case as Lonnie Johnson. Three of the people who attended the party, Johnson would not offer them to provide an alibi. One of them, was allegedly his wife (name unknown), and another one, Grover or Jeff Adkins, was also arrested and charged for being an accomplice in stealing the Sodder's chain blocks.

It was very odd, that according to newspapers, tens of thousands of West Virginia men were being discharged from the various branches of the military, Adkins chose this time to enlist. Some speculation must be made based on the information available.

Another possibility that could explain what happened to the ladder could be that it had been moved by one of the children. One of the children could have moved the ladder before the fire for some purpose and then later became afraid to admit it for fear they might be somehow blamed for the death of their brothers and sisters. However, this would not explain why it was located some 75 feet away from the house in a ravine. If one of the missing children moved it, it would likely have been either Louis or Maurice. But the question still remains why.

There is yet another possibility about the missing ladder. There is a prevailing theory that the Sodder house was burned as a result of a pre-planned arson because of perceived slights made by Mr. Sodder against the local Italian leadership, or what is also known as a *sgarro*.

Another aspect of this theory is that the fire was intentionally set on Christmas day to maximize the impact of the tragedy. Part of this theory is that either the whole family should die in the fire or at least the children to cause George and Jennie Sodder as much pain as possible, or to satisfy a "vendetta" against the Sodders. If the ladder was moved to inhibit the Sodders from getting to their children, then it worked. This theory could have also included the possibility of disabling the Sodder trucks.

If the arson theory is valid and if the fire was started on the roof as a result of the fireballs being rolled onto the roof described by the late-night bus driver, then it would be logical to assume that the ladder was intentionally removed to keep anyone from being able to fight the fire. And, during the confusion it was used to cut the phone lines to the house so they could not call for help.

The Rubber Object

In the spring of 1946, about three months after the fire, while young Sylvia Sodder was playing, she found a small, strange object that was green and described as possibly being made of plastic or rubber and appeared to be burned on one end.[124] The object was found where it could have rolled off the roof of the Sodder house. If this was correct, it would match up to the eyewitness account of the late-night bus driver who saw "fire balls being rolled onto the house."

One question that remains is that if this individual did see something strange, why didn't he stop and report it or go to the Sodder house and try to ascertain what was going on. This man may have been a passenger on the bus and could not get the driver to stop. But since his name is lost to history, anything here would be speculation.

Thinking the rubber object found by Sylvia had a military appearance, it was shown to a local military official. They reported that the object had the appearance of a military device called a "pineapple or napalm device."[125]

The use of this term by whoever this person was is very unfortunate. "Pineapple" was the name given to the MK 2 grenade by the troops in WWII probably because its shape and texture resembled a pineapple. But the MK 2 device had a cast iron casing and was heavy. It was an explosive device rather than an incendiary that produces fire. Also, the MK 2 made a very loud noise that would have awakened not only Mrs. Sodder, but all the neighbors for miles.

Rubber grenades were not manufactured for the military until after WWII and were called MK 47s. These were used for riot control. They were considered non-lethal. And, in terms of the original description obtained by the Sodders using the term "napalm", the US military did not make a hand-held grenade that used napalm. They did make a tubular-shaped thermite device that was widely used in disabling vehicles or artillery. These devices were made of metal strong enough to contain the heat reaction so the device could do its job. This meant the device got very hot when it was activated. And the metal tube would be left in the debris, but may have been tough to be recognized by a civilian.

One explanation for the presence of this rubber device would be that it was a toy bought for the children for Christmas but if this were the case, it would appear that Mary Ann would have recognized it since she purchased the toys. Or perhaps the toy had been one of the presents still wrapped and waiting to be opened on Christmas morning. But, if this were the case it would seem unusual that it could have survived the fire. Realistically, the plastic object surviving the fire would not be unusual since many other objects were found including a dictionary, a piece of a coat, and a piece of linoleum from the kitchen.

Also, this object could also have been brought in by any one of the hundreds of people who had visited the site in the months following the fire and perhaps just fallen out of their pocket. Like all of the potential physical evidence related to this case, this object has since been lost to time. Without being able to inspect it, any ideas on it are just speculation.

Another fire

In the spring of 1947, Mr. Sodder read about another fire where seven people had died, including small children. While the bodies were burned severely, there were still full skeletal remains of everyone, including a three-month-old infant.[126] It was said that when Mr. Sodder read this story, combined with all the other strange occurrences, that he then decided that his children had not burned up in the fire. Despite exhaustive research, I could find no newspaper articles about this fire.

Chicken Bone Experiments

As time passed, doubt grew in the minds of the Sodders about the death of their children. More and more of the strange occurrences, both before, during, and after the fire, caused the seeds of this doubt to continue to grow.

In her frustration with the local officials who continued to refuse to take the Sodder's repeated requests for a more thorough investigation seriously, Mrs. Sodder felt she had to do something. She had no training in police investigative techniques but she had been raising ten children as well as being the bookkeeper for the family business. So to say that she was intelligent, resourceful, and obviously loaded with common sense is an understatement. She decided to conduct some experiments using the resources and materials she had at her disposal.

Mrs. Sodder began placing animal bones left over from meals into her coal fired kitchen stove. At the time, many families kept the fire in a kitchen stove burning throughout the day. Through all of her experiments, she was never able to cause the bones to turn to ashes. There were always still left in the remains of the fire in her stove.[127]

Try to imagine the tenacity and resolve of this woman. In order to try and find answers regarding the disappearance of five of her children, she has to set aside her grief and pain to recreate the same conditions that may have caused their death.

In some happier events, in June of 1947, George and Jennie's oldest son, John married 18-year-old Margret Meadows from Hico. Later that same year, Joe Sodder married Clarice Louise Buckland from Harewood.[128]

Fireballs

Regarding the "fireballs being rolled onto the roof" there could be a possible explanation. Some descriptions of the fire inside the house describe it as being inside the walls or "running" along the walls. If this was the case and the fire was electrical in nature, it would be "running" inside the walls, all the way from the basement, through to the attic.[129] Then it is possible that what the bus driver saw was the flames shooting out of the walls on the outside of the house, possibly running toward the roof. Of course this is just speculation.

If the intentional arson theory is to be believed, the fireball could have been a typical Molotov cocktail. A glass bottle or jar has a wick inserted and is thrown on its target. But why try to throw the cocktail onto the top of the house? Why not start the fire at ground level?

Five Children and Five Children

The probability that the same five children who stayed up and played were the exact same five who either died or disappeared is difficult to explain away. There were a total of 11 people in the house that night, and using statistical analysis and probability and combinations, the odds of this occurring are roughly 438 to 1.

It makes the odds even more difficult to assume the selection of the children taken was made while they slept in their beds. If the five children who were already downstairs playing were lured out of the house this better explains how they could have been taken without anyone else in the house knowing. They were taken before going to bed.

As part of this possibility, private investigator Troy Simmon's theory on the disappearance of the children could be modified to fit the available facts:

First, the children never went to bed, they were still on the first floor. They may have been lured out of the house by someone who entered the still unlocked doors, perhaps promising them something relating to Christmas, or telling them that the house was on fire. The older boy Maurice may have resisted and was killed. They would have had to have done this very quietly since Mary Ann was still asleep on the couch nearby.

This modified theory could explain the following:

1. Mrs. Sodder said that none of the children's chores were completed.

2. The same five who stayed up playing were the same five who disappeared.

3. That only a few remains were found (if they were actually remains).

4. The bones that were found in the 1949 excavation were found on the opposite end of the house to the boy's bedroom. Maurice may have been taken into another room and killed away from the other four so they would not panic and wake the others in the house. But this is countered by the fact that the bones found in 1949, showed no evidence of ever being exposed to fire. This will be covered in a later chapter.

5. A woman in Fayetteville told Mr. Sodder that four of the children were taken.

6. Mrs. Ida Crutchfield, operator of the Alderson Hotel in Charleston, said that only four of the children were in her hotel on Christmas morning.

7. If the children went to bed, why would they not have awakened Mary Ann from the sofa so she could have gone up to bed as well? Did she normally fall asleep there?

8. If someone came into the house and they either lured the children out of the house, or killed them in their beds and then carried them out, how could that have been done if the children had gone upstairs to sleep and Mary Ann was asleep on the couch?

If the children were still playing downstairs and someone came to the door, they could have quietly and easily lured them out the door with the promise of presents or a party. It could have taken less than ten seconds.

A question that has come up frequently is that if the children were taken, why would they never have come back home once they became adults? One answer is that they may have been shown the burning house and told that everyone died in the fire. Or they could have been taken out of the country. Or, they might have been killed as part of a vendetta.

There is another possibility. In the 1950 Fire Marshal Report, there is a reference to Mr. Sodder being questioned about why he believed the children were still alive. Sodder mentioned that a girl from Fayetteville told him that she had heard that four of the children had been taken out of a window the night of the fire.[130]

One thing about this is that there were two separate bedrooms upstairs. Was the Sodder ladder used to remove the three girls from one bedroom, then moved to the other bedroom and the two boys removed?

Could the movement of the ladder explain the noise that Mrs. Sodder heard shortly before the fire? Doubtful, because she said she listened intently for any additional sounds and heard nothing more. It would seem that if one or more people were in the upstairs bedrooms walking around and carrying five children out of two separate windows, especially if they were resisting, she would have heard more sounds.

John Sodder

There were different newspaper accounts of John Sodder's claim of trying to wake the boys.[131] John later revised his statement to say he thought he heard one of them reply but it may have been Ted who answered him. John later claimed he was misquoted and that he did not see or hear the other boys. John's grandson, Jonathan Bandy also referred to his great-grandfather, George Sodder concerning his beliefs about the circumstances of the fire:

I know he did not blame himself for whatever happened

*to them. He did not want to pursue anything because he did
not want to know if they were killed in the fire or murdered.
He just wanted to believe that they were still out there. He
was also a little scared to look into it. He did not want to put
his family in any possible danger (which I believe he was too
skeptical).*

Late Night Phone Calls

Another mystery is the phone call that Mrs. Sodder received around midnight. An investigation identified the caller as Mrs. Frank Harding, a local resident. When questioned, she at first admitted to making the call saying that she simply called the wrong number. Later, when questioned further by the West Virginia State Police, Mrs. Harding denied even making the call.

This became one of several statement reversals that would later call into question if there was some sort of conspiracy. Some investigators referred to this call as a possible warning to the Sodders. Others have said it was possibly a call just to check and see if the phone lines had been cut yet.

One interesting note was that as the house was burning, people were trying to reach the fire department but failed because the phone operator was not on duty or just didn't respond. The local phone system was the type where an operator had to place the call for you.[132]

Mrs. Harding would have had to have specifically asked the operator for the Sodder home when she called at around 12:30. She could not have dialed a wrong number because the phones did not allow dialing by the caller. They would have had to have told the operator with whom she wanted to speak. Then we are back to the original question, was the call a warning to the Sodders to awaken them before the fire? Or, did the operator, in a sleepy state, place the call to the wrong number herself? Or, was it simply a prank call placed by a bunch of intoxicated locals? If this was the case, would it not discourage you from making a crank call, knowing you had to go through an operator to do it.

There are no records available as to the identity of the phone operator. In 1942, while America was deeply involved in World War II, officials in Fayetteville made plans in the case of an enemy attack. The civil defense program was called the Blackout Committee. It involved many citizens performing various duties including fire watchers, medical staff, public works, food and housing, and emergency phone switchboard operations. The operators named in the August, 1942 *Raleigh Register* newspaper story were Mrs. Helen Smith, Mrs. Ethel Radford, and Miss Lillian Smith.[133] It is possible that one of these operators was on duty at the phone switchboard the night of the Sodder fire. A search for these people through census records and vital statistics yielded no further information.

Regarding the series of phone calls and the fact that some calls were completed and some were not, the following is a summary of the calls known to be made and attempted and approximate times for each:

12:30 a.m.   Phone call to Sodder home (Mrs. Frank Harding). Call was received.

1-1:15 a.m.   At Mary Ann Sodders urging, Mrs. Gar Davis tries to call the Fayetteville Fire Department and cannot get the operator.

1:15-1:30 a.m. Thomas Smith tries to use the phone at Crass's Park beer joint and is told it is out of order.

1:30-2 a.m.   Smith drives on to Fayetteville and reaches Fire Chief Morris and alerts him regarding the fire.

Lonnie Johnson Statement

Jumping forward briefly, most of the discussion about Lonnie Johnson will be in a later chapter. But there were two interesting admissions that Johnson first included in his statement, and then left out of his statement. Johnson, who was around 30 years old,[134] failed to mention that during the night of the fire, he admitted that he cut the phone lines. He then stated in the coroner's inquest hearing that he meant to cut the power lines, thinking that if the fire was electrical in origin, it may help stop it. This, of course, is ridiculous. And, if Johnson had cut the power lines, as he said he intended, he may have inadvertently killed himself. It is hard to understand how he could have not realized that, and it seems to discredit his whole statement.

To me, the obvious question is if you know Johnson is not telling the truth, why not question and investigate further? Why was he carrying wire cutters after a party? Did he get them as a Christmas present? The only other possibility would have been if Johnson was able to climb the pole himself to cut the line. But no statement, report, or letter says this.

If he used the Sodder's ladder, it would have had to have been before George Sodder tried to find it. Which calls into question what time the line was actually disabled. It is known from the Harding call that the phone was working at approximately 12:30. And that by the time the fire department was called, at around 1:30, the line had been cut by Johnson.

Janutolo Statement

One of the most antagonistic, intimidating, and yet prophetic statements alleged to have been made was by Fiorenzo Janutolo about three months before the fire. As already described, after Mr. Sodder declined to buy insurance from Rosser Long, and Janutolo was alleged to have come to Sodder's house and tell him that his house was going to go up in smoke and his children would be destroyed. He also added that Sodder would be paid back for his dirty remarks about Mussolini. In addition, he mentioned the fact that Mr. Sodder would not let Mrs. Sodder sign the papers to settle her father's (Joseph Cipriani) estate.

Mr. Janutolo's comments concerning insurance policies and Benito Mussolini could be interpreted to relate back to some of the organizing principles of the Order of the Sons of Italy in America (OSIA).

In its early years the OSIA was criticized for its support of Italian dictator Benito Mussolini. In the years after WWII, the

67

OSIA officially moved away from its association with Mussolini. But there were still many who believed in what Mussolini stood for and they felt that they would be betraying their homeland if they turned against him. Considering the statement made to Mr. Sodder about his dislike for Mussolini, and who said it to him, this is an important part of the story and will be covered in more depth in a later chapter.

The man who approached the Sodders about buying life insurance was Armistead Rosser Long, but he went by Rosser Long. The 1950 Fire Marshal Report mistakenly referred to him as Russel Long. Long was the president of an insurance agency in Fayetteville by the same name and was highly successful. Rosser Long was very active in local organizations such as the Rotary Club, Ancient Free and Accepted Mason, Lions Club and others. His wife was also active in the Women's Club and other organizations.

In addition to the Longs, there were many other prominent Fayetteville citizens who participated in these organizations. These included:

Cleante Janutolo – The Foreman of the coroner's inquest on the Sodder children's fate.

Fiorenzo Janutolo –George Sodder's former employer as well as the beneficiary of Sodder's home owner's life insurance which was apparently held through the Rosser Long Insurance Agency.

Forest J. Morris – the infamous fire chief who arrived eight hours after the fire was reported. Morris also worked as a bookkeeper for the Janutolo Company.

Carl Vickers, Fayette County Prosecuting Attorney. Vickers is likely to be the Fayette County politician who told George Sodder that he could not "bring a case against people with whom he had to live and eat."[135]

John Duval Schultz – Another member of the Coroner's Inquest. And a man who would later say that no matter what evidence he was shown, he would never change his mind about the children dying in the fire. [136]

In the 1930s through the 1950s, these men ran Fayetteville. There are nearly a thousand articles in local newspapers over a thirty-year period that detail various social events in which these men and their wives all socialized together.

Long approached the Sodders about buying insurance at the recommendation of Fiorenzo Janutolo, but was turned down. When Long reported this back to Janutolo, he was not pleased. Why Janutolo would ever suggest Sodder as a client is still unusual since they did not part well when Mr. Sodder went out on his own. But something did not please Janutolo and as described earlier, he made his feelings clear to Mr. Sodder.

What does this list of names have to do with the Sodder fire and the missing five children? I am not exactly sure. When I started researching each of the names in the reports, I found these men named in countless articles together. They were all community leaders of one sort or another. People of power and authority.

At the time this happened with Long and Janutolo (approximately sixty days before the fire), two of Mr. Sodder's children were still serving in the military. I find it odd that one can be accepted as a candidate for life insurance while fighting overseas in a war.

No explanation can be found regarding Janutolo wanting the settlement of Mr. Cipriani's estate to occur, or why he involved himself in this at all. A review of estate documents for Joe Cipriani would need to be made to see who benefited from the estate being settled.

In terms of pure speculation, it could be that Janutolo was considered an Italian community leader and the Ciprianis went to Janutolo to get some kind of relief, thinking that since he once employed George Sodder, he could convince Sodder to settle the estate, which would be a financial gain to the Ciprianis and Janutolo would then get a cut.

Fiorenzo Janutolo died in 1966 in Montgomery of heart disease.[137] In one newspaper article, I found a quote from his wife, who stated that during their marriage, they had made 22 trips to Italy.

Concerning the Fire Chief, he made many excuses about why the fire truck was not brought out earlier. One of these claims was that most of the fire department were away at war including those who knew how to drive the fire truck. It would seem that the chief of a fire department, even one made up of all volunteers, would take this into account as part of his job. And as a result, the remaining members, including the Chief himself, would be cross-trained on any and all the requirements needed for properly responding to a fire.

Imagine if a fire occurred and the person who knew how to operate the fire hose, or knew how to open a fire hydrant were away. The point is that there should be no excuses for a fire department not responding to a fire two and a half miles from their station, and one that they had been told involved the lives of children.

Fire Chief at the Coroner's Inquest

Try to imagine for a moment that you are the Fire Chief of Fayetteville. You are sitting in a coroner's inquest, which is essentially a court trial, or at least it is supposed to be. Five children have been declared dead and the statement has been made that no verifiable trace of their bodies have been found. Their parents are sitting in the audience brimming with grief and trying to find answers.

As the fire chief, you are not called as a witness in the inquest even though you were one of only three or four firemen who responded and one of about a dozen who searched the debris for human remains. At one point, you were actually in charge of the search. Reports state that the basement of the Sodder house was searched throughout the day and into the evening. You will later claim to have found this "body part" in the evening when no one else was around, after all the other searchers found nothing. You sit there through the inquest and say nothing. There is possibly a second inquest a few days later and you still say nothing.

What would compel you to remain silent through this proceeding? And later, when it finally comes out that you had found this "body part" and you were asked why you had chosen not to say anything about your find, you reply, "because no one asked me."

I have been called as a witness in several court trials and it is a very intimidating situation where you feel a kind of compulsion to tell the truth for fear of the wrath of the law. For fire chief Morris, to be a county official, and a father himself, he chose to say nothing,

Or, if you choose to believe the second report from 1951, there were several people who claimed to have seen the "body part." All totaled, six people are named in that supplemental report claiming to have seen the heart. But in the second coroner's inquest held several days after the fire, again, no one mentioned it.

Chapter 4

The Mass in the Box

Whenever, therefore, people are deceived and form opinions wide of the truth, it is clear that the error has slid into their minds through the medium of certain resemblances to that truth

Socrates

The Sodder family became reluctantly reconciled about the fate of their children until the middle of 1947. It was then that several of the strange events described caused them to change their minds. The final straw was the supposed human organ(s) referred to as a mass, in the cartridge box found buried at the site of the fire.

There are two official versions of what happened. Both of these versions come from reports from the West Virginia State Fire Marshal's office, supposedly written by the same man, C.R. Cobb, Assistant State Fire Marshal. The first version came out in 1950 and the second, approximately eighteen months later, in what was called a supplemental report.

The first version states that initially, nothing was found after the fire was extinguished, but the Fayetteville fire chief admitted he did find a mass somewhat later in the day. The second 1952 report in many ways contradicts the original version. The first version is recounted here:

The story begins the day of the fire. After an hour or two of searching the debris, Fire Chief Morris told the Sodders that no remains could be found. Four days after the fire, Mr. Sodder, as he had been advised by his friends and family, turned the black hole into a cemetery filling it up to ground level with about six feet of fill dirt.

C.R. Cobb, WV Assistant State Fire Marshal. Source: Family Member

Oscar Tinsley, Private Investigator, Source–Charleston Gazette

There were several reasons why this was done and none of them as mysterious as have been described in other accounts. After four days of waiting, Mr. Sodder concluded that the State Fire Marshal was not coming back to investigate further, as he had promised the day of the fire. Also, at the time, they had been convinced that the children had died.

Additionally, the time for the children's funeral was drawing near. The service was held at the site of the fire and Mr. Sodder obviously did not want their friends and family staring into a hole in the ground during the ceremony. So, he filled it to give the spot a semblance of dignity.

According to the 1950 report, around mid-July 1947, about a year and a half after the fire, James Frame heard that the Fire Chief was telling people around town that he actually had found something in the ashes. He was describing the object he found as a human heart. It was reported that Reverend Frame told Chief Morris that "the human heart would resist fire." The idea that the human heart contained some sort of special magical qualities regarding the existence of a human soul which made it resistant to fire was a local colloquial peculiarity.

Morris also told Frame that he had placed the mass in a wooden cartridge box and buried it in the debris. Thinking it was important that the Sodders were aware of this development, Frame contacted the Sodder parents and relayed the conversation he had with Chief Morris.

What is not contained in the 1950 report is that it was around this same time that Mr. and Mrs. Sodder were becoming less and less satisfied with the conclusions regarding the fate of their children. With their growing frustration, around 1947, the Sodders hired a private investigator named Oscar Tinsley from Gauley Bridge who, working with his brother C.C. Tinsley,[138] began exploring leads into the possible kidnapping of the children.

The Sodders had begun to consider having the basement of their old house excavated to search again for any remains. As Mr. Sodder made arrangements for excavating equipment and manpower, his intentions became common knowledge around Fayetteville. Some believe that it was not until Morris learned that the basement was to be re-excavated that he decided to finally tell someone about the existence of the mass in the box. In addition, in a 1948 *Charleston Gazette* story discussing the advantages of further excavation states that most officials saw no benefit to it. It further stated that "Chief Morris is among those holding that point of view."[139]

Upon hearing Reverend Frame's account, the Sodders were puzzled that it was the first they were hearing about it nearly eighteen months after the fire. Secondly, why had Chief Morris not chosen to speak to them directly? What he had told them the morning of the fire was now apparently not true and that some remains had been found. Thirdly, when Mrs. Sodder called chief Morris and asked him to come to the scene and show them where he had buried the "heart," he came but did not make his prescence known.

Mrs. Sodder called him again and Morris told her that he had been to the scene and placed a stake in the ground where the box containing the heart was buried. This seemed very unusual in that the new Sodder home is only about 100 feet from the scene of the fire. Morris had still not bothered to come to the Sodder's door and tell them he was on the property and still did not visit the Sodders personally or discuss the matter with them. Considering the sensitivity of the whole situation, this behavior seems highly unusual.

It is unclear from the 1950 report how many phone calls it took to eventually get Morris to the site for a face-to-face meeting, but it was finally accomplished. Once he was there, Mr. and Mrs. Sodder asked him why he had not told them before that he had found parts of their children when, on the day of the fire he first said that he was unable to find anything. He replied, "I thought I told you, but maybe I didn't." There is nothing that indicates he even offered any kind of apology.

Morris went on to say that he had found the mass sometime after everyone else had left. He said he placed the mass (possibly human remains) on a shelf in the Sodder garage. He further stated that he returned either later that same day, or the next day, he could not remember which, found a wooden box—either a dynamite or cartridge box he found on the site.

He then wrapped the object in brown paper, placed a lid on it and nailed it shut. The box was then placed in the debris of the basement and covered with a piece of tin roofing material. Then on Saturday, December 29th, the site was filled with dirt and the object was covered. In this version of the Fire Marshal's report, Morris was quoted as saying that he was unable to name any person who also saw the mass or the box he placed it in. At the time (in 1947), this was the extent of Morris's explanation.[140]

On the following day, after finally getting Morris to admit to everyone that he had found some remains, George Sodder, private investigator C. C. Tinsley, his brother, O. C. Tinsley (Oscar Cole Tinsley) gathered at the site of the fire. Interestingly absent from the gathering (or left out of the Fire Marshal Report, if they were there) were any officials from the County Sheriff's office, the State Police, the Fire Marshal's office, or any other state regulatory office. They spent the morning digging up the box in question from the place previously identified by Chief Morris by his stick in the ground.

Morris appeared while the digging was being done and by his direction, the crew began digging where he indicated. It was reported that the crew "dug a hole about six feet square and five feet deep" when a box was found. And, as was described, the box was found under a piece of tin roofing at the bottom of the basement.

As described in the 1950 report, "The box was well preserved and identified by Mr. Morris as the box containing the heart or what he had found in the debris and in the same position and general condition as it was when he placed it there." Morris was then asked if what was contained in the box was, to his knowledge, the only remains that had been found after the fire. He indicated that it was.

It is significant that this question and answer indicate that the box was either open when it was found or opened when it was unearthed. In yet another strange action, when the box was removed from the debris, Chief Morris demanded and was given a receipt for the box and its contents by C.C. Tinsley.

The 1950 report states that when Morris was later questioned about the box, he admitted that he did not tell the Sodders or any official about what he had found. He also stated, "the mass in the box is the only thing found by him of similar or like character or that may have been any parts of the missing children."[141]

Regarding the actions of the Fire Chief, in C. R. Cobb's 1950 report is the following statement:

Mr. Morris cannot or will not offer any explanation for his peculiar and apparently secret handling of the matter in not reporting and presenting to the proper persons and authorities and things he may have found in the debris such as has been described. Representatives of this office (State Fire Marshal), an Assistant Prosecuting Attorney, State Police and other officials were present on the site throughout the day and none were informed of the mass he allegedly found and replaced in the debris.

He (Chief Morris) states that he was present at the coroner's inquest and did not make any mention of what he had found, stated in any way of explanation that he was not questioned.[142]

In other words, he is claiming he did not say anything because he was not asked. He did not mention the disposition of the remains of a child after a horrific fire taking five lives, because he had not been asked.

A note included in a later part of the 1950 report states:

Note: the box and mass could have been placed in the ruins where it was found anytime between Tuesday and Saturday before the basement was filled.

If this were the end of the peculiar story of the mass in the box, it would be strange enough and to even the most untrained observer would raise enough questions to warrant further investigation. But the story, and the peculiarities associated with it, would continue.

After removing the box from the ground and having the fire chief verify it was the same one he had buried a year and a half earlier, it was taken by Mr. Sodder and Mr. Tinsley to a funeral home in Montgomery, some twenty-five miles away. Mr. Sodder did not trust anyone in Fayetteville so he took the box to the Gaye Funeral Home to allow the mortician to examine the contents of the box.

The Gaye Funeral Home in the original incorporation papers filed with the state of West Virginia, had two names. The first, of course, was Harold Gay, whose name was originally spelled G-A-Y, no "E" at the end. It was reported that when the funeral home was founded, Mr. Gay felt that to create an establishment called "The Gay Funeral Home" was in bad taste considering the type of business it was and that his potential customers would be in any type of mood, other than a gay or happy one.[143] So, the business was incorporated as the Gaye Funeral Home.

Perhaps even more interesting is that the second name on the incorporation papers of the Gaye Funeral Home was someone already well connected with the Sodder case. Mr. C. I. Dodd, who ran the Dodd Funeral Home in Fayetteville and another person who claimed to have gone through the ashes of the Sodder house fire and said they found nothing.

It is not unusual for men of similar professions to know each other. However, to say that it is nothing more than a coincidence that Dodd is the owner of one funeral home associated with the Sodder case and a part owner of a second associated with the Sodder case, would simply be naive. It may be mere speculation to say that Mr. Sodder, or one of his investigators, was given the name of Harold Gay by C.I. Dodd as a possible out-of-town, independent source to examine the mass and someone who could give an impartial analysis.

Through whatever means or referral, the box did eventually end up in the hands of Harold Gay. Mr. Sodder and Detective Tinsley showed him the box, but Gay was not told what was supposedly inside or the circumstances of the case. Mr. Gay opened the box and examined the contents while the other men watched. He was said to have noted that the mass was wrapped in newspaper and contained in a "cartridge or powder box" and had the lid nailed shut. He also added that the box was wet and appeared to have been underwater.

From his examination, Mr. Gay was able to say that the mass had no bones or other hard objects in it. He further stated that the mass weighed between four or five pounds. Gay then stated that it was his opinion that the object in question was, "definitely a portion of an animal beef liver which he further stated had never been exposed to any heat." He added that the object was well preserved and had not decayed.[144]

The on-lookers were likely stunned at the surprising turn of events. Mr. Tinsley then told Mr. Gay that he wanted to preserve the object for analysis by someone he knew who worked in a lab in

Baltimore, Maryland. The name of this person was not mentioned in the records.

Gay advised Tinsley that the mass should be placed in a refrigerator, but that he did not have one at his establishment. Tinsley then asked if he could keep the object at the funeral home until other arrangements could be made for it and a portion of it could be sent to Baltimore. Gay agreed and is said to have placed the object in jar with embalming fluid, he replaced the lid to the box and placed it outside on the back porch of the funeral home because it had begun to give off an offensive odor.

The men then left the box with Mr. Gay and then went their separate ways. However, Mr. Tinsley did not return the next day as he said he would. Saying the object had an offensive odor that could hurt his business, Mr. Gay instructed his brother, Mr. W. L. Gay to bury the object in the back yard of the funeral home. However, the brother did not do as he was instructed saying he was too busy. He placed the object in a corner of the rear porch, but he never did remember to bury it. This being mid-July, it would be a good assumption that the weather was warm.

Around ten days later, Mr. Tinsley finally called Mr. Gay to tell him he would be coming to collect the box "in a short time." Harold Gay then instructed his brother to dig up the box and place it where Mr. Tinsley could retrieve it when he arrived. But, since his brother had never buried the object in the first place, he recovered it from the place he had secured it and then set it out in the open so Tinsley could easily find it.

Once again, Tinsley did not come to Mr. Gay's funeral home the following day. By the time he did arrive, the box was missing from the porch. Neither of the Gay brothers could remember when it turned up missing. Despite a search of the property and questioning the owners of the funeral home, no trace of the box could be found and it was never seen again.

The fact that the box turned up missing after being placed on the back porch of the funeral home was not as mysterious as has been previously reported over the years. The 1950 report states that between the time that Tinsley last called Mr. Gay and the time that he eventually returned to pick up the box, the regular garbage pick-up service had removed the weekly refuse and possibly picked up the box since it had probably been placed nearby. Considering that it had been sitting out in the heat for more than ten days, it probably gave off a garbage-like odor. At the time in this part of West Virginia, there was no requirement that garbage had to be placed in trash bags as it is the case today.

No records exist to explain why Tinsley took so long to return to the Gaye funeral home. Perhaps if he had acted a little more expeditiously one of the strangest aspects of this case might have been explained. This would have proved the Fire Chief had misled the investigation into the death of the Sodder children.

If this had been proven, and the Fire Chief forced to admit his true actions, it could have been the beginning of the collapse of a series of inconsistencies and story reversals. But as it stands, the mass in the box is probably buried under tons of garbage in the old Montgomery city dump.

Several sources state that Tinsley did remove a piece of the mass and sent it to his contact in Baltimore for analysis. He later stated that this same person, whom he never chose to identify, corresponded with him and confirmed Mr. Gay's identification of the mass as a beef liver.[145] There is also a reference in the 1950 report that quotes Tinsley as saying:

C. C. Tinsley, states that he, upon request of Mr. Sodder conducted the investigation in the beginning. He states that he intended to take the mass and the box in question to a friend of his for examination and analysis. He states that he did not notify the proper state and County officials because of a lack of faith in them.

Version Two

The second version of the official story of the mass in the box comes primarily from a supplemental report by the State Fire Marshal's office filed on January 25th, 1952.[146]

The reason a second report was prepared is unclear but could have been due to Mr. Sodder's insistence that the case be reopened after the 1949 excavation of the site and the lack of human remains found at that time, as well as other strange occurrences and incidents that had happened both before and after the fire.

Another possible reason a second report was written could have been to clarify the statements made previously by certain individuals or to hear from some witnesses who had not been interviewed for the 1950 report, or even for the initial West Virginia State Police report. And, one of the central questions related to this case is again, why people changed or embellished their stories in relation to this case.

In the 1952 report, Reverend James Frame now claimed that on the morning of the fire after he had led the Sodder family in prayer, one of the searchers going through the debris handed him an internal organ which he described as about the size of his fist. He further stated that it appeared to him to be part of a lung and it was water-logged. He then placed the object on a section of stove pipe laying nearby.

Mr. Carl Vickers, the prosecuting attorney, was also interviewed for the 1952 report where he stated he also saw a "mass of internal organs." He further stated that he instructed Fire Chief Morris to "dispose of the remains." Vickers was also interviewed by the *Charleston Gazette* in 1948. Vickers stated in this article that he saw remains on the morning of the fire.[147] These are obvious and significant differences between these two reports prepared by the same man, approximately eighteen months apart.

In the 1952 report, Fire Chief Morris once again claimed to have put the mass in a cartridge box and deposited it in the debris under a piece of tin roofing. One part of Morris's 1952 version is that now he also claims that when the box was to be opened it was still wet. This part of the story was also confirmed by Mr. Gay when he later examined it in Montgomery several hours later that same day. It is impossible to tell if Morris added this detail later to make his statement match up with those of others included in the new report.

Another difference between the two reports in relation to Morris is that the writer of the 1952 report claims that he (Morris) "poured water on the fire for two hours before being able to search for the remains of the children," twice the amount of estimated time that he gave in the 1950 report. Also, Morris claims that when he and his department members arrived at 8 a.m., the basement was a glowing bed of embers. In the 1952 report, Reverend Frame, who apparently arrived at the scene before water was applied to the fire, described the basement as "a raging inferno."

It should be again pointed out that in the 1950 report, the original searchers of the debris were each interviewed and no one admitted to having seen anything that could be classified as human remains.

During this time, if the story in the 1952 report were true, all Morris had to do was mention that Vickers had told him to dispose of the mass as described in the 1952 report. And, if this was true, when questions were raised, all Vickers had to do was confirm Morris's story. But from the time of the fire in 1945, through to the issuance of the 1950 report, up until the 1952 report, some seven years after the fire, it appears that Morris said nothing to indicate a change in his initial story.

Common sense would indicate that possibly the author of the two different reports, separated by eighteen months, was either mistaken or had been given false information. But this is unlikely in the context of a thorough investigation, especially considering that the lives of five children had been lost and considering the 1950 report repeatedly indicated there had been no remains of the children found. These are not minor details.

Accounts of Morris describe him as arrogant, hard-headed and bossy. F. J. Morris, in addition to being the chief of the local fire department, was a veteran, a leader of the local VFW post,[148] a past-master of the Fayetteville Masonic Lodge, and a captain of the Fayetteville Civic Defense League.[149] He was also a community leader during the Second World War and in charge of city-wide black-out drills that served to prepare Fayetteville in the event of an enemy air attack.[150] Morris was accustomed to being in leadership roles and could have been of the mind that since he was a local government official with some level of importance, he did not owe anyone any kind of explanation and let it go at that.

Morris simply refused to speak of it for his own reasons, at least officially. He did state that he did talk to his friends about it.

When viewed from this context, Morris's silence is not so strange but it is what in some cultures would be considered the only acceptable action. Either way, remaining silent did not enhance his credibility with the Sodder family.

Also, there is a direct contradiction here. The 1950 report states that the county prosecutor was present the morning of the fire and saw nothing. However, In the 1952 report, it states:

> *Mr. Carl B. Vickers, Prosecuting Attorney for Fayette County, was interviewed at his office in Fayetteville on 1-25-52 and he states that he saw the mass of internal organs recovered from the debris and instructed Mr. F. J. Morris, Volunteer Fire Chief, from Fayetteville, West Virginia, to dispose of the remains,*[151]

The differences in these two reports are not trivial details that do not lend any relevance to key individuals connected to this case:

- Whether or not human remains were, in fact, found at the site the day of the fire.

- Why an object, later identified by several people, as a beef liver, was purposely buried in the ashes of the Sodder house by the Fire Chief and initially reported to be human.

- Why this object, if it was human, was not turned over to a funeral home or other proper authorities.

- Why officials changed their stories in conjunction with these facts, or they simply left important facts out of the official reports either because they did not have a way to explain them or they chose not to investigate further because of what they may uncover.

- They did not think it was worth the time and effort to make a more thorough investigation because the Sodders were Italian immigrants.

- Why were the parents not told about what was found? If your children were dead, you need to know. If there were no remains in the ashes of a fire, you should be told about that too. There was no need to place an object that was not human in the ashes and claim something was found.

There has to be a reason why Morris did not explain this. One of the obvious reasons is that the particular explanation given in the 1952 report did not exist in 1950. It was conjured up in the time following the initial report. The reasons could have been because initially, the explanation offered by the first report was thought to be enough to satisfy those involved. In other words, the answers were obvious, even though every little detail was not thoroughly explained, like why there were no bones of the children remaining. But as the Sodders began to ask questions, hire private investigators, who, in turn, began contacting newspapers and magazines, more and more light was shed on the case and something had to be done.

The private investigators actually began to uncover information that the police and fire marshal had either missed or ignored. The original half-baked explanations in the various reports were not going to work anymore. Even if they had been developed for no other reason but to cover up a shoddy, half-baked investigation. So they had to come up with something else. The trouble is, someone did not destroy the original 1950 fire marshal report as they should have. Either that, or they did not know what it had to say and they couldn't count on someone to alter the original report to match the new explanation. Or, did they make an attempt?

Modified Report

During the author's research, something odd was discovered about the 1950 report. There are two different versions of the same report. The author originally obtained a copy of the 1950 report in 1992 from an unnamed source and then received a second copy during the writing of this book from a separate source. Upon examination of the second copy, differences were noted in terms of, 1) the number of pages, 2) several corrected typographical errors, 3) paragraph spacing, and 4) possibly a different typewriter font (which means at this time in history, a different typewriter).

The following two pictures are snippets of two different versions of the original 1950 report. In the first version, included in a paragraph located on page 11, there is the phrase "no direct evidence."

Next, the same paragraph is located on page 10 of a different version of the same report.

> The cause of the fire has not been determined. There is no direct evidence or facts that would definitely establish the fire as incendiarism. The fire may have been of accidental origin.

> The cause of the fire has not been determined. There is no direct evidence or facts that would definitely established the fire as incendeerism. The fire may have been of accidental origin.

Differences between the two versions of the 1950 Fire Marshal Report

It can be seen on the top picture, the term "no direct evidence" appears on the first line but it carries over to the next line in the following picture.[152] And again, in the top picture, approximately half of the next sentence is on the middle line and continues on to the third line. Whereas in the next picture, it is all on the bottom line. This, along with the other points I cited, leads me to believe the various versions of this report have been retyped.

What could be a reason why someone would take this report, retype it, and it still seemingly be the same report as when they began? One reason could be that an agency may have loaned the original report to another agency and the second one wanted to make a reproduction of it. In the early 1950s in rural West Virginia, many smaller offices had no method of reproducing reports except re-typing them or sending them away to be reproduced.

There is evidence to show this and several other documents were shared among the several agencies involved. This included state and United States senators, congressmen, governors, and even U. S. Presidents. When many of these officials were contacted by the Sodders and asked to look into the case for them, the officials usually began their inquiries by contacting either the West Virginia State Police or the State Fire Marshal's Office for information. This may have resulted in these officials reproducing the report in some way that may have included retyping it.

A more sinister explanation is that the reports were re-typed to cover up something originally included in them that later, someone decided should be removed. Conversely, it could have been to add details that had been left out of the first report, and now that the Sodders were asking legitimate questions, some answers had to be provided.

There are other surreptitious possibilities as to why the report was retyped but what would have been accomplished by doing this in the form it ended up for any other reason is unclear. If it was retyped to add or omit certain facts that could change the complexion of the case, only the person who did the retyping, or directed it to be done, would know that.

One thing that is clear is that during the writing of this book, a Freedom of Information Act Request to the Fire Marshal's Office for copies of files related to the Sodder case was filed and the author was told that officially, the Fire Marshal no longer has any files related to the case in their archives. It brings to mind, considering all the reports, documents, letters, etc, that were available at one point in history and are now officially gone, what else was available at one time but was never revealed.

The confusing differences between the two reports could be attributed to someone having a conversation with one or more of Mr. Sodder's private detectives, then, later, when the authorities follow up with the same person, they get a different answer. I believe the differences were created by the writers to intentionally create confusion and to make Mr. Sodders private detectives look bad so they would stop the investigation. This theme can be seen in many letters and reports from both the State Police and Fire Marshal's Office.[153] The state and local officials had already made up their minds that the children had died and that was that. To change that position could have been embarrassing to some. Also keep in mind that it was assumed at the time that none of the official reports or correspondence related to the case would ever be seen by the public. This was all before the Freedom of Information Act.

Reverend Frame

Another one of the figures in the case whose statements seem to conflict in relation to the two Fire Marshal Reports is Reverend James Frame of the Fayetteville Baptist Church. In the 1950 version, he is mentioned as being at the property the morning of the fire offering comfort. He is later mentioned as the one who in 1947, Fire Chief Morris tells that he did find something in the debris. The 1950 report states that Frame contacted the Sodders and told them what Morris had said. And, according to that version of the report, that conversation set into motion the events previously described regarding discovery of the mass in the box.

In his statement to the state police, C.I. Dodd, a Fayetteville mortician, stated that he received a phone call from Rev. Frame saying that they (the searchers) had found something in the debris that Dodd should come and deal with.[154] Dodd assumed that for Frame to call him, what must have been found was human remains. But, when Dodd arrived with a hearse to transport what was found back to his funeral home, he was told there was nothing to transport.

However, in the 1952 report, Frame denied making any call to Dodd that morning. He also denied making a call to a neighbor of the Sodders, Mrs. Garfield Davis, where he was supposed to have told her to put the object that was found on ice. The neighbor's statement was also taken for the 1952 report and she denied receiving any phone call from Frame. This had all been asserted by Mrs. Sodder herself, in which she stated that she had received the information from Detective Troy Simmons. This is all very strange because it is obvious that any claims regarding various phone calls or objects that may have been found, or for that matter, not found, would be checked by the police and therefore, why would someone lie about it?

Whatever version of Frame's statement is to be believed, it is well documented that George Sodder was very unhappy with Frame. In a pamphlet published by Mr. Sodder in 1953, around the same time he erected the first billboard, he asks the same questions as to why Frames' statements differ between the two reports.[155] There is no record of any reply to Mr. Sodder's questions. While this document is obviously Mr. Sodder's side of the story, the reader can draw their own conclusions regarding this information.

There were also several other statements taken by the State Police and private investigators. C. E. Dodd, the son of C. I. Dodd, gave a statement 17 days after the one given by his father, in which he states that when driving to visit his father for Christmas, he passed the site where the Sodder fire had occurred hours before. He also stated that he and his father returned to the site around 10:30 or 11 a.m. but was not prompted by any phone call.[156] This statement makes it obvious that the question of whether or not a phone call had occurred, or if the trip to the Sodder Fire site was prompted by a phone call, had already been discussed by those conducting the interview.

The other question here is why C. E. Dodd's statement directly conflicts with that of his father concerning the alleged phone call. And, again, why was this so significant, that it was repeatedly brought up in police statements?

This whole conflict surrounding the Frame phone call may have been just a way to discredit Sodders private investigator, Troy Simmons, who was raising questions and keeping the case alive.[157] The earliest mention of the phone call came from a statement from Mrs. Sodder in which she says she first heard about Frame's call from Simmons.

A simpler possibility could be that Simmons lied about the call to keep the case alive and Mr. Sodder paying his bill. This was alleged by the police and the Fire Marshal in numerous reports. They felt Simmons, and the many other private investigators were unfairly taking advantage of the Sodders' emotional state and willingness to spend any amount of money, just to find a trace of their children.

But, Simmons alleged that Frame made a phone call about the possibility of someone finding remains of the children. This would obviously indicate that if remains had been found that one or more of the children died in the fire and had not been kidnapped as earlier private investigators had claimed. The kidnapping scenario is what was keeping the case alive and made it financially viable for the multitude of investigators. So, for Simmons to take the dangerous step of lying to authorities about something as simple and easy to investigate as a phone call seems implausible. It would seem that he would rather pick something that served his own financial interests, instead of something that did the opposite. This alone is conclusive enough to say that Simmons did not lie about Frame's phone call.

Conclusions

All descriptions of the mass claim that it had not been exposed to fire. A liver or other organ that had been exposed to fire should be readily identifiable as opposed to one that had not. What constituted the identification of the mass in the box as a "beef liver?" Which, if it was an animal liver, it had to be a small section of one rather than the whole thing. This mass only weighed about three to four pounds. A whole cow liver weighs about thirty-five pounds. The identification of the mass as a beef liver comes from three different sources separated by two states.

The first source is a little questionable. The 1950 report, which very carefully chronicles the discovery of the mass, all the way through to where it was lost, does not mention if the box was immediately opened and examined. Several newspaper and magazine stories do describe the box being opened when it was dug up but do not describe the contents other than to say they appear to be wet and fresh.

The second identification is from Harold Gay, funeral home owner. As far as Gay's qualifications, he was a mortician for many years and saw many bodies. He was sure enough of his identification to be willing to give a sworn statement.

The third identification comes from an individual who worked at a lab in a hospital in Baltimore. Private Investigator George Swain knew this person and sent a section of the mass to him for identification and analysis. However, Swain refused to identify this person other than saying he was very qualified to make the necessary determination.[158]

The informal analysis may create more questions than it resolves. Assuming the object found in the box was placed there

90

by Morris, and it was a beef liver, the central question is obviously why would Morris do this? What would he hope to accomplish with this deception? If the children's remains were not in the debris of the fire, was this piece of liver brought to the site in order to intentionally convince those who were there, that the children did die there? Again, why? What would be the motivation to do this?

Assume that everyone's conclusions about the mass were true. It was a piece of beef liver and had not been exposed to fire. Think for a minute what that means. Someone, probably Morris, brought a piece of liver to the location of the fire. If it was some kind of symbol about taking away the good food of life and leaving the Sodders with just liver, why not tell them about it to make it hurt more? Or, was it a symbol for the people who had done this, rather than for the Sodders? They knew it was there and what they had directed to be done. So it gave them the sense of winning the vendetta. Kind of a trophy.

Motivation

Cui bono is a Latin phrase that means "to whose benefit?" It is commonly used to suggest that the person or people guilty of committing a crime may be found among those who have something to gain. But the party that benefits may not always be obvious or may have successfully diverted attention to a scapegoat.

The Sodder fire may be a mixture of all of these. There may be no traditional motive here. This could be what the police and Fire Marshal missed the whole time. They were looking for an accident, robbery, simple arson, and may have put little to no emphasis on revenge. In this case, in terms of a financial motive, there was no life insurance on the Sodders or their children. There was insurance on the house but was payable to the man who had co-signed the loan. They were not looking for someone who was trying to make someone else show respect.

This would also have to assume that the person who arranged for the burning of the house to be the same one who ordered the removal of the children. The initial implication is that there are two separate crimes involved here. Since the Fire Chief admitted to placing the object into the box and burying it at the site of the fire, it has to be assumed that he is part of the crime. But, again, it comes back to motivation. If the motive is to benefit in some way, how does that apply here?

On his part, it would have to come back to money in some form. Another possible motivating factor would be if he were being blackmailed or threatened into participating. Obviously, there is no evidence available today to justify a claim such as this. Here, over seventy years later, there is only circumstantial speculation. All that is available are the multiple strange actions of the Fire Chief in connection to this case. Namely:

1. Waiting eight hours to respond to the first notification of a fire at the Sodder home. Then, offering multiple excuses as to why it took so long to respond.

2. Supposedly finding some remains in the fire debris but then specifically telling the Sodders that nothing had been found.

3. The question of this object turning out to be an animal liver rather than human remains which had to have been placed there by Morris.

4. When the box was removed, Chief Morris demanded a receipt for the object that was uncovered, almost as if he felt it belonged to him.

5. Morris's failure, or refusal, to explain his actions to any officials, at any of the Sodder inquests, or meetings of any kind. Almost like it is no one else's business.

Another possibility would be if Morris took these steps to create the illusion of human remains being in the debris. Again, why? Morris told his Masonic Lodge brother, James Frame about the remains being found. It could be that Morris did this knowing that Frame would tell the Sodders. By doing this it would either convince the Sodders that the children did die in the fire and they would then not look any further. Or he did it, to somehow give them comfort. But again, he never mentioned finding what he called "human remains" to the Sodders. So they received no comfort from Morris's actions.

With all other explanations set aside, and in all fairness, Morris may have known nothing as to the "why" he was told to place the liver in the ashes. He may have just been told to do it and say nothing about it, which he certainly did for several years.

Still another aspect about the mass that comes from the 1950 report on page 15:

He (Morris) states that he found the mass (liver) in question sometime in the evening.[159]

At this time of year it was dark in the "evening" (after 6 p.m.). Morris found this object in the dark?

There are just too many contradictions in all of the written descriptions and accounts surrounding the mass (liver). There is no single, steady, fluid account of the discovery of the mass. There are many perspectives documented at various times. But there is just something about the entire story that rings untrue. Some kind of planned deception. The liver placed in the fire debris is just something I have tried and I cannot get past.

Another factor that limits where the liver came from comes from Mrs. Sodder, herself. In the 1952 report, she is quoted as saying:

Mrs. Sodder states that she had no such meats or animal organs in her house. She also states they sold their hogs and cow on foot after the fire and had not butchered any animals previous to the fire.[160]

Chapter 5

The Excavation

"It was the most completely burned-up place that I have seen in the course of my 18 years with the fire department"

Forest Judson Morris, Charleston Gazette, 11/14/1948

The Girl from New York

Another episode in the mystery occurred in the early months of 1949. It began with a magazine article that Mrs. Sodder saw about a young girl's beginner ballet class in New York City sponsored by the New York Children's Aid Society.[161] The photo showed several young girls practicing ballet. The Sodder's immediately recognized their daughter. Mr. Sodder was said to have exclaimed, "That's Sis," referring to Betty Sodder, the youngest of their five missing children.[162] (It is assumed the girl in question is the one shown in the right side of the foreground).

The picture in question of the New York Children's Aid Society Ballet Class. (Source is the Internet)

Two days after seeing the photograph and making some initial inquiries, Mr. Sodder boarded a train for the trip to New York City. He went by himself and without any identification that could prove who he was. Remember this was at a time when there were no photographs on driver's licenses and most everything was paid for in cash.

Mr. Sodder was said to have gone to the offices of the magazine to learn more about the story. He was given the name of the photographer who, in turn, gave him details about the location where the photos were taken. One version of this story says that upon reaching the building where the ballet class was held, Mr. Sodder asked to see the girl he saw in the picture. However, since he had no identification and his request was considered strange, the teacher of the class refused to name the girl.[163]

Another, more questionable source says that with the aid of the photographer, he somehow made it to the home of the girl's parents in Washington Heights. After explaining his reasons for being there, the parents produced a copy of the young girl's birth certificate. After seeing that the child truly belonged to the New York parents' Mr. Sodder was said to have told them, "I'm sorry I troubled you," and was ready to leave. At this point, the mother woke her young daughter and introduced her to Mr. Sodder. It was a confirmation that he had been mistaken.[164]

While this is an interesting sidebar to the story and has been retold by nearly every writer of this story, it, never-the-less has been discounted, almost from the time it occurred. Every assurance was given to Mr. Sodder that the young girl was not one of the missing children and he accepted it.

Asking for Help

George and Jenny Sodder had gradually become convinced their children did not die in the fire. They also believed the fire was intentional, and that the children had possibly been kidnapped as part of a vendetta against the family.

At one point in the late 1940s, Mr. Sodder was employing two private detectives at the same time to chase down clues as to the whereabouts of the children. The first was Oscar Tinsley from Gauley Bridge and the other was George Swain from the American Detective Agency. A *Charleston Gazette* newspaper article from November 1948 contains statements from both detectives about their theories.[165] Swain was noted in several official reports as seeking the help of the West Virginia State Police and the State Fire Marshal's Office. According to the 1950 report from the Fire Marshal's office, George Swain had visited their office several times, sometimes with Mr. or Mrs. Sodder.

In February of 1949, C. A. Raper requested a copy of the WV State Police Report prepared weeks after the fire in 1946. A surviving transmittal letter sending the report (apparently the only copy) back to the State Police states that the report "served our purpose."[166] The possible significance of this letter showing the Fire Marshal borrowing the State Police report is that the Fire Marshal did not do what he said he would when the fire first happened.

The State Police were the first law enforcement agency on the scene and had already begun preparing their report when the Fire Marshal arrived. Raper stated then that he would not prepare a report since the State Police were well underway with the investigation.[167]

This 1949 letter shows that either the Fire Marshal did not follow up with the State Police as he said he would around the time of the fire or that he perhaps wanted to compare his own report with that of the State Police. Either way, it is evident that Raper is reviewing the case with all of the publicity in the newspapers at this particular time.

In early 1949, the Fire Marshal's Office had apparently grown tired of Swain's visits and told him so. In the 1950 report it says,

> *On Swain's fifth visit to the Fire Marshal's Department, he was informed that if he had any information that pertained to the solution of the case in question, he was to make a report giving all the information and that if he had such information and did not make the report, he would be cited for withholding evidence. After this, Mr. Swain's visits ceased, for a while.[168] He did not stop investigating, he just stopped sharing his information with the Fire Marshal's office.*

97

Undaunted, the Sodders continued to look for help and eventually moved up to the West Virginia Governor's office as well as the sitting West Virginia Senators Harley Kilgore and Matthew Neely.[169]

Probably after consulting with each other, both of these senators offer the Sodders the most valuable resource they had at their disposal. They referred the matter to the FBI, since it was being proposed that kidnapping was involved. But FBI director J. Edgar Hoover called the case a local one and out of the jurisdiction of the FBI. But in a letter to Senator Kilgore, he did offer the availability of the FBI laboratory, "If the scientific examination of any evidence in this connection is desired by local authorities, I will be happy, of course to make available the facilities of the FBI laboratory, and if there is any other way within the scope of our authority in which we can assist local police officials we will be very glad to do so."[170]

The FBI

The lack of involvement of the FBI is highly significant because if they had become involved early on, it is much more likely that any evidence or potential witnesses may have been brought out.

But the FBI did not become involved in the early stages of the case because:

- They were not invited to participate by local officials.

- George Sodder received no ransom note, which in the eyes of the FBI was key to defining the case as a kidnapping.

- When the Sodders contacted the FBI and they then questioned the local officials, instead of investigating the case independently, they were referred to the Fire Marshal who told them there was no merit to the Sodders claims.

- And finally, there was not enough publicity to bolster the reputation of the Bureau and its power-hungry director.

Thomas Brophy

The first recognized expert contacted by Detective Swain was retired New York City Chief Fire Marshal, Thomas Brophy. Brophy was considered a legend in New York in the field of fire investigation.

Swain made the trip to New York and visited with Brophy at his home. After hearing the details of the case, Brophy agreed to come to Fayetteville, but he also estimated that for him to do so, it would cost approximately $125 a day for him and an assistant. Swain estimated that Brophy would be able to make his evaluation in Fayetteville in no more than three days, but to be conservative, he set out to raise $1,000.

At the time, the Sodders did not have enough money to pay for an excavation of this magnitude, so a Sodder Fund was created by Dewey E. S. Kuhn of Charleston, a concerned citizen who read of their plight in the *Charleston Gazette*. Although Mr. Sodder was not delighted about having to resort to what he assessed to be charity, he nevertheless was willing to try. "We are willing to do almost anything toward locating the children," Mr. Sodder said in 1949.[171]

The Sodder Fund

During the spring of 1949, several citizens wrote to the *Charleston Gazette* expressing their feelings regarding the case and making small contributions:

> *Let's solve this mystery by starting a fund for the Sodders to raise approximately $1,500 to finance a thorough investigation of the case by Thomas P. Brophy of New York City. Providing these children are living and can be found this idea is certainly worth a little consideration. Just try to imagine the joy which would be experienced this Christmas which has been missing for the past three, if their children are recovered.[172]*
>
> *Lawrence R. Smith*

*I believe with all my heart they need a helping hand from
every citizen of West Virginia. We don't have much of this
world's goods. But we have our children that we love and we
sympathize with the Sodder family so much that I am sending
our contribution to the fund for the service of an able man like
Mr. Brophy.*[173]

Mr. and Mrs. W. M. Price

*I think that anyone in a position to help should do so. So
that the anxious hearts of the Sodder's might be relieved. It is
a burden hard for them to bear. It is a fate worse than death
and I only hope and pray that everyone will help. Every donor
will receive his reward from God.*[174]

Mrs. George D. Miller

But, by May 1949, the Sodder fund had only raised about
$51.[175] The rest of the summer was spent on trying to raise additional funds but by August, contributions had all but stopped.

Perhaps the most unfortunate aspect of this part of the case is
that being a nationally recognized expert, Brophy's involvement
would have most likely produced a verifiable solution of some
sort, at least from the standpoint of the fire being arson or not. His
opinion would likely have been accepted by the Sodders and the
officials as well. If he had concluded that the fire was arson, and
that the lack of remains of the children indicated they were not in
the house at the time of the fire, it could possibly have forced state
and local officials to begin a serious investigation into the case.

With Brophy's refusal to become involved, Detective's Swain
and Hill once again contacted the Smithsonian and informed them
of the situation. They attempted to locate the services of a second
expert and they were eventually put in touch with Dr. Oscar Hunter. Dr. Hunter became involved and was present at the excavation
in August 1949 along with an agent from the William Burns Detective Agency.

The Excavation

Mr. Sodder was determined to find answers, and a new excavation began around 8 a.m. on Thursday, August 18, 1949, and lasted until about 7 p.m. A newspaper article from the time listed about 14 diggers. Some were employees of Mr. Sodder's trucking business, as well as some neighbors and friends. Also present were Earl W. Pierce, Assistant Chief of the Fire Department at the U.S Naval Ordnance Center in South Charleston, and three Charleston firemen, Joseph P. Huddleston, Mike Cunningham, and Harold C. Pierce. Detective George Swain and two of his assistants, Frank Hill and C.W. Mooney were there.

Dr. Hunter arrived in the early afternoon. He had said when he arrived at the site that, "according to information furnished to him about the case, that there is a good possibility that all of the bones were not destroyed if the children were victims of the almost three-year-old fire." Mr. Sodders two oldest sons, John and Joe, assisted with the digging. Mr. Sodder was overseeing the whole excavation while his wife dropped by occasionally.

Reports state that a large scoop had been attached to the end of a tractor and by using this scoop, large amounts of material could be removed in a short amount of time. It is assumed this method would be used for the fill dirt where no remains were anticipated to be found.[176] Also, in preparation for the excavation, it had been suggested that large sieves be prepared so as to not miss any small pieces. Later, when Dr. Hunter arrived, he stated that these "would not be necessary because they would find large bones if any are there."

When Fire Marshal Raper arrived, he was quoted as saying that he agreed with re-investigating the site in order to help give the Sodders some answers, but he strongly disagreed with the methods being used. The mechanical excavator could have caused some smaller items to be missed. Raper was quoted in the *Charleston Gazette* as saying, "All of the dirt should have been slowly and carefully removed with hand tools," and that "every shovel full of dirt should have been sifted and checked."

George Sodder, in a letter later written to the head of the West Virginia State Police said Raper "didn't like their method of digging."[177] In his defense, it would seem that Mr. Sodder was given conflicting instructions in how to prepare for and conduct the excavation. This may explain Dr. Hunter's quote in the newspaper

101

about the number of bones they were expecting to find. It seems based on what they found that he was already second guessing him, telling the diggers that they would not need the sieves.[178]

A photograph from the day of the dig shows about eight people in the foundation digging and about ten people looking on. Another photograph shows Dr. Hunter holding the bones that were discovered with Mr. Sodder, Fire Marshal Raper, and others looking on. Reporters and a photographer from the *Charleston Gazette* were also on site.

George Sodder, Earl Pierce, and three unidentified men (All Standing) excavating the family's basement. (Source-Charleston Gazette)

It is well documented by several sources that many items were found during the search that would indicate the fire was not as hot or intense as had been reported earlier. The searchers found, scorched coins, several pieces of tire inner tube, pieces of roofing material (the asphalt shingles, not the tin roofing), part of a dictionary normally kept in an upstairs bedroom, Pieces of linoleum flooring, un-melted glass jars and bottles, pieces of furniture upholstery, and a piece of a coat belonging to Mrs. Sodder.[179] Finding coins and other small items show the searchers, at least some of them, were being very careful and diligent in their work.

C. A. Raper, Earl Pierce, and Smithsonian Pathologist, Oscar Hunter examine human bones found during the 1949 excavation. (Source - Charleston Gazette)

After several hours of digging, bones were found in two different locations. In the northeast corner, a total of eight pieces of bone were found. The pathologist concluded rather quickly that these eight pieces had the characteristics of animal bones. Several of them were cut in sections and he concluded that they, "have all the aspects and appearance of the thoracic vertebrae of animals together with a few ribs and one femur."

In the southeast corner of the house, a total of six bones were discovered. Two of these bones were small fragments that were later determined to be the leg bones of a chicken. But again, it is important to note that while these were animal bones, they were also described by the pathologist as being "fragile long bones" that had survived the fire. In this same location, four other bones were found that were immediately identified as human bones by Dr. Hunter.

Once these human bones were found, the area where they were located was thoroughly searched for others but no more were found.[180] It is noted in the 1950 report that once the human bones had been found, George Sodder stopped all further digging.[181] A newspaper article of August 19, 1949, states that this order by Mr. Sodder was given only after considerable excavation. Mr. Sodder was then quoted as saying, "There would be no more digging," and this was only said due to the fact it was the end of the day and the foundation had been thoroughly searched.[182]

Dr. Hunter said he considered the search a very thorough one and expressed surprise that it revealed such an "amazing scarcity" of bones. He further said that it was most unusual that no skulls or pelvic bones were found in the ashes of a fire that apparently had insufficient heat and duration to consume them. He said that he was certain that the quality of the soil would not cause decomposition during the time they would have been underground.[183]

Dr. Hunter also said that although there was little doubt that the four vertebrae bones were of human origin, he would confirm this once he returned to his laboratory in Washington. He also said that if it was necessary, he would be able to determine the approximate age of the person.[184]

Once he returned to the Smithsonian Institute, Dr. Hunter examined the bones and issued his report. The following is a reprint of the major portion of the pathologist's report.[185]

In the excavation, bones were found in the northeast corner of the basement and in the southwest corner of the basement. In the northeast corner eight fragments of bone were found. All of these were cut in sections and have all the aspects and appearance of the thoracic vertebrae of animals together with a few ribs and one femur.

In the southeast corner of the house 6 bones were found 2 of which are fragments. These 2 fragments are fragile long bones which have the aspect of a chicken's femur. In this same location, however, there were 4 bones which are definitely identified as human bones. These 4 consist of lumbar vertebrae. They all belong to the same individual and their articulations fit precisely, one with the other. These 4 vertebrae are discolored by the earth and adjacent metallic substances. They show no evidence of charring, however, except perhaps for deposition of charred material on the surface of the bones. The bones themselves, however, show no evidence of having been burned. The uppermost vertebrae and the second vertebrae show some chipping of the dorsal spine and lateral processes.

Conclusions:
From studying these bones it can be unequivocally stated that these bones are identical with known human bones of the age group 14-15 years and it is probable, with room for very little doubt, that they belong to a child of this age.
The bones show no evidence of actual charring which would indicate that they were not free within the fire and subject to high temperature. They, of course, could have been in the fire covered by flesh and consequently insulated from the higher temperature associated with the fire.

The question immediately arises as to why these bones should be found without the associated bones of the remaining portions of the skeleton and consequently it would lead one to believe that the remaining portion of the skeleton necessitates the conclusion that they were forcibly removed from the remaining portion of the skeleton. Such a forcible dismemberment during life or even after a body has been subject to fire of the intensity described would necessitate a considerable amount of force and dexterity on the part of an individual planning such a dismemberment.

It would seem more reasonable that the remaining bones had been removed from the skeleton subsequent to the death of the individual at a time when the interlacing ligaments and fibrous tissue had undergone degeneration. This feature, therefore, suggests that these bones were separated from the remaining portion of the skeleton at some later time and that perhaps these bones were overlooked at the time of the removal.

> *Reported*
> *Oscar B. Hunter, Jr. MD*
> *Pathologist*

One of the more immediate results of Dr. Hunter's report

pertained to Private Detective George Swain. According to C.A. Raper's 1950 report, Swain contacted the Fire Marshal's office again after the excavation and informed them that he, "was satisfied regarding the origin of the fire and the death of the children and was withdrawing from the case."[186] Detective Swain's full statement printed in the *Charleston Gazette* on September 8, 1949, read as follows:

It has come to my attention that Mr. and Mrs. George Sodder of Fayetteville, the distressed parents of five children who supposedly perished in a fire that destroyed the Sodder home on the Christmas morning of 1945, are to pursue investigation of the mysterious circumstances surrounding the tragic event. I therefore wish to inform the public that neither I, nor any member of the American Detective Agency I represent are taking part in pursuing the matter further.

Since the basement of the home was excavated Aug. 18 of this year, under the supervision of a competent pathologist from Washington D.C. (Dr. Benwood Hunter, Jr.), and this eminent authority reported the bones found were human bones, it becomes my duty to accept these findings x x x.

My three years work on this mystery leaves the matter unsolved in spite of the fact that I worked diligently in probing every known lead in the face of utter frustration met at every turn. Many mysterious circumstances will puzzle me forever. My efforts, in a large measure, were prompted by sympathy for the bereaved parents and I regret that I was unable to bring them even a crumb of solace in their bereavement.

My heart goes out to the Sodder family, but in justice to the agency, I must say that any further investigation is not being done by anyone connected with this agency or in conjunction with me personally. Throughout my investigation I have been guided by advice from some of the nation's most noted experts on arson, pathologists, and criminologists, and I feel that many of the mysteries surrounding the fire never will be solved. I believe it is utterly foolish to spend any more money on a search that is bound to prove fruitless. As I see it now, the question is not whether the children perished in the flames, but what became of the bones following the fire.[187]

Within a month of Swain's departure from the case, the Sodder's had engaged a new private detective, Mr. Troy Simmons, President of the West Virginia Merchant Police. In an article in the *Charleston Gazette* from October 18, 1949, Simmons states, "I want it to be clearly understood that the case has not been dropped. Detective George T. Swain of Charleston did not resign from the Sodder case but was discharged."[188]

Troy Simmons had been an investigator for nearly 30 years. Simmons claimed that his agency was state of the art because of three major innovations he helped to implement. First, Simmons was one of the first to import bloodhounds into the United States for tracking suspects. He also said his agency was the first in West Virginia to make use of fingerprints in criminal detection. And he pioneered the use of polygraphs in questioning suspects.[189] He was well qualified to investigate the case of the Sodder children.

Simmons took immediate charge and after coming up to speed, he announced that he believed "the children were the victims of a grudge murder and their bones never left Fayette County." Simmons, and his assistant, A. D. Roberts first step was to assemble a group of 15 men to search approximately 20 coal mine shafts and water wells in the vicinity of the Sodder house in an effort to locate the bodies.[190]

Marshall Newman

After Dr. Hunter's analysis of the bones, for some unknown reason, the bones were examined by a second pathologist at the Smithsonian Institute, Dr. Marshall Newman. Why this second analysis happened is lost to history. Speculating, perhaps it was at Dr. Hunter's request so that a second opinion could be offered to the Sodders. Or, maybe Dr. Hunter simply wanted a colleague's review on a case with so many mysterious circumstances in question.

The following is an excerpt from Dr. Newman's report:

107

The human bones consist of four lumbar vertebrae belonging to one individual. Since the transverse recesses are fused, the age of this individual at death should have been 16 or 17 years. The top limit age should be about 22 since the centra, which normally fuse at 23 are still unfused. On this basis, the bones show greater skeletal maturation than one would expect for a 14 year old boy (the eldest of the Sodder children missing). It is however possible, although not probable for a boy 14 1/2 years old to show 16-17 maturation.

The vertebrae show no evidence that they have been exposed to fire. In view of this it is very strange that no other bones were found in the allegedly carefully excavation of the basement of the house. Since the house was stated to have burned only for half an hour or so, one would expect to find the full skeletons of five children, rather than only four vertebrae. It is however impossible for me to make a conclusive judgement of this point since I was not present during the excavation.[191]

The archives at the Smithsonian Institute also contained a shipping invoice signed by George Sodder on September 20, 1949. The Smithsonian sent the bones back to him when the analysis was complete. George Sodder denied ever signing the shipping receipt.

It is generally assumed that because of the age of the bones, they belong to the oldest Sodder boy, Maurice. Mr. Troy Simmons stated in a newspaper interview in October 1949, that in order for the oldest boy's bones to have been found in the basement corner where they were, he would have to had left his room in the attic, gone downstairs, through the raging flames, then gone through several rooms on the first floor before reaching the corner of the house where the four bones were found.[192] (See the floorplan that illustrates this position).

George Sodder soon made it clear that he was not convinced. Shortly after the excavation, he was quoted in a local newspaper as saying:

I am still not convinced they (the children) are dead. Only three or four bones, which may or may not be human, were found even though the men had dug to the very floor of the basement. The pathologist tells me if the children had been caught in the fire, at least their skulls should have remained.[193]

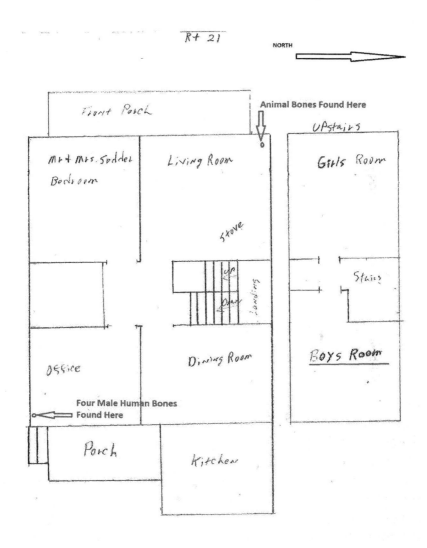

Sodder floorplan with locations marked where human bones were found in proximity to where the boys slept

In another article a week later, Mr. Sodder continued:

The absence of other bones is proof that none of the chil-

dren was in the fire. Those four bones may have been placed there soon after the fire or at some other time.

To make his point further, Mr. Sodder pointed out that the reason the bones were found in this excavation (1949) and not found the morning after the fire (1945) is that they were not there in 1945. The nine-man search party, originally led by the Fire Chief Morris told the Sodders that they had "searched "with a fine-tooth comb."

Other facts that disputed the idea that the bones excavated were those of one of the Sodder children included:

- The age of the bones did not fit the age of the oldest boy, Maurice. Dr. Newman's report set the minimum age at 16 years old.

- The bones were found at the opposite side of the house from where the boys slept.

- No other remains were found nearby, not even larger femur bones or skulls

- The bones that were discovered showed no evidence of ever being burned or charred.

- The letter sent to Troy Simmons stating that the bones came from a cemetery in Mount Hope, WV where a young boy had been buried.[194]

Fill Dirt

The importance of the dirt Mr. Sodder used to fill in the ruins lies in the assumption that some people (mostly Mr. Sodder) have made the claim that the bones found in the 1949 excavation were contained in the fill dirt. There is one reference to the possible origin of the fill dirt in a newspaper article from 1995.

The Sodders came to believe the four vertebrae arrived in fill dirt, possibly from a cemetery in Mount Hope, used when they filled the basement...[195]

I believe the author of this article has mixed up two separate points about this Mount Hope cemetery. First, there is the article as written implying that fill dirt came from a cemetery in Mount Hope. Another reference to the cemetery comes from an anonymous note left on the desk of one of Mr. Sodder's private investigators. It refers to several aspects of the case but it specifically refers to the fact that the four bones came from the grave of a young boy who was buried in the Mount Hope cemetery. This same note implied that someone robbed the Mount Hope grave and planted the four bones to make people think that the Sodder children died in the fire.[196] So it is likely that the writer of the 1995 newspaper article has mistakenly mixed up the events related to the Mount Hope cemetery and the fill dirt did not come from there.

The piece of equipment used to fill the basement of the Sodder house is referred to several times as a bulldozer. This detail alone could possibly answer the question of the origin of the fill material. Since there is no mention in any surviving documents of a truck used to haul the material from another location, a possibility is that the fill material was scraped off in small layers from the Sodders yard and pushed into the hole. But, from having seen the site, I doubt this is true. The house was atop a small rise on the property which would have made scraping dirt difficult and left parts of the property unusable and possibly unsafe.

Another indicator that may show that the bones might have come from the fill dirt could be found in the other bones that were found in the 1949 excavation. Dr. Newman's report mentions some animal bones and bone fragments that were found in the north-west corner of the ruins. This was the opposite side of where the human bones were found and where the living room was located. After a fire, animal bones would have normally been found in or around the kitchen. But the kitchen was located on the opposite side of the house. Obviously, the Sodder's would not have had any animal bones in their living room. So, it is a valid assumption that these bones were not from the house. Since they were found within the remains of the concrete floor of the basement, they had to have come from the fill dirt.

The 1950 report continues regarding the bones discovered in the excavation,

The origin of the bones was not established at the time and has not been to this date. It is not known whether bones

111

present in the basement before the fire or were present in the
filling material used to fill the basement. Their presence at the
site is unexplained and where they came from may never be
known. From reports of the examiners and by using common
sense they could not be considered of any significance in the
solution of the case.[197]

This is a powerful statement coming from a state official involved with the case from the beginning. By saying the bones that were discovered in the excavation have no meaning, he is indirectly validating that the bones were not of the missing children.

If George Sodder still had questions about the origin of the bones, and all the diggers, experts were there, on site ready to continue, it would make sense to remove all doubt and continue. But again, when a man sees what may be the bones of his child, it is impossible to understand what could have been going through his mind at the time.

For those believing that the bones found in the excavation could be those of one of the male children, it is very difficult to reconcile how the body of a child sleeping in an upstairs bedroom could end up on the opposite side of the house while the house is burning and collapsing.

Additionally, the four bones that were discovered were found almost mechanically separated as well as never being exposed to fire. It is very improbable that the bones found in the foundation were severed from the rest of a spinal column as a result of falling through the fire from the upper floors to the basement. Where are the rest of the children's bones? Five bodies of children, containing as many of 206 bones per body, gives over 1,000 bones total.

Chapter 6

The Bones

*What is remarkable is that so little is known about the
physiology of burning human remains, especially that which
would interest fire investigators and homicide detectives.*

*Elayne J. Pope, M.A., O. C. Smith, M.D.,
Timothy G. Huff, M.A.*

After the excavation, the Sodders inquired to the Cincinnati
Cremation Company asking what is involved with the basic cremation process in an effort to learn about the destruction of a human
body. The letter the Sodder family received back startled them. In
December of 1950, the company responded:

*It has been our experience that human remains being
placed in our crematorium chambers for a period of about two
hours with an average temperature of 2,000 degrees Fahr-
enheit will completely disappear except for the bones which
remain intact of sufficient size that parts therein can be recognized as parts of the human skeleton.[198]*

This letter only served to further convince the family that their
children had been removed from the house before the fire began.

Modern Cremation Process

The time required for cremation varies depending on the size
of the body. In modern furnaces the process may be as fast as one
hour per 100 pounds, but this is also dependent on the amount of
fat on the body. Let's say five bodies at an average weight of one
hundred pounds each. It would take a coal, natural gas, or coke

oven fire, completely enclosed, burning constantly for approximately five hours, to burn them all to a point of normal cremation and that would only be true if they were in a cremation chamber. But even after all of this, there would still be bones remaining.

After the incineration is completed, there are still large bone fragments remaining. These fragments are swept out of the retort and pulverized by a machine called a Cremulator. This is essentially a high-capacity, high-speed blender which uses an impact process to break up the remaining bones into ashes. The grinding process typically takes about 20 minutes.

The heat from a house fire is generally released into the air. The laws of thermodynamics state that heat energy will move from a hotter source to a colder source as fast as possible. The colder air draws the heat from the fire and causes it to consume fuel. For the Sodder fire, it lasted roughly 40 minutes, although the ashes probably held heat in the basement for a while.

In this case, the direction of the heat transfer was straight up to the frigid cold night air. These facts do not lend themselves to producing a sustained level of heat to totally incinerate five human bodies to ashes.

Bone forensics

A leading expert in what can be termed "burned bone forensics" is Dr. Elayne J. Pope. She currently holds the position of Forensic Anthropologist and Autopsy Supervisor for the Office of the Chief Medical Examiner for the City of Norfolk, Virginia. Her research over the past 15 years has focused on recognizing the changes a body goes through while it is burning. Her research has been invaluable to arson investigators and law enforcement officials.

One article related to burned body research was written by Dr. Pope and two of her colleagues, Dr. O. C. Smith and Timothy G. Huff. The April, 2004 article is titled *Exploding Skulls and Other Myths About How the Human Body Burns*. It is a comprehensive study of the effects of fire on the human body through the experimental use of human cadavers. The next several pages will go into graphic detail on burned bodies and using some of the information from this article in an effort to offer a possible explanation as to what might have happened to remains of the Sodder children if they did die in the 1945 fire.

Odor of Burning Bodies

There were many reasons cited by the Sodder's why they did not believe their children died in the fire including that there was no odor of "burning flesh." A colleague of Dr. Pope's named John Dehaan states that the odor of a burning body has been described as "the most revolting odor, and it stays with you forever."[199] Many firefighters confirm this is true.

In the case of the Sodder fire, some have said the reasons there was no burning body smell could be attributed to the high winds the night of the fire and that obviously any spectators would have been standing up wind to avoid flames, ashes and cinders. But according to many modern investigators, there would still be the residual smell left in the basement after the fire was out. No one ever mentioned the presence of such an odor.

Transformation of the bone

When bones are burned, they change both in physical appearance as well as in chemical composition. For a completely burned bone, the organic material that originally made up the interconnecting fibers and which makes the bone hard is destroyed and what is left is referred to as "calcined" bone, which has a similar texture and consistency as a stick of chalk.

After being subjected to a fire, bones undergo a transformation from being hard and firm to being very brittle and easily crushed. If the bones are struck with high pressure cold water, it can cause the same effect as cold water to hot glass, the bones can literally crumble.

Absence of Remains

It is common to think that the human remains left after a fire will include the larger bones such as the pelvis, large leg and arm bones, and especially the skull. There has been a common belief that the absence of a skull after a fire can be attributed to the "exploding skull" phenomenon. It has been believed that during the intense heat of a fire, the brain fluid within the skull begins to boil. When the pressure becomes too great within the confines of the skull, the fluids of the brain can cause the skull to explode and fragment.[200] This action is analogous to a potato or an egg exploding in a microwave.

The research of Dr. Pope, and her colleagues has shown that this phenomenon does not bear out under extensive experimentation. Fragmented skulls found in the aftermath of a fire can be the result of falling debris from a house fire, or the falling of a body from upper to lower floors. This can actually crush the brittle remains of the bones.[201]

All told, this is one possible explanation as to what could have happened to some of the remains of the Sodder children, if all of the variables fall into place. This includes:

- Location of the remains relative to the hottest point of the fire
- Availability of enough fuel to consume the body
- Type of fuel available
- Time exposed to the heat source
- Contact with water
- If the remains were/were not crushed by the searchers
- Overall temperature of the fire

But, all five bodies? All of these conditions fall into place at the right time to accomplish this? The odds would have to be astronomical.

Types of Fuel Available

It is more difficult to say with certainty what could have been completely incinerated without knowing specifically what was stored in the basement, as far as flammable materials and in what

116

quantities. At least part of the basement was used as a repair shop for Mr. Sodder's trucking business.

There is mention in some reports that George Sodder stored what was known as drip gasoline in the basement. Aside from being very dangerous and highly flammable and explosive, the problem with the idea of storing drip gas, or any type of gasoline for that matter, is that it evaporates rather quickly.

Mr. Sodder strongly denied having any drip gasoline but there was found in the ashes, two large metal barrels. Here again, for a fire to be as hot as this one was supposed to be, it would have seemed that metal barrel drums themselves would have melted in the heat of a fire hot enough to also incinerate 1,030 human bones. Mr. Sodder claimed these were two empty barrels in the basement at the time of the fire.

Next, it is known from the Fire Marshal's report that there were three wood and/or coal burning stoves in the house that were burning the night of the fire. This could possibly necessitate storing coal or firewood in the basement. Or, the coal could have been stored outside in what used to be called a "coal crib."

No documentation exists saying if it was stored inside or outside and no family members can recall how the wood or coal was stored. But many houses of the same area and time had coal chutes to the basement. The presence of coal would certainly have created a much hotter fire that would have burned longer. But since there is no mention of it specifically, this is just speculation.

The same report stated that Mr. Sodder also stored a large number of rubber tires in the basement for his trucks. But again, no mention of how many might have been there.

Let's speculate and say that all of these various materials were in the basement–coal, wood, rubber tires, drip gasoline, and all the other materials a normal house may have on hand. This basement foundation would have amounted to a crucible of sorts where everything would have combined to burn.

But even with all these various materials, the coal would be the one thing, in large enough quantities, that would have reached the highest temperature. So, in terms of incinerating the bones into ashes, it would not have mattered how much wood or other materials were there. Nor how much the wind fanned the flames; the coal and or the drip gasoline would have had to be of sufficient quantities to reach the combustion temperature of a human body for sufficient time to completely incinerate five bodies. And the fuel would have to be located in the right part of the basement where the bodies would have fallen. And all five bodies would have had to have fallen near where the coal was stored.

Any way you look at it, trying to come up with explanations as to what happened always ends up with a lot of speculation and assumptions regarding the correct conditions that may have existed to cause the total incineration of all of the bones.

There was some argument that because two or three chimneys of the house collapsed and fell into the basement, the fire transferred heat to these three sources. While this is true to a very limited extent and duration, this level of heat transfer would just render the bricks of the chimney hot for just a short time.[202]

If sufficient heat was generated in the basement to completely incinerate all five bodies, the bricks and mortar of the chimneys would also be turned to dust. What could have happened with the chimneys is that if they did, in fact, collapse into the basement, they could have covered some of the remains of the children. It is unknown if the searchers removed old chimneys and searched under them.

Outside Bones

Private investigator Troy Simmons reported after the excavation that a letter arrived in his office that offered some explanation:

W. Va Merchant Police

Charleston, W. Va.

I just read your reward in the Fayetteville paper in reference to the Sodder fire and their children on Dec. 25, 1945. Arnold Jacobs knows all about the fire. He was in charge of the fire truck that night. He cut the phone lines with tree clippers and put the bones in there after the fire. Check with the phone company. These bones came from an old cemetery at Mount Hope. His mother lives in Virginia.

118

I will watch the results of the letter. If it turns out, I look to be paid.

A Miner who needs money[203]

This not only refers to or gives an explanation as to why the bones were found the way they were, but it once again brings the actions of the Fayetteville Fire Department, under the supervision of Chief Morris into question. The writer of the letter mentioned a name at the fire department who "knows all about the fire."

This all seems too bizarre to be realistic. And the steps described above to acquire the bones, not only seems ghoulish, but too daunting to be practical.

Using Find-a-Grave.com, I discovered that the old Mount Hope cemetery had been transcribed years ago listing all known graves of which there were only 25. Separating out females and men who were of the wrong age and date of death, there only remained one name. Frank Fedele was a 19-year-old marine who was killed in WWII and buried there. I also discovered that Frank Fedele was initially buried in Beckley but later moved to Mount Hope. This dis-internment could have presented someone with the opportunity to acquire the bones.

The strange question is why choose the spinal bones, instead of an arm, or leg or ribs which are right there facing you? This would involve turning the body over to get at them, not to mention removing the clothes. Then, these bones would have to be pulled apart or hacked which may account for the hacking marks noted by the pathologist.

Next, whoever removed the bones would now need an opportunity to take and place them in the ruins of the Sodder house. Since the four bones were found in the basement according to the story in the *Charleston Gazette* of August 1949, it would at first appear that is where they ended up after the fire. In terms of the Mount Hope theory, that they were placed there, after the fire, but before the site was filled, this gives a window for placing the bones between December 25 and four days later when Mr. Sodder had the site filled.

What could the Sodders have possibly done to make someone

mad enough to first burn down their house, either intending to kill them all (or alerting them to the fire by calling thirty minutes in advance)? Then to help cover it up, extract bones from another body to be planted just to confuse them. Not to mention spiriting the possibly still living children away to be adopted by someone else. What would be the motive?

So to summarize, right after the fire there is a statement that one or two people saw something that looked like a mass that had bones in it. On the other hand, you have statements from several other people who say they saw something but specifically say, they saw no bones. Then you have statements from others who saw nothing. Then, several years later, an animal liver that had never been exposed to fire, was dug up at the site.

Also, George Sodder stopped digging when the first bones were found in 1949. He had gone to all the trouble and expense of bringing in experts and when the first evidence of the bones was uncovered, he stopped it? The only documentation of him stopping the process is a comment in the 1950 report by Fire Marshal C.A. Raper. Raper and several of his assistants were present so some validity must be given to this account. But, if Sodder did stop them and no other excavations were done, this leads to the possibility that more bones could be there.

To date, there have been no further official excavations, even after the Sodders sold the property when Jenny Sodder died in 1989. There was mention several years ago of one of George Sodder's grandchildren wanting to do a new excavation. If it happened, nothing was ever made public.

If the digging was stopped after four or six bones were found, there is still the question as to whether or not there are more there. But what are the few remaining facts? George and Jenny Sodder spent the rest of their lives following up every clue, every possible shred of a rumor that might have led to finding their children. Why would they have done this if the basement had only been partially excavated and searched? Would it not have been in the back of their minds that some of the answers they were searching for could be in their own backyard?

The bones located in 1949 were of no value in terms of providing answers to this case. With all of the variables surrounding not only the discovery of these bones, but also witness statements, the current location of the bones, chain of custody, who handled them and why, by the time they were mailed back to Mr. Sodder, their value as evidence was lost forever.

The only real use of the bones discovered in 1949 would be for DNA comparison. If they were still available, they could be compared to a member of the Sodder family and this could at least prove a connection. This could show that at least one of the children could have died in the fire.

George Sodder was convinced that the two pathologist's reports proved that the children were taken from the house before the fire. This made all of the strange occurrences begin to make sense. The next step was passing on the results of the analysis of the bones to the local and state officials who would have the authority to pursue the individuals responsible. Sodder believed this would motivate those in power to seek out the ones who had committed this injustice. But Mr. Sodder would soon learn, this would be easier said than done. Fayette County was a small but concentrated conglomeration of cultures and power structures that, like anywhere else, was based on who controlled the money.

Chapter 7

The Second Investigation

Motive – Means - Opportunity

Traditional Methodology of Criminal Investigation

Armed with the reports of the two forensic pathologists, George Sodder was confident he now had enough ammunition to get the authorities to take him seriously regarding the possible kidnapping of his children.

Harold Gay Statement

Private investigator Troy Simmons took a statement on November 2nd, 1949 from Harold Gay, the funeral home manager in Montgomery. Mr. Gay identified the mass as a beef liver wrapped in newspapers and estimated that it weighed between four and five pounds. Gay also said that the liver he saw had never been exposed to fire.[204]

By this time, Assistant State Fire Marshal Carlisle Alonzo Raper had been appointed State Fire Marshal. He had been acting Fire Marshal since the resignation of Robert Kidd who had held the post for several years. Shortly thereafter, Carleton R. Cobb was promoted to Assistant Fire Marshal specializing in arson investigation.[205]

Meanwhile, Sodder private investigator Troy Simmons was doing his part to keep the case in the newspapers to gain public support and as a possible way to put pressure on officials. In November of 1949, a story appeared in the *Charleston Gazette* stating that Simmons had been working closely with Fire Marshal Raper and the arrest of several suspects was only a few days away.

Simmons expressed his opinion in the story that he believed the children were the victims of a grudge murder and that "their bones never left Fayette County." He also stated that the search for the children's remains was continuing in several coal mine shafts located near the Sodder family property.[206]

A similar story appeared in the *Gazette* nearly four months later on March 3rd, 1950. This story stated that five suspects were about to be arrested for conspiracy in relation to the missing Sodder children. Simmons was again mentioned in the story and was said to be working not only with Fire Marshal Raper but also Smithers Police Chief Mike Aquino. The police chief was said to be accompanying Simmons and George Sodder to Grace, Maryland to follow up a lead concerning a couple who lived there but were in Fayetteville on Christmas day, 1945. Simmons was also quoted in the article as saying he was "well satisfied with the progress of the case."[207] There was no mention of what this lead was in Maryland and whether or not anything became of it.

Despite the claims in both of the *Gazette* stories of arrests being imminent, no one was ever arrested.

In March of 1950, Mr. Sodder contacted Rush D. Holt, a former U. S. Senator and at the time, a member of the WV House of Delegates. Holt, in turn, did the same thing that most other officials did when contacted by the Sodders. He contacted Fire Marshal Raper who explained they had thoroughly investigated the fire.[208]

Raper claimed that his office had cooperated with Mr. Sodder and his private investigators but he added that it was his opinion that Mr. and Mrs. Sodder were the victims of unscrupulous private investigators who were only out to take the couple's money.[209] In his response of April 8th, Holt thanked his dear friend and for his handling of the matter.[210]

June, 1950 Fire Marshal Report

The 19-page 1950 report is for the most part, written towards the belief that the children died in the fire. For example, it mentions the finding of the bones, but it does not mention any part of the two pathologist reports that indicated that the bones were of the wrong age. In other parts of the account, it states that the origin of the bones is unknown, that their presence at the site is unexplained, and that they cannot be "considered of any significance in the solution of the case."[211] A highly significant admission.

Pages 12 through 14 go into detail about Mr. Sodders relationship with Fiorenzo Janutolo, his former employer, and the man who was the beneficiary on Mr. Sodder's homeowner policy. It goes into detail about some of the inflammatory remarks allegedly to have been made by Janutolo.[212]

Mr. Janutolo was reported to also take Mr. Sodder to task for not allowing his wife to sign papers that would settle the estate of her father, Joseph Cipriani who had died earlier that year. It was at this point, according to the report, that Mr. Janutolo was reported to have told Mr. Sodder, "Your goddam house is going to go up in smoke and your children are going to be destroyed." And, he was reported to have added, "you are going to be paid back for the dirty remarks you have been making about Mussolini."[213]

The most curious and fascinating part of the report is that it states, "Mr. Janutolo has not been questioned about any of the remarks or actions mentioned above at this date." Nearly five years after the fire and remarks such as these, and no one had taken the time to ask Mr. Janutolo to explain himself? Of course, that does not mean that he was not questioned, just that there is no record of it.

It seems that for such an incriminating and threatening series of statements by Janutolo, that someone of authority would have taken the time to question him regarding his intent and motives, or even allow him an opportunity to deny that he made such a statement in an effort to clear up a misunderstanding.

There is a paragraph on Page 13 of the report where the writer makes a mistake that has been carried through to the present day. Right after the paragraph where Mr. Cobb writes about Mr. Janutolo never being questioned, Cobb then writes:

An inquest was held on December 26, 1945 before Mr. H. C. Level, Justice of the Peace of Fayette County, W. Va. Mr. Janutolo was foreman of this jury. Mr. Janutolo reported to the Squire that no parts of the five missing children were found in the debris.

The way this paragraph is written, it implies that Fiorenzo Janutolo was the jury foreman because it comes right after another part of the report that specifically mentions him. A man named Janutolo was foreman of this jury but it was, in fact, Cleante Janutolo, Fiorenzo's uncle, business partner, and next-door neighbor. For proof of this fact, see the death certificates of the five children.[214]

Overall, while the 1950 report is a key document because of the vast amount of information it contains, it is also a narrow document because of the amount of information it contains. It covers a lot of topics but often just skims the surface.

Some examples of topics that were covered in a way that seemed to emphasize that the children were not kidnapped include:

The Sodder's missing ladder – the 1950 report mentioned the fact that the ladder was missing on the night of the fire. But it was also mentioned that the moving of the ladder "was not taken too seriously because one of the children could have moved it."[215] There is no mention of the fact that the ladder was found shortly after the fire some 75 feet from the house in a ravine.[216]

The man who saw fireballs – In nearly every newspaper article, magazine story, and letter (written by the Sodders) concerning the case, there is the mention of the man who on the night of the fire saw fireballs being rolled onto the roof of the Sodder house. He was located by one of Mr. Sodder's private investigators around 1948 but never named in any surviving document. There is no mention of the fireballs or this mystery man in the 1950 report.[217]

Fire department delay in arriving – the report mentions that fire chief Morris claimed his reason for not arriving at the fire for more than eight hours was due to bad weather. However, other documents indicate Morris also claimed his delay was due to his not knowing how to drive the fire truck and that the Sodder house was located outside the department's jurisdiction. While this excuse may have been technically true, it would seem that considering there were no other departments responding, and the fact that the lives of five children were involved, the Chief could have made an exception regarding his department's jurisdiction. And, since the 1950 report mentions the comings and goings of many witnesses to the fire, in vehicles, the Chief's claim of bad weather keeping him from responding to the fire appears odd.

It could be that the writer of the 1950 report created his summarization from notes in the "voluminous" file, as C.A. Raper once described it. Also, this report was probably never meant to be seen by the general public.

Governor Patterson

In July of 1951, George and Jennie Sodder wrote a letter to then West Virginia Governor (and former Fayette County resident) Okey Patterson asking for help. Mr. Sodder wrote:

Proof was established two years ago that the children did not perish in the fire. We had the site excavated and though four human vertebrae were found, they had never been exposed to fire. They were said to have come from a cemetery in Mt. Hope. The bones are those of a boy whose mother was at the time of said excavation, living in Virginia. The question now is what became of these children.

Now that we have proof that the children were not in the fire, we come to you for help. We believe you have at your disposal intelligent officials who can solve this mystery.[218]

Governor Patterson responded nine days later stating that he was forwarding Mr. Sodder's letter to W. E. Burchett, Superintendent of the Department of Public Safety's Division of the State Police[219] who then answered Mr. Sodder on the 19th of July:

Our department conducted the initial investigation that began about 8 o'clock a. m. on the morning of December 25, 1945. Later, members of the Fire Marshal's Office investigated the same case. I am advised that you have employed, at considerable expense, private detectives to look into this matter for you. Yesterday I talked to Mr. Raper, State Fire

Marshal, who has a voluminous report on this case and he informs me he has talked with all the investigators employed by you. Mr. Raper advises that all evidence obtained to date leaves no doubt but that your children met their death in the fire that destroyed your home. This department reached the same conclusion a number of years ago.

I am sorry that a difference of opinion exists in your mind and wish to advise you that if evidence is ever obtained which would cause us to believe otherwise, we will be glad, at that time, to reopen the investigation.[220]

This, of course, was not the response Mr. Sodder was expecting. With his news about the un-burned bones and lack of human remains, he thought the State Police would be clamoring to come to his property to investigate. When this did not happen, he turned again to his private investigators to try and gather more direct evidence.

The Florida Connection

Somewhere along this same time, Mr. Sodder somehow became convinced that his five children may have been taken by members of his wife's own family, the Ciprianis, and spirited off to Cortez, Florida where several members of the Cipriani family lived.

Mr. Sodder's private investigators had found someone in Charleston who had come forward claiming they had seen the Sodder children in a car being driven by people of Italian descent and having a Florida license plate.

In 1951, private investigator, T. C. Simmons secured the services of the Tampa Patrol and Detective System, a private investigation company. The company was owned by Joe Carter and over the next week, Carter provided several reports back to Simmon.[221]

In an initial report from July 24, 1951, Carter outlines his approach to the case which is to slowly infiltrate the small fishing village and ask around to see who knows anything about the Ciprianis or the missing Sodder children.[222]

*There is no doubt plenty of work that can be done there,
but you would have to have an agent or two to work into this
bunch before they are going to get any place much with low
down results.*[223]

In the second report he dives into the investigation by naming
one of his sources and their take on the situation.

*Our agents went to Cortez Florida and upon arrival there
they located the property of Cipriani, consisting of a pure oil
gas station, and several cabins, also they have a drag line and
several trucks, Jimmy Capriana (sp) is here now, he and his
brother Frank are in business together operating a drag line
and some trucks. We found out all we could by talking in a
around about way from some people who lived here for a long
time by the name of Mr & Mrs W. J. Evers, they own a house
across the street. They told us Frank had a sister drowned
on the bridge just before the fire in Fayetteville, which From
reports in the States Attorneys(sp) office shows that it was
accidental. Also a week or two after this tragedy, Frank came
into the tavern and told them he was going up there as his family seemed doomed that his Sisters whole family was burned
up. He was gone about two weeks before he returned and
has never talked about it since, as he never came back any
more. Also the Evers stated that they had seen the little boy
in the picture but they could not say where but were certain
it was the same one this Louis Enrico Sodder the 10 year old
in the newspaper but did not recall seeing the others. We also
checked with the States Attorneys(sp) office and found that he
was laying in on this case and he had his file brought out for
us to examine but we found nothing that we didn't know. This
man Frank was a regular visitor at this Tavern mentioned and
they think it funny that he never comes around anymore.*

Agents Wyly & Carter.[224]

The next day, agents Wyly and Carter re-interviewed the
Evers but stated they found out nothing new from the couple.
They also interviewed the Bradenton Beach drawbridge operator
and his wife, Mr. and Mrs. G. W. Bennett, who confirmed that the

Ciprianis had 5 or 6 children living in the village with them.

The oldest is a girl of 18 years and she is in college now and they were positive they had seen the Jennie Irene Sodder and they also stated they believed the children had visited here before the fire. They knew about the telegram. It seems he took exceptional pains to let the telegram be seen around here. We questioned several other people and there seemed to be a hesitation to talk about this family. This family also has a little boy living with them now that was borned here according to the statement of the Bennetts and their little granddaughter. The trucks and drag line are busy all the time they seem to be making money. No West Virginia License seen around the place.

Agent Wyly & Carter[225]

A few days later, another report arrived from Joe Carter.

We are not yet convinced that these children are here but circumstances have a tendency to make you feel like they may be or some where that they might have sent them, if there is anything further that you wish we will do our best for you, The Tampa Morning Tribune has contacted us with a desire as your suggestion of running something in the papers about the case, what ever is done I will let you know and send you a copy under a separate cover, you will find our bill inclosed(sp) for the 2nd day and necessary expense.[226]

Another report came in three days later from Carter.

As you can see by our reports, there is enough evidence to tend to substanuate(sp) the fact that the children are here or at least have been, as you well know if we go to these people with no more than we have they will have time to cover up.[227]

In August, Mr. Sodder replied to Superintendent Burchett's letter of July 19th where the Superintendent made it clear that he and the Fire Marshal's Office had no reason to believe the children had not perished in the fire. Undaunted, Mr. Sodder provided him with a synopsis of the case, this time, from his viewpoint.

1   We received your letter of July 19, 1951 and are surprised that the Department of Public Safety could have come to the conclusion you say they did.

2   To say that if evidence is obtained you will be glad to reopen the case. We can give you evidence, though at the time it happened we were very confused and thought ourselves that the children were in the fire. So we had the site covered and made into a cemetery. But later too many suspicious things occurred which caused us to know that our children were not in the fire.

3   For instance, a passerby called the Fire Department at Fayetteville and told Fire Chief Morris that the Sodder's house was burning down. He said "Yes, we know about it." Yet he did not come to the scene of the fire until the next morning at eight o'clock. He denied knowing anything about it.

4   Fire Chief Morris conducted a preliminary search of about two hours with six men and said there was nothing to be found.

5   Later on he changed his statement and told some of the people around that he found something.

6   Spectators say this piece of matter that was found looked like a hambone. It was kept in our garage for about two days, then it disappeared. We asked Morris what he found and he said it was the upper part of a human body, heart and lungs, etc.

7   All these conflicting statements caused us to contact Chief Morris and ask him where he buried this matter. We excavated the place and found the piece of flesh. We took it to a mortician to have it analyzed. He said it was beef liver. Later this beef liver was confiscated. This happened the day we were supposed to take it to the Department of Public Safety.

8   Now, Morris tries to say that we stopped him from search-

ing the place thoroughly, although he told our detectives that he searched as "with a fine toothed comb."

9   *We excavated the site of the fire and found four human vertebrae. Dr. Hunter, a pathologist from Washington D. C. said that the bones had been forced apart by an expert. Hunter stated that there should have been a basketful of bones found.*

10 *Fire Marshal Raper did not like our method of searching the soil from the excavation. He said that it should have been screened. However, Dr. Hunter said this was not necessary that the larger bones would have been found if they were there.*

11 *The bones were analyzed by the Smithsonian Institute in Washington. The report stated they had never been exposed to fire. They would probably have been from the body of a youth of about nineteen or twenty-two years of age.*

12 *We had a report that the bones came from a cemetery in Mt. Hope from the body of a youth whose mother now lives in Virginia.*

13 *Two of our detectives were told by lawmakers in Fayetteville to stay out of the case and keep out.*

14 *The Prosecuting Attorney in Fayetteville said he did not wish to open a case against people with whom he had to live and eat.*

15 *We could not hire a lawyer in Fayetteville because all of them were afraid they would be put out of their office building if they took over our case.*

16 *We heard nothing of an investigation being made by the State Police. They merely said that the fire was caused by defective wiring, which is not true, since the lights were still burning when we came out. Expert electricians said*

this could not have been the cause.

17 *We have given you a good bit of evidence and have still more if you wish it. We can back up any statement we have made.*

18 *The only thing we can not tell you is who did it or where they took our children,*

19 *Please, can't you help us now?*

Mr. and Mrs. George Sodder and Family[228]

There is a lot of information contained in this letter that can be characterized as a summation of contentious points of the case up to that date. There are also several points Mr. Sodder makes that are in conflict with other accounts. Because of this, I have numbered the paragraphs in this letter so the reader can follow along with the explanations I am going to offer.

Paragraphs 1 through 5 are just a rehashing of information already covered in this book so far. In paragraph 6, Mr. Sodder refers to the mass as a hambone. It is unknown where that terminology was first used and why since most previous accounts state that the mass was soft and there were no bones in it.

In paragraph 7, Mr. Sodder says the mass was confiscated. The account in the 1950 report says that the mass was likely taken on the regular trash pickup.

In paragraph 8, Mr. Sodder is correct here. Chief Morris did say initially the site had been thoroughly searched and nothing was found. The earliest documentation where he said otherwise was a November-1948 *Charleston Gazette* article that read:

Chief Morris admits that he did not search the ruins of the fire. He looked thoroughly where the beds should have been and looked over the majority of the whole site but he did not finish the job to his satisfaction.[229]

This is in direct opposition to what Morris said the first morning when he claimed the ruins were searched as if with a fine-toothed comb.[230] I am more inclined to believe the mass was never in the ruins of the house for the following reasons:

133

- Morris' first statement was the morning of the fire where he said that nothing had been found. It is generally true that the first statement someone makes about something is usually the most truthful. As time goes by, they have a chance to think about it and change their account to either match other accounts or to rid themselves of fault.

- When later interviewed by the WV State Police, the nine other searchers from December 25th, 1945, all stated that they found no human remains in the debris.

- The fact that the so-called mass was described by several different people as being soft and never having been exposed to fire, which would describe the consistency of raw, uncooked liver.

- Mrs. Sodder stated previously that the family had no beef liver in the house before the fire.

Paragraphs 9 and 10 are true. No differences here from previous statements.

Paragraph 11, actually Oscar Hunter estimated the age of the owner of the bones to be 14-15 years old, while the second pathologist to examine the bones, Marshal Newman, gave a range of between 16 to 22 years of age.

Paragraph 12 is a reference to an anonymous note that was mailed to T. C. Simmons concerning the bones found in the basement of the Sodder house.[231]

Paragraphs 13 and 14 is hearsay and cannot be attributed to any one person.

Paragraph 15 seems like an odd thing to say if no context can be applied to it. But when the fact that many of the buildings along Fayetteville's main street were constructed and owned by the Janutolo Company, it begins to make sense. However, it is also well known that Mr. Sodder had in his employ as many as three different attorneys. All three of these attorneys were from Fayetteville and all three stated that Mr. Sodder needed to have more evidence to prove his case in court.[232]

Paragraph 16 - it has been well documented that the suspected cause of the fire was listed as "unknown, but probably due to faulty wiring." When the State Police were confronted with the fact that the lights in the house were still on during the fire, they changed their theory saying it somehow started on the roof. However, no official document has been discovered documenting that change of theory.

Paragraph 18. Notice the wording here. "The only thing we cannot tell you is who did it…" Does that mean they cannot tell them because they do not know, or because they are not allowed to tell, or afraid to say? Are the Sodders clinging to the Italian tradition known as omertà in the hopes that if they remain quiet, the persons who did this might be willing to give the children back at some point? Or, that if the Sodders can do nothing against the people who did this but perhaps the State officials could.

When he received no reply, Sodder wrote again..[233] Still receiving no answers, Mr. Sodder apparently made a trip to Charleston to see the Superintendent and had a short conference with him. There is no record of what was said in this meeting but a follow-up letter from Burchett a few days later gives some idea.

> *When you came to my office some few days ago you mentioned that a detective agency in Florida was investigating the possibility that your children might be found in that state. You also stated that you had received some correspondence from this agency in which they describe their attempts to locate your children and, at the time, mentioned some possible connection with the Federal Bureau of Investigation in this investigation.*
>
> *I would appreciate it very much if you would send me this letter so I can examine it for the purpose of expediting the investigation or determining whether or not the detective agency has made certain allegations which are not true. I shall return the letter to you as soon as it has served its purpose.*
>
> *W. E. Burchett*
> *Superintendent*[234]

Meanwhile, on September 17, 1951, C. R. Cobb sent an internal report to Raper giving him notification that T. C. Simmons had informed him that he has information that the missing Sodder children are, "in the custody of Mrs. Sodder's sister at Vera Cruz, Florida." Cobb was informing Raper that Simmons, through a detective agency in Florida, had attempted to locate the children in Vera Cruz. Cobb seemed to enjoy telling Raper that no trace of the children had been found other than one of the Cipriani children shared the name Martha with one of missing Sodder children. He also seemed very concerned that Mr. Sodder had spent a lot of money on these private investigators.

Cobb continues:

Numerous persons and agencies have been employed by Mr. Sodder in this case at great expense to him. The case has been investigated by this office, county officials, and the State Police. All information has been thoroughly investigated and there has not been any evidence produced that the children did not perish in the fire; however, the paid investigators declare from time to time that they have obtained certain information regarding their whereabouts.

It is respectfully requested that the proper procedure of the law be put into effect to cause the production of all papers in the hands of the investigators employed by Mr. Sodder so that information in them may be investigated without further cost to Mr. Sodder.

If these children are now or ever have been in the possession of Mrs. Sodder's sister or anyone else in Vera Cruz, Florida, this fact will be established through law enforcement agencies there and no expense will be necessary. Your investigator will await the production of the necessary information to proceed in the investigation.[235]

It would seem that at some point, Mr. Sodder's allegations of kidnapping were taken slightly more seriously. None of the public agencies wanted to have it appear they were ignoring the Sodder family's claims. So, a campaign of documentation began, possibly on both sides. Mr. Sodder's detectives began interviewing witnesses and those associated with the case. The State Police and Fire Marshal did the same and began investigating the Florida angle of the case due to the information that Mr. Sodder's investigators had discovered.

The Fire Marshal's Office wrote to several police officials in Florida requesting an investigation of the Cipriani's living there. And the content of these letters makes it clear that Mr. Cobb had once worked in those areas.[236] In this letter from 12-27-1951, he jokes with Deputy Sheriff Culbreath by calling him a rookie and tells him to "give my regards to all the boys."

Dear "Rookie";

I wrote "Heinie" on November 27, 1951 after Mr. Raper had talked to him about five (5) children alleged to have been removed to Cortez, Florida after their home burned here in West Virginia on December 25, 1945. He has the correspondence between Mr. Joe Carter of your city and Mr. Troy Simmons of Charleston, West Virginia concerning these children which is self-explanatory.

Since writing "Heinie" another operator D.D. "Dave" Fisher has entered the case here. Fisher reports that a Mr. Barnette, County Commissioner of Cortez, Florida, said he definitely saw the Sodder Children in Cortez after the date on which the fire occurred.

Later in the same letter,

I will consider it a personal favor if you can find out for me definitely whether or not these children ever have been in Cortez or locality since the date of the fire, December 25, 1945, so that we can corroborate or disprove this report.

C. R. COBB[237]

I know that if I was a private investigator working on this case and somehow saw a copy of this letter, I would have Mr. Cobb up on charges for accusing me of "manufacturing evidence" and being shady, assuming I was not guilty of those accusations.[238] It also appears that Mr. Cobb's "thorough investigation" and general familiarity with the case does not extend to knowing the sex of all five Sodder children. In this letter he refers to the oldest boy, Maurice, as female. Additionally, in contrast to his statement that, "not a single bit of evidence has been found that would indicate that the children did not die in the fire," the same can be said regarding the existence of evidence showing that the children did die in the fire. There was none.

A day later, N. C. Reger of the WV State Police writes a short report for the purposes of inserting it in the Sodder file regarding a call he received from an operative of T. C. Simmons, named Dave Fisher. This letter covered much of the same ground as the previous letter but here it was documented so it could be part of the file as directed by the head of the State Police.

Resume Report

One specific report from the fire marshal was titled "Resume of the Sodder Fire" and was produced around this same time. In this report, there is no mention of the fact that the two pathologists that examined the bones found that they had never been exposed to fire. There is always discussion in any Fire Marshal document about how there is no evidence that the children were kidnapped. What is always missing is any evidence that the children did die in the fire.

There is a paragraph about the Sodder belief that the fire was "of incendiary origin" and that it was the result of trouble between Mr. Sodder and Frienzo(sp) Janutolo. But there is no mention in the report of what reasons there might be for trouble between the two men like Cobb included in the 1950 report. There was also no mention of questioning of Mr. Janutolo regarding this "trouble". This report, like all others, is slanted to the Fire Marshal's opinion.

Raymond Wise and Mrs. Bree

Mr. Cobb's recommendation was accepted. Either that or it

was a result of Mr. Sodder's efforts to get help using private detectives and the newspapers. A meeting was finally held in December, 1951 with the Superintendent of the State Police, Colonel Burchett. The following is a report summarizing the meeting written by State Police Sargent N. C. Reger two days later:

> *Three hours were spent discussing this case and the only possible lead developed from this talk was that a Mrs. Bree of Smithers was the woman who was supposed to have seen the Sodder children after the fire, and to have kept them at her home the night of the fire. The next morning it was reported that the children were taken away in a car bearing Florida Registration Plates. This information was reported to have been obtained by Troy Simmons, Private Detective, who received it from Mrs. Raymond Wise, who learned it from her husband, Mr. Wise, who was alleged to have been told by Mrs. Bree.*

> *On December 19, 1951, Sergeant Reger called Sergeant Callaghan at Montgomery and was advised that he, Sergeant Callaghan, and Captain C.L. Walker had previously interviewed Mr. and Mrs. Bree and had been told that none of this information was true, but that Mrs. Sodder's brother, driving a Florida car, had stayed there some time before for a brief visit with Mrs. Bree's husband. Sergeant Callaghan was asked to submit a resume of Mrs. Bree's statement so that we could include it in the Sodder File.[239]*

I believe that the idea of the children being taken to Florida by the Cipriani's was first discussed here. After Cobb interviewed Wise concerning Bree's alleged comments about the Sodder children, he reported the results back to Raper:

> *As requested, your undersigned investigator, interviewed Mr. Raymond D. Wise, of 211 Ferndale Drive, Charleston, West Virginia, in regard to the allegations that a Mrs. Tony Bree of Smithers, West Virginia, had made certain statements to him concerning the Sodder children in question.*

> *Mr. Wise states that he knows Mrs. Bree, but that she nev-*

er, at any time, made that statement or any similar statement to him. He is at a loss to know how the informant obtained such information.[240]

Shortly thereafter, on January 8th, as directed, W. R. Callaghan interviewed the Brees of Smithers and reported back to Superintendent Burchett.

Dear Sir:

On the morning of the 19th of November, 1951, Captain C.L. Walker and I contacted Mr. and Mrs. Tony Bree of Smithers, W. Va. in regards to the following story or information furnished by Mr. George Sodder of Fayetteville, W. Va. Mr. Sodder stated, "On the night, that his children were supposed to have burned up in his home near Fayetteville, W. Va. about Christmas Time of 1945, that Mr. and Mrs. Tony Bree of Smithers, W. Va.

Both, Mr. and Mrs. Toney Bree denied that the Sodder children had been there at the time specified, or any other time to the best of their knowledge. They did admit that they were close friends with Mrs. Sodder's brother Jimmy Cipriani of Smithers, W. Va. and the other brother, who lives in Florida. The Bree's advised that the Cipriani family from Florida had been to their place somewhat earlier the year of 1945.

I have known the Bree family personally for several years and personally know that Toney Bree is honest and well respected by the people of his neighborhood. I believe she along with her husband have been truthful in the matter concerning the Sodder Children.

W.R. Callaghan

1st Sergeant, Company D, D.P.S.[241]

Mrs. Bree denied making the comments, Mr. Wise denied saying that Mrs. Bree made the comments. As it says above in N. C. Reger's letter, the origin of this information came from Mrs.

Raymond Wise (Mayme). But in all of the statements being taken and letters being inserted into files to make it appear that the investigation was thorough, no one bothered to take Mayme Wise's statement or make a record of what she had allegedly said.

A 1944 record shows 26-year-old Raymond's occupation as salesman, and at one time he was a truck driver for Imperial Ice cream. That may be why someone who lives in Charleston knew Mrs. Bree who lived in Smithers with her husband, Tony, where they operated their popular restaurant for many years.

If her husband did not tell her, then how could she have found out about the story concerning the Sodder children possibly being at the Bree home after the fire? And how or why would she have come in contact with Troy Simmons, the Sodder private investigator?

Why would Mayme Wise make up such a bizarre accusation that still contained the level of detail she included? How could she have just come up with the name "Bree" out of thin air for it just to be a coincidence that the Bree's were friends with the Ciprianis? Or, why would T. C.

Raymond and Mayme Wise, around 1950

Simmons lied about something that could so easily be checked and verified as being false. Once again, it is another situation where someone supposedly makes a statement only to find that when it is investigated by an authority, they claim they made no such statement.

The obvious question is what kind of conversation did Raymond have with his wife after being interviewed by the State Police since Mayme had told Simmons the story she had to tell about Mary Bree and her comments about the Sodder children? There are several possibilities here. He either told her that she was mistaken, and he (Raymond) had never said anything about Mrs. Bree. Or he might have told her that he had repeated the story to her (Mayme) in confidence and now they were all in trouble with the State Police, because of her repeating what she had been told.

Interviews with descendants of the Wise's indicate that Mayme was a person of very good character. They do not feel that she was lying about what she repeated concerning this conversation. Of course, none of this literally means that the Sodder children were in the Bree's house the day after the fire. It just means someone said it happened. Many times, in events such as this, some people like to insert themselves into the happenings just to give themselves a sense of personal importance.

Shortly after the police interviews with Mrs. Bree and Mr. Wise, Mr. and Mrs. Wise left to live and work in the steel mills of Northern Ohio. Why then the sudden exit from West Virginia?

The Re-Investigation

By the beginning of 1952, Mr. Sodder was able to convince the Fire Marshal and the State Police to hold a second hearing concerning the case. This was also with the agreement that during this period of preliminary investigation, that Mr. Sodder would curtail the activities of his private investigators, which he did. A list of names compiled by Mr. Sodder and his investigators was given to the state officials who promised to question them and investigate their possible role in the fire.[242]

January 2, 1952[243]

On December 31, 1951 at 10:15 a.m. a meeting was convened in the office of the Fire Marshal for the purpose of discussing the Sodder Case and to determine what course

*of action to assist Mr. Soddard in his quest and to eliminate
private detectives from an investigation. Mr. Soddard gave
various names that had been suggested as suspects by various
private investigators which indicated that each investigator
had one or more suspects in this case. Mr. Soddard gave what
he believes to be reasons why the children are alive and told
of places he had traveled on the case and the approximate
expense. He gave possible clues to be checked, most important
of which is the lead in Cortez, Florida and which is now being
investigated by the Florida Authorities at the request of Mr.
Raper's Office.*

*As a result of the meeting, it was decided that the Cortez
angle should be investigated; Lonnie Johnson is to be interviewed in Fayette County regarding remarks he is reported to
have made; Mr. Frame, the Minister who made the remark that
the human heart would not burn is to be interviewed and Mr.
Morris, the Fire Chief of Fayetteville when the fire occurred is
to be interviewed. All of these leads will be checked by the Fire
Marshal's Office with the exception of Lonnie Johnson who is
being interviewed by the State Police in D Company.*

N. C. Reger[244]

When mentioning that the basement of the house was excavated, there is no mention acknowledging the fact that only four bones
were found. This fact concludes that there were no remains of the
children found in the excavation. No document that I have located
that comes from the State Police ever acknowledges this fact or
offers any explanation as to why no remains were found.

Lonnie Johnson Revisited

One of the people that was to be re-interviewed was Lonnie
Johnson. In January of 1952, Johnson was first interviewed by T.
C. Simmons and based on his responses, later by the State Police.
The following letter from State Police Officer Reger is to State
Police C.L. Walker concerning interviewing Johnson.

December 28, 1951

Dear Captain Walker:

Fisher called Major Boyles (of the WV State Police) and wanted to have Lonnie Johnson, interviewed and determine whether or not at one time he talked to Troy Simmons and made the remark, "he was getting damn tired of taking the rap for those people at Fayetteville." It is alleged that he did make such a remark to Troy Simmons concerning the Sodder case.

After Johnson has been interviewed, I would appreciate it very much if you would send to the Bureau a brief statement covering the interview with Johnson. This is requested only because we will have it in file and thus show that all possible angles have been covered by our department. I have written this letter at the direction of Major Boyles.

N.C. REGER[245]

After Johnson's statement was taken, the following letter was written a few days later.

Sir:

As directed by you, a statement was obtained from Lonnie Johnson, of Gatewood, West Virginia, in regards to the George Sodder case, and is attached in triplicate, to the back of this letter. Johnson in his statement stated that a deputy sheriff accompanied the detective to his home, on the date he was interviewed. This deputy was interviewed, and he stated that he was not present when the detective interviewed Johnson, so he could not state what was said. The name of the deputy sheriff is W.E. Stull – Fayetteville, W. Va.

H.D. Gibbs, Corporal, Company D[246]

As one of the earlier letters stated, the police were only doing the investigation to placate George Sodder, and make sure a record of the questioning could be inserted into the file. The results of their questioning of various individuals was just to prove they had done it. So, when it was proven that Lonnie Johnson basically lied to the State Police, there is no indication that the lie was investigated, or any follow-up of any kind was taken. To do nothing more than take a statement from Johnson, stick it in a file, and leave it at that, seems to justify Mr. Sodder's expression of concern over the depth of the investigation.

Additionally, the man who was with Johnson on the night of the fire, Dave Adkins, was apparently never questioned about anything and possibly still serving in the Army.

Lonnie Johnson was no stranger to run-ins with the law. He was arrested in September 1938 for public drunkenness and in February of 1974, Johnson was indicted for four counts of grand larceny. Even regarding the arrest for stealing from Mr. Sodder, Johnson failed to appear to answer the charges (twice) and a second arrest warrant had to be issued for his failure-to-appear. Lonnie Johnson died in Fayette County in 1988.

Fire Marshal Supplemental Report

At around this time, M. M. Arthur and C. R. Cobb, both of the State Fire Marshal's office compiled what was titled the Supplemental Report (1952 report) for the case.[247] This was either designed to clear up mistakes and misrepresentations from earlier reports or it was designed to fit the aspects of the story the officials chose to focus on or create.

After the flurry of letters sent by the WV Fire Marshal's Office and the State Police to various officials in Florida, an answer was returned in February of 1952. The following letter from Deputy L. G. Swann to C.R. Cobb gives the results of their investigation. The most important part of the response is shown below:

There is definitely no foundation for any report coming from that county in regards to the Sodder children. Mr. Baden informs me that he contacted all the persons who you named in your letter and there is definitely no foundation for the report of the private investigator hired by Mr. Sodder to make the investigation at Bradenton. Sheriff Baden also informs me that he has good contacts in Cortez and they were interviewed along with the others you mentioned both by himself and the FBI. (Agent McVey)

Deputy L.J. Swann[248]

Also in February of 1952, a report was filed by FBI Agent John Woodruff that effectively nailed the coffin closed on the Florida angle of the investigation.

SODDER CASE

The following information was received at Department Headquarters, February 18, 1952, from Mr. John Woodruff, Special Agent, Federal Bureau of Investigation:

On September 20, 1949, George Sodder was in Washington, D.C., and at that time reported this matter to the FBI. He related all the facts and background in the case, which are already known, but in conclusion he stated that he had received no threats, no ransom notes and no evidence of kidnapping, and at that time nothing was said about the possibility of the children being in Florida.

On September 10, 1951, Mr. Archie L. Wyley, a private Detective of the Tampa Patrol Detective Association, Tampa, Florida, reported this case to the Miami Office of FBI, and gave the background of the case, which is already known.

Information had been developed which indicated that these children had been kidnapped and were now living with the family of Frank Cipriani. He believed the children had been kidnapped and taken to Florida.

On continued questioning, Wyley finally admitted that he was confident two of the children who reside in the home of Cipriani, and that Martha Lee Cipriani was actually a daugh-

ter of Frank Cipriani instead of being Martha Lee Sodder as originally reported.

The FBI investigation included a check of birth records and school records dating back to Christmas, 1945, and in some cases back to 1940 and 1941. These checks reflected that the four children in Florida living with Mr. and Mrs. Frank Cipriani are all natural born citizens of the Ciprianis.[249]

There is one large discrepancy in this report and an earlier letter. In Woodruff's report above, he states:

None of the Ciprianis went to West Virginia for the funeral and they had no direct contact with the family until about a year later.

In the report issued on 7-24-1951 by the Tampa Patrol and Detective System agents Wyley and Carter described earlier, they state that at the time of the fire:

Frank (Cipriani) came into the tavern and told them he was going up there as his family seemed doomed that his Sisters whole family was burned up, he left and was gone about two weeks before he returned...

Also in Agent Woodruff's report, he states that Archie Wyley, "reported the case to the Miami Office of the FBI and gave the background." So, Woodruff knew Wyley and had read his report(s). While this may not seem like a major breakthrough in solving the case, it is yet another example in how the reporting or investigating of so-called experts or officials can be mismatched, incorrect, or just wrong.

It should also be kept in mind that all of the letters being reproduced here were probably never made available to the public or even the Sodders, themselves. At this time, there was no Freedom of Information Act.

Withdraw of Troy Simmons

In late February of 1952, the Fire Marshal received a letter from private investigator Troy Simmons notifying him that he was withdrawing from the case. Simmons cited that he was upset that

147

Mr. Sodder was bringing in what he termed "amateur investigators" with whom he could not work.[250] There was no word at the time as to who these amateurs were and what specific issues there were that were causing friction between the investigators.

This reward poster appeared in the June 11, 1952 Charleston Gazette.

Sodder Reward Poster

With T. C. Simmons leaving, Mr. Sodder decided to take a different approach. He offered to post a reward for information related to the recovery of the children. He approached Charleston attorney W. C. Haythe. Together with Dr. Walter Goff of Dunbar and Doral Chenoweth, a reporter for the *Daily News Digest*, formed a committee that would evaluate information that came in. The value of the information would be determined before any payment would be made. Each man agreed to serve on this committee without compensation.

The reward poster states that Mr. Sodder posted a surety bond, a legally binding contract that ensures obligations will be met. Mr. Sodder essentially placed $5,000 with someone who would pay it out to anyone the committee deemed had provided important information as to what may have happened to his children. There are no surviving records of the committee or whether they actually gave out any money.

Ida Crutchfield

In June of 1952, and possibly as a result of the publication of the reward offer, Mrs. Ida Crutchfield came forward stating she had seen the children several days after Christmas in 1945.

I did see four of the Sodder children in my hotel (Alderson Hotel) the immediate week following December 25, 1945. The children were accompanied by two women and two men, all of Italian extraction, to the best of my knowledge. I do not remember the exact date; however, the entire party did register at the hotel and stayed in Room 25, which is a large room with several beds.

They registered between 11 p.m. and 1 a.m. I tried to talk to the children in a friendly manner, but the men appeared hostile and refused to allow me to talk to the children. After registering these people, I made a friendly remark to the small boy. He answered me and one of the older girls began to talk to me.

One of the men looked at me in a hostile manner; he turned around and began talking rapidly in Italian. Immediately, the whole party stopped talking to me. I sensed that I was being frozen out so I said nothing else. They left early the next morning. At the time, I had not heard of the Sodder fire.

In August of 1946, a young man who seemed to be of Italian origin came to the Alderson Hotel accompanied by a small boy, whom he said was his ward. He stayed in Room 8 for two days and three nights. The child was not allowed out of his sight. On reflection, I realized that this child was the same one as had been here the winter before. I still did not connect those occurrences with the Sodder case until I saw the pictures in the paper.

I did see the three Sodder girls and the young Sodder boy (Louis) once and I did see the youngest boy a second time. I do not remember seeing the older boy.[251]

An article from this time stated that after a short investigation, the State Police did not consider Mrs. Crutchfield's statement believable and disregarded it. A few interesting facts included in this statement are:

- Mrs. Crutchfield states that only four of the children were in her hotel, the oldest boy was not with them. There was some speculation at the time that if the children had been taken from their house that the oldest boy might have fought back and killed.

- She gives the room numbers where the people stayed. This level of detail almost seven years after the fire has to indicate that she has records of the adults registering at the hotel and must have their names. This information had to have been turned over to the State Police.

- The fact that Mrs. Crutchfield was willing to give a signed statement to the police shows that at least she believed she was telling the truth.

Ida Crutchfield was the owner and operator of the Alderson Hotel located at 512 Virginia Street in Charleston.[252] If her statement is true, then whoever took the children was definitely traveling West. If the children were to be taken to Italy, the kidnappers would need to travel east.[253] Mrs. Crutchfield died in 1965 and research has shown no further documents exist to support her claims, or if she received any of the reward money.

The Crutchfield statement once again inflamed Mr. Sodder to no end. He considered this some of the best evidence so far as to what happened to his children. He made the rounds again, trying to drum up interest in his case but all the same officials still held the same conclusions as before.

Governor W. C. Marland

Seven months after the Ida Crutchfield statement was taken, it was Mrs. Sodder who wrote a letter to Governor W. C. Marland, asking for more help from the State Police now that Superintendent Burchett had resigned. She specifically cited the Crutchfield statement as evidence that the case should be revisited.

Dear Mr. Marland,

After eight years of Police Service I see that Mr. W.E. Burchett resigned. For all he has done for me I wish he had resigned seven years ago. He said he wanted to stay on the job to stop crimes. If he didn't stop crimes or investigate them better than he did my case we gave him because a arson and kidnap case is here in Fayette County. Because some criminal set my home afire and then kidnapped 5 of my ten children in the year of 1945. We have a signed affidavit that the immediate week following Dec 1945 my children were accompanied by two men and two women. They stayed one night at a hotel in Charleston W. Va. in the month of August in 1946. A young man accompanied my small son who he said was his ward. stay in the same hotel. The first time, yes. Mr. Marland the criminal sleep and rest right in our state capital.

Three hearings has been forced in Mr. Burchett office. But what has Mr. Burchett done. Nothing. He did not even try to investigate and as for Mr. Patterson or our Fire Marshall Mr. Raper they have done no more than Mr. Burchett. Why are they hiding from the truth they know very well this crime has been committed. But we are not going to give up looking for them. After all we should get some justice. Mr. Marland you and Mrs. Marland have children and I know you love them more than anything in the world. I hope you can understand how we feel. There will be no rest until we find out what they did to my children. I will appreciate hearing from you.

Thank you.
Mrs. George Sodder[254]

But as usual, the response was the same.

Dear Mrs. Sodder:

I have your letter of February 13, in which you make charges relative to the inaction of certain law enforcement officials sometime in 1945. I am sorry to advise that there is no way in which I can help you in this matter, but it is my sincere hope that in time you will be reunited with your children. With best wishes, I am.

Sincerely,

WILLIAM C. MARLAND

Governor

And with the letter from Gov. Marland, the final chance at reopening the case for a formal investigation was over. This was at a time when circumstantial evidence was not considered valid for criminal prosecution in a case concerning possible murder, arson and/or kidnapping. The officials wanted direct evidence to justify going forward because they knew that to go into a court room without it was a waste of time. But it even went further than that.

Mr. Sodder complained many times that it appeared the extent of the second investigation was simply cursory and the officials involved already had a predetermined end in mind. He complained that officials basically contacted the people in question and asked them if they had any knowledge of the events of the case. When they said no, the state investigators returned saying the potential lead was a dead end. No follow-up, no back checking, just anxious to get in and get out and move on to something else. Sodder complained about this lack of in-depth investigation, especially concerning leads in connection to the Florida branch of the case.[255]

There were also complaints about the people who were interviewed or re-interviewed. At one or more of the meetings held there was a list of people compiled who would be questioned. However, this apparently was not the total list. In her statement of 1968, Mary Ann Sodder complained:

We asked the Prosecuting Attorney to call in some people who were considered suspects in this case. He said he could not question these people because they were personal friends of his. At another time he said, "Today they burned your house, but tomorrow they may burn mine and I have children too."[256]

While her statement is very accusatory, it does not say who the additional people were that the Sodders wanted questioned. It must have been someone in a position of power to cause this Prosecuting Attorney to make a statement such as this. It is likely that this is the same prosecutor that Mr. Sodder referred to in his July 19, 1952, letter to Superintendent Burchett where he stated:

The Prosecuting Attorney in Fayetteville said he did not wish to open a case against people with whom he had to live and eat.[257]

By the middle of 1953, frustrated to no end, Mr. Sodder would take the investigation into his own hands using a unique method of gaining support, and at the same time provide a proverbial slap in the face to those who had ignored his requests for help.

Chapter 8

The Billboard

*Anger is directed not toward the crime, nor the criminal,
but towards those who failed to halt the criminal's actions.*

"The Nation," 1964

As the Korean War was ending, a new battle was just beginning for George Sodder and his family. Mr. Sodder had decided that he would take the fight to the rest of the world.

Mr. Sodder erected a full-sized billboard on his property on U. S. Route 21. On September 10, 1953, Mr. Sodder and his sons finished what would become a Fayette County landmark for the next 36 years.[258]

The photographs of the five children that appeared on the billboards, as well as the "wanted" posters were their school pictures from the year before. Since the Sodders lost everything in the fire, the photographs on the billboards came from either from family members, or possibly from the school photographer himself. Some people have said that all of the Sodder children look very emotionless or even sad in the photos, but at the time, this was the look that photographers asked for. Children weren't asked to smile for the camera. It was a different time.

In all, there were at least three different billboards. A part of the first board, added as a kind of supplement, directly called for the removal of the state fire marshal, Mr. Raper.

First Billboard

Original billboard which offered a $5,000 reward. Source: The Charleston Gazette.

On Sunday morning, September 13, 1953, *The Charleston Gazette* carried a story announcing that despite the fact that the West Virginia State Police had closed the case, George Sodder was renewing the search for his five children with the erection of a full-sized billboard in front of his Fayetteville home. And to prove his point, he was now offering a reward of $5,000 for information that may lead to their recovery.[259]

The text of the first billboard read as follows:

WHAT WAS THEIR FATE? KIDNAPPED-MURDERED? OR ARE THEY STILL ALIVE?

$5,000 REWARD IS OFFERED BY GEORGE SODDER FOR INFORMATION LEADING TO THE RECOVERY OF ANY ONE OR ALL FIVE OF HIS MISSING CHILDREN.

THESE CHILDREN DISAPPEARED ON CHRISTMAS EVE, DEC. 24, 1945; WHEN THEIR HOME WAS DE-STROYED BY FIRE. A COMPLETE INVESTIGATION OF THE BURNED PREMISES FAILED TO PRODUCE EVI-

DENCE OF HUMAN BONES OR FLESH...

*AN AFFIDAVIT HAS BEEN SIGNED BY A PERSON
THAT SHE SAW FOUR OF THE FIVE CHILDREN IN
CHARLESTON AT HER HOTEL TWO OR THREE DAYS
LATER. THEY LEFT THE NEXT DAY ACCOMPANIED
BY TWO MEN AND TWO WOMEN. ALTHOUGH LATER,
5 DIFFERENT PEOPLE SAW THE SAME CHILDREN IN
CORTEZ, FLA.*

Another story the same day in *The Charleston Daily Mail*
pointed to four main reasons why the family still believed the children were not in the fire:[260]

1. No bones or other remains were found by searchers.

2. Telephone lines that went to the house were found to have been cut.

3. The step ladder usually kept near the house was later found a short distance away.

4. The notarized statement from Ida Crutchfield saying she had seen four of the children in her Charleston hotel days after the fire.

When the billboard was erected, the story was carried in more than 23 newspapers across the country. In one Raleigh County paper, the Sodders explained that they were "not particularly interested in punishing anyone." They would waive any charges or sign any kind of release asked for. If they could only regain their children or learn what happened to them.[261]

Second Billboard

While the first billboard asked the question, "What was their fate, kidnapped or murdered?" The second billboard made it clear what the family had come to believe.

*THESE CHILDREN WERE KIDNAPPED ON CHRIST-
MAS EVE 1945 AND THE HOUSE SET AFIRE TO COVER*

THE CRIME. FOR THE SAFE RETURN OF ANY OR ALL OF THE CHILDREN, $10,000 IS OFFERED BY MR. AND MRS. SODDER.

The second version of the billboard was erected around 1960 with the reward now doubled. Source: Charleston Gazette.

Second Section

Sometime before 1966, a second section was added to the right side of the billboard. There are very few, if any pictures surviving this second section of the billboard. I think many newspapers were reluctant to print pictures of this section because the wording was so inflammatory. This new section read as follows (partial):

IT IS INCONCEIVABLE TO THE HUMAN MIND THAT ANYONE COULD BELIEVE, THAT THESE CHILDREN

PERISHED IN THE FIRE.

WE WOULD WELCOME

………………………WE ARE INTERESTED IN…….

ALL EVIDENCE LEADS TO THE CONCLUSION THAT THE CHILDREN WERE KIDNAPPED AND THE HOUSE SET AFIRE TO COVER THE CRIME. IT IS OUR BELIEF THAT THE PRESENT STATE FIRE MARSHAL SHOULD BE REMOVED FROM OFFICE

WE FEEL THAT THE FIRE MARSHAL & MOST…….

RESPECTABLE CITIZENS…..ADMINISTRATION OF JUSTICE…….

The second billboard with the right hand section in view.
Source: Charleston Gazette

The second billboard saw the wording changed somewhat but the central theme remained the same. The reward was increased to $10,000. And the right -hand section that was on the first billboard was still there with the very inflammatory language, but it was reworded. Sadly, there are no surviving legible photographs of this section.

Third Billboard

By the mid-1970s Mr. Sodder had died, and the billboards had been up for nearly 20 years but the family was no closer to reuniting with their missing children. Undaunted, the family took on an even greater task by erecting a more permanent billboard than the previous two. The text at the top of the third billboard, referring to the number of years since the fire, dates the billboard to sometime after 1975:

AFTER THIRTY YEARS IT IS NOT TOO LATE TO INVESTIGATE

(This time there are six pictures of children)

ON CHRISTMAS EVE 1945 OUR HOME WAS SET AFIRE AND FIVE OF OUR CHILDREN AGES FIVE THROUGH FOURTEEN KIDNAPPED. THE OFFICIALS BLAMED DEFECTIVE WIRING ALTHOUGH THE LIGHTS WERE STILL BURNING AFTER THE FIRE STARTED.

THE OFFICIAL REPORT STATED THAT THE CHILDREN DIED IN THE FIRE HOWEVER NO BONES WERE FOUND IN THE RESIDUE AND THERE WAS NO SMELL OF BURNING FLESH DURING OR AFTER THE FIRE.

WHAT WAS THE MOTIVE OF THE LAW OFFICERS INVOLVED? WHAT DID THEY HAVE TO GAIN BY MAKING US SUFFER ALL THESE YEARS OF INJUSTICE? WHY DID THEY LIE AND FORCE US TO ACCEPT THOSE LIES?

(PICTURE NO. 6 RECEIVED IN 1967. LOUIS ONE AND THE SAME NOW LIVING IN ANOTHER STATE.)

This was the third and final version of the billboard, was erected in the 1970s. Source: Sodder Family

This new billboard was built after 1975, six years after George Sodder's death, meant that it was either built by the Sodder children or Mrs. Sodder paid someone to build it for her. Why move the billboard from one side of the entrance gate to the Sodder property to the other? I believe the original billboard was placed within a utility right-of-way and it is possible they were told it had to be moved by a local utility company. Photographs of the older billboards do show a powerline directly over the billboards.

This third billboard was not made of plywood and paint as the others had been. It was made from cinder blocks placed on a concrete foundation. The cinder blocks were then coated with a layer of smooth mortar and then painted white with several coats of thick enamel which made the surface even more smooth and made it easier to paint. As the photo above shows, this billboard was recessed and had a small roof on it. No doubt, the earlier billboards were greatly affected by the weather and eventually had to be replaced. This third billboard was built to last.

A 1980s newspaper article states that Becky Thomas from Alloy was commissioned by Mrs. Sodder to do the lettering on this sign since she had also lettered the sides of the trucks owned by the Sodder Trucking Company.[262] The author had many conversations with Mrs. Thomas who described Jennie Sodder as a kind lady who firmly believed her children did not die in the fire.

Sixth Photograph

One distinct difference in this third version of the billboard is that it carried six pictures instead of five. This sixth photograph was reported to be of a 17-year-old Louis Sodder that had been received in the mail in 1967 from a postmark in Central City, Kentucky.

Photo purported to be Louis Sodder at Age 17

Actual Louis Sodder Photo at Age 10. Source: Sodder Family)

On the back of the photo, it read:

Louis Sodder
I love brother Frankie
ilil boys, A90132 or 35[263]

Over the years, there has been an enormous amount of speculation as to what this means. In comparing the two photos above, there are some obvious similarities such as the shape of the chin, coloring, and slight hook of the left eyebrow. Some of the identifying characteristics listed in one of the reward posters for Louis was; a small scar in the right eyebrow, and a small mole in the corner of the side of the mouth. However, none of these features appear on the photo of the adult Louis, or even on the younger version of Louis, for that matter.

As far as the letter and number, these have been interpreted many different ways. One way was to call it a date, September 01, 1932 or 35. Nothing of significance here in terms of family birthdays or similar dates.

Some identified the numbers as a postal code in Palermo, Italy. (90135). If the children had been kidnapped, perhaps this was a location where they ended up but then why mail the letter from Kentucky?

The Sodders took the photograph to Charleston in an effort to convince Attorney General Donald Robertson that this, combined with all the other circumstantial evidence was enough to reopen the case. But the Attorney General was not convinced of the identity of the young man. So, the Sodders once again employed a private detective whose name is not available. The Sodders gave the PI $400 in advance and sent him to the town listed on the postmark of the letter with instructions to bring Louis back home.

It was reported that Mrs. Sodder was afraid that if the letter or the name of the town was published it could bring harm to this man who might be her son. The photograph was enlarged and placed in a frame in front of her fireplace. Eventually the sixth photo was added to the billboard and labeled, "Picture No. 6, received in 1967, Louis (one and the same) now in another state."

Sylvia Sodder Paxton, the youngest of the 10 children, stated that she remembered the writing on the back of the photo was different for the last part:

lilil boys (George and Jennie Sodder always thought this was possibly slang terms for "little boys"), Age 32 or 35.

Several years ago, Jennie Henthorn, a daughter of Sylvia Sodder and granddaughter of Jennie Sodder stated on Webslueths.com regarding the sixth photo:

*Mom and Dad were involved with much of my grand-
parents' investigations. Dad went with my grandfather when
he met with the private investigator. Mom and Dad went to
Central City, KY, on a Sunday to look around and ask whether anyone knew the man in the photo. They were not able to
find anyone who knew the young man. My grandparents were
afraid that harm might come to Mom and Dad, so they did not
want my parents to go to the newspapers or anything. They
wanted that work to be done by the private investigator. Dad
called and spoke with the private investigator sometime after
the initial contact, and he gave Dad the "these things take
time" speech. My parents' impression is that he took the money and never followed through.*

A part of this quote could answer the question as to why
George Sodder chose to use private investigators so often, which
cost him so much money. By using private investigators, he felt he
was keeping his family members out of possible danger.

Along these same lines, Mr. Sodder made an interesting
comment in a newspaper story about the missing children about
a year after receiving the picture from Central City. He stated,
"That letter, like all our others, had been opened, and then resealed,
meaning that someone was opening their mail."[264]

The Reward

When the first billboard was erected in 1953, the Sodders
advertised a reward of $5,000. Over time, the reward was doubled.
What most people did not realize was that there were other ways
to obtain smaller parts of the reward. In various publications, the
Sodders described what they were willing to offer: *two thousand
dollars is offered for information leading to the arrest and conviction of those who took the children, and another one thousand dollars reward is offered for the conviction of the person or persons
who set fire to the house.*[265]

Virtually any law enforcement agency can describe what happens when the promise of free money is made. It can cause some

people who have valid information to become motivated enough to come forward. But most of the time, it brings out people who have nothing valid to offer.

It was reported that due to the number of newspapers and magazines that published stories, there were sightings of the five missing Sodder children from as far away as Texas. The results of the billboard advertising such a large reward produced some strange letters.

The A. L. Amey Letter (All spelling errors left in place)

From A. L. Amey

Waverly, WV

Oct. 23 – 1954

Supt. Of Public Safety

Dear Sir,

I want to clear up the Sodder case and the murder of Stephans of Wirt. I have oferd (sp) everything reasonable. And by not being told the news by the Law of what they know or have done or are intending to do, I have been made to suffer every evil thing. Sir my reason and only reason for being instered (sp) was and is that I started the case by taking up the subject of finding the Mr. Sodder children that were lost. Then he found them by my efforts. He offered 5000 reward. That's why the case turned out as it did. For some people here did meet with him at once when he came to see me. They black mailed me. To defraud for the reward. And they had many people to help with it. I spoke to you about the funeral at sea. That man that was buried at sea was one of Sodders sons 21 He was the one that I refered (sp) to Mr. Sodder the father an Italian.

Sir please answer giving (sp) me all knolidge (sp) you have at once. So I can setle (sp) the case. Remember, I tried to help your society.

Resp. A. L. Amey
Excuse mistakes.

The Whipple Letter
Apr. 9/54
Supt. R. W. Boyles:
W. Va. State Police
Charleston, W. Va.

Dear Sir:

I have been interested in helping to locate one or all 5 of Geo. Sodder children. It is certain, these 5 children did not perish in the fire. I have good source reasons to explain as to why all these children did not burn up nor were they directly kidnapped. I have sent source data to Mayor Hereson & DA of Fayetteville, but no reply. However, I have not sent the real clincher which proves these children didn't perish in the fire. I write to Mr. and Mrs. Sodder often and I would like to ask you this:

1. *Did Sodders send their children away?*

2. *Were there a grand _____ before or after the house burned down?*

3. *If 2 was positive Sodders didn't send children away (But I heard John Sodder did) I think I could locate one, Lee Martha Sodder, by and by.*

But as goes, truth serum is the fastest and surest bet to get facts from all the Sodders, but those children didn't burn up. Please let me know if or not you are interested.

Sincerely yours,

> *Mrs. G. Whipple*
> *1224 Harrison St-*
> *K. C. W. Va. (Kanawha City)*

Aside from the spelling and typing errors, they are riddled with factual errors as well. No doubt if they had something other than hearsay information or speculation, a break would have been made in the case. Especially in the case of the "Miner" letter.

At first reading of this letter, one might think Arnold Jacobs is the possible mastermind behind the fire but there are several problems. We already know that Lonnie Johnson confessed to cutting the phone lines. We also know that Chief Morris was one of the firemen who answered the call and since he was chief, it is assumed that he was in charge of not only the truck, but also the whole operation.

Other sources say that there was a man named Arnold who was part of the group of firemen but these sources specify that it was Arnold Dempsey, rather than Arnold Jacobs.[266] A search of various records failed to turn up anything for an Arnold Jacobs living in the area but there are a significant number of records for an Arnold Dempsey. This includes a 1940 military draft registration that states Mr. Dempsey worked at the Dempsey Transfer Company, the same failing company that George Sodder purchased in 1942.[267]

His father, Joseph B. Dempsey, was the owner/operator of the Dempsey Transfer Company until his death in 1940.[268] Since Mr. Sodder bought the company in 1942, it is possible that Mr. Sodder bought the company from Arnold Dempsey and three years later, Arnold responded to a fire at his former home/place of business.

The other fireman who answered the call for the fire was James Roles. Nothing connected to the Sodders could be found about Roles, except like Arnold Dempsey, he was married and divorced three times. Oddly both Roles and Dempsey had been married at different times to the same woman. Arnold Dempsey was married to Vesta Mae Beck in 1935 and James Roles was married to her in 1948.

Front Page Detective Magazine Story

It is not clear how it was initiated but somehow the writers of *Front Page Detective Magazine* contacted Mr. Sodder and they wrote a story that appeared in their March 1954 issue titled, "Where are They?"[269] It appears that the author likely just used newspaper accounts to get the basic facts. However, other parts of the story were so misconstrued that the true case was almost unrecognizable. It was like the writer just wrote whatever came to his mind.

An article was written in *The Raleigh Register-Herald* in January 1954 titled, "Sodder Story in Magazine Resented in Fayetteville." The main points of resentment cited were that the response from the people of Fayetteville, after the fire, was surprisingly little, that no funds were collected to help get the family back on their feet, and that little in the way of food was given to the family in their great time of need.[270]

The truth is exactly the opposite. From the moment the fire was extinguished, local citizens went into action. They established a place for the family to sleep temporarily in a small building on their property. Then they collected beds, mattresses, sheets, pillows, etc., nearly everything the family needed to survive. A stove was donated from the Fayette County Board of Education and pots, pan, utensils were sent over. At the same time, the Fayetteville Catastrophe Committee started gathering clothes, furniture, and other necessities. In addition, some civic leaders had begun to collect cash to help with other incidentals.

George Sodder was contacted by the Beckley newspaper and asked for his comment on the magazine article. He was quoted as saying that about 75% of the article is incorrect. He added that the story favored, "those who would prefer to see the investigation bungled rather than see a clear-cut investigation." Word had also reached Mr. Sodder that if what had been written in the magazine article came from him, that some people possibly regretted their donations to the family. Mr. Sodder added that, "At the time, we took the aid in good faith and appreciation, but if there is anyone who regrets contributing, we are willing to repay them."[271]

In another newspaper article a few weeks later, Fayetteville Mayor Ben Keller took issue with the magazine story directly because of a number of letters he had received, some as far away as Illinois, were critical of the town and their perceived treatment of the Sodders. His statement contained a six-point statement:

1. *The fire did not occur in Fayetteville.*

2. *Over $1,400 was collected for the family within two weeks.*[272]

3. *Other donations were collected at the door of a church.*

4. *Hot meals were delivered to the family three times daily for a considerable time.*

5. *Beds and bed-clothing, plus clothes for the family were furnished promptly.*

6. *A small house on the premises was scrubbed and cleaned and made habitable by volunteer workers.*[273]

Sally Smith

In September of 1954, Mrs. Sodder gave a statement regarding a conversation she had with one of her neighbors. The daughter of her neighbor, Sally Smith (pseudonym)[274] was very upset and wanted to speak to Mrs. Sodder. Mrs. Smith asked her to come and see her daughter, Sally, who was "bad off" and so upset that she thought she was going to die.

Mrs. Sodder accompanied Mrs. Smith back to her daughter's house. Sally Smith was "certainly glad" to see her and that she had something she had to tell her about her missing children. She proceeded to tell Mrs. Sodder a story about Mrs. Blake Sugerwell, a woman with short, red hair who lived across the road from the Sodder house. Mrs. Sodder stated that she did not know who Sally was referring to. Sally continued that this Mrs. Sugerwell had murdered the children and buried them in the old well that was located in the woods about a half mile away. Obviously, no such person existed.

When she finished telling Mrs. Sodder this story, Sally's parents and husband all told her that she "didn't know what she was talking about and that she was just upset," all which Sally denied. She then asked her mother, "what about the freshly dug grave behind the house." When her mother did not answer, Mrs.

Sodder stated that maybe a dog had been buried there. Sally said it was not a dog and, "she could tell the difference between a dog and person."

Superintendent Boyles stated that from Mrs. Sodder's statement, it was obvious that Sally was "mentally off" but he wrote, "we are trying to keep this file complete and up-to-date and it will be necessary to interview" Sally and her family. Upon receiving this order, Walker then directed Sergeant W. R. Seal to contact Sally's family. Sergeant Seal learned that on the night of the fire Sally was, "not out of the house and knew nothing of the death of the children." Her mother also told the officer that Sally had been confined to Spring Grove Mental Hospital in Maryland from December 1953 to February 1954. During his visit, Sergeant Seal also attempted to speak to Sally, herself, but in his letter to Captain Walker, he confirmed that she was "mentally off" and "not responsible for what she said."

Sally was later committed to the State Mental Hospital located in Spencer, WV. The meeting Mrs. Sodder had with Sally has been included in this book to show some of the wild stories the Sodders had to endure. This was not the only claim of this type either.

One thing to note is that after hearing Sally's story, the Sodders, as usual, did contact the local authorities and offered to have her protected by the law. This story of Sally Smith is yet another sad chapter of an even sadder story.

Second Reward Poster

Another reward poster was also created around this same time. This one carried much of the same information as the first poster but also had a very detailed list of identifying characteristics of each child such as hair and eye color, complexion, scars or moles, and which hand they favored. A property bond was posted by Mr. Sodder which pledged real or personal property of sufficient value to cover the cost of the reward.

Some critics said that Mr. Sodder did not have enough money to post for what was considered to be such a massive reward at the time. Even George Sodder admitted he did not have that much cash at hand. But to get his children back, he was willing to sell everything he owned. Mr. Sodder also stated that he would be willing to take out a second mortgage on his house.

W A N T E D
$5000.00 (five thousand) REWARD
MISSING PERSONS
FIVE CHILDREN - Brothers and Sisters
Were they KIDNAPPED - MURDERED? MYSTERIOUSLY DISAPPEARED
Missing since December 24th, 1945
MR. and MRS. GEORGE SODDER
of Fayetteville, West Virginia, Offers $5000.00 REWARD
FOR ANY INFORMATION LEADING TO WHEREABOUTS OF THEIR FIVE MISSING CHILDREN, OR EVEN ONE MISSING CHILD /

MAURICE SODDER

Male, white, age 14 when he disappeared. Age now about 23 years of age. Scar on the back of head in hair, also another scar on the top of his head near the top of his head near the forehead, also scar on left side of chin. Black hair, dark brown eyes.

MARTHA LEE SODDER

Female, white, age 12 years when she disappeared. Age now about 20 years of age. Scar, a very small scar on the forehead in the hairline, a scar kiss on the right leg on the shin bone. Brown hair, large brown eyes, full lips.

LOUIS SODDER

Male, white, age 10 when he disappeared. A about 19 years of age, then small in the brown mole, a small mole in the corner of the of the mouth. Black wavy hair, brown eye dark complexion. He used his left hand as more than his right hand.

JENNIE IRENE SODDER

Female, white, age 9 when she disappeared. Age now about 16 years of age. Long dark brown hair, large brown eyes. Dimple in right cheek only.

BETTY DOLLY SODDER

Female, white, age 6, date when she disappeared. Age now about 14 years of age. Scar under the ear on right side. Hair naturally black, curly hair, eyes black. Mole on right arm above elbow.

FIRE WHICH DESTROYED THEIR HOME CHRISTMAS EVE 24TH, 1945. NO BONES OR IDENTIFICATIONS OF ANY MARKINGS RE
OF FIVE MISSING CHILDREN WERE NOT FOUND IN THE ASHES AND RUINS OF SMOKING EMBERS OF THE BURNT HOME OF M
MRS. GEO. SODDER'S FAMILY. THE PARENTS PERSIST THEY STILL REFUSE TO BELIEVE THEIR FIVE CHILDREN DIED IN TH
WHICH TOTALLY DESTROYED THEIR HOME. THERE WAS NO EVIDENCE OF ANY HUMAN FLESH OR BONES.
TO ALL LAW ENFORCEMENT: FEDERAL, STATE, COUNTY, AND CITY—PLEASE BE ON THE ALERT FOR THE ABOVE FIVE MI
CHILDREN, WHO DISAPPEARED DEC. 24TH, 1945.
IF YOU ARE IN POSSESSION OF ANY INFORMATION REGARDING THE WHEREABOUTS OF FIVE MISSING CHILDREN Named: MA
MARTHA LEE, LOUIS, JENNIE IRENE, BETTY DOLLY—SODDER FAMILY, PLEASE COMMUNICATE WITH THE UNDERSIGNED

Second Sodder Wanted Poster, Sodder Family

The Pamphlet

While it may seem strange or out-of-date today, pamphlets back then were a frequently used way of spreading information about an occurrence, a person's experiences, or perhaps their personal manifesto or political positions.

While believed to have been produced around the time of the first billboard's erection, the pamphlet was first mentioned in a July, 1957, letter sent to WV Governor Cecil Underwood's office. A copy was enclosed to the Governor, who forwarded it to the Office of the State Police. State Police Captain N. C. Reger then sent the pamphlet to the Superintendent of Public Safety, who by this time was a Colonel Fair.

Reger, who had been involved in the case back in the early 1950s briefed Colonel Fair in a very abbreviated way that slants the story toward the belief that the children died in the fire. Reger concludes his synopsis with the statement:

> *Almost twelve years have elapsed since the fire and during that period, no evidence has been found which would indicate anything other than death by burning.*[275]

Some of the initial statements in the pamphlet made by George Sodder are listed below and give the reasons for creating both the billboard and pamphlet:

> *It seems that all hope of getting help from local, State or Federal Law enforcement agencies are fading away. At times we seem to be overcome by a wave of hopeless frustration.*

> *If we only had half the interest the police put behind the finding of the kidnapped Marcus child, in finding our own children, we could have found out what happened to them long ago.*

> *If there is anyone who still insists that the children perished in the fire, we would like to have an open discussion with them, not hush-hush behind closed doors as it has been so far. We still insist they don't have, never had, and never will have any vestige of evidence of what they say.*

Some of the questions in the Pamphlet related to the Fayette-ville Fire Chief, Forest Morris:

Why did he (Morris) state the next morning that he knew nothing about whose house it was (on fire) and that he had to ask the neighbors about it? Then when he was confronted with the man who called him, he said it was out of the city limits. The man who called also said that Morris answered the phone and said, "we know about it," when he (Morris) was told that Sodder's house was afire.

Why did he tell us that he searched the site of the fire "as with a fine-toothed comb," and did not find a thing in the ashes?

Why if he didn't find anything, did he put this piece of beef liver in a box and bury it in the ashes and tell everyone that it was part of a human body?

Why, since Mr. Morris was a member of the inquest, did he not show the piece of beef liver to anyone except his closest associates? Why did he not show it to the coroner?

Some of the questions in the pamphlet related to the Fire Marshal, Raper:

Why did he say he was at the scene of the fire the day it happened when he really did not come to the scene until three days later?

Why did he go ahead and make a report to the Department of Public Safety at Charleston that all the investigators that he had talked to had come to the conclusion that the children perished in the fire?

Why then when faced with facts and asked to produce once single investigator of ours who would say he believed the children perished in the fire, did he fail to find even one of those persons to back him up?

Why, when he went to Florida thinking that there might be some of the children there, did he not go for information to the County Commissioner and four other persons who saw the children at that particular residence. Why didn't he go with the private investigators whose names he knew? Instead he went to the residence of the people where the children were seen. According to his word, they denied having the children and he considered this sufficient for his investigation. This is a true example of his investigations.

If this is true, it does, in fact, show a very one-dimensional investigation by Mr. Raper,[276] just as Mr. Sodder complained. It begs the question, what did the Fire Marshal expect the Ciprianis to say? "Oh, yes, we have the children. They are right here. And we burned the house down too."

Other more general questions in the pamphlet are:

Why did (Rev.) James Frame call the mortician and say there was something at the scene of the fire that he should take care of?

Why did the Rev. Frame deny it later and say that he did not call the mortician? The mortician says he did, and according to record, the mortician is more truthful, more trustworthy, and a man of greater integrity than James Frame.

Why does Frame deny calling a neighbor of ours and telling him to put the liver on ice?

Why did Duval Shultz (A member of the Coroner's Jury) say he would never change his mind about the children perishing in the fire, even though the piece of flesh he saw was proved to be beef liver and not part of a human body?

Why did a neighbor couple who came to the scene of the fire, saying it was God's will that our house burned, suddenly turn at once and leave immediately, when my wife told them that someone had set our house on fire? They acted as if we accused them?[277]

In 1957, a copy of this pamphlet was sent to West Virginia Governor Cecil Underwood's office. As usual, nothing constructive happened.

Death of Troy Simmons

Troy Simmons, the president of the West Virginia Merchant Police died on July 18, 1957, from a massive stroke (his fourth).[278] Simmons made some progress on the case but withdrew in 1952 citing Mr. Sodder bringing in "amateur" detectives into the case.[279]

Doyle Wiant

In 1959, another memo was written from a Major Jack to Colonel Fair at the West Virginia State Police about yet another private investigator who had entered the case. A gentleman named Doyle Wiant had written a letter to Governor Underwood on behalf of the Sodder family asking that the State reopen the investigation into the missing children.

Mr. Wiant informed the Governor that he had "made seven trips into the state" and he had, "received statements from people who had never been questioned by any investigators who were the very first at the scene of the fire." He further stated that he had, "interviewed 20 persons who were at the fire while it was burning at its peak."

In his memo to Col. Fair, Major Jack stated that it was his recommendation that Mr. Wiant, "should furnish the State Police with the names of those persons with whom he had talked in order that our members could investigate…" He added that while his department stood ready to reopen the Sodder case, "should there be sufficient evidence to justify its reopening," but that, "I do not think it would be in the Department's best interest, or to the interest of any investigation conducted to furnish officers to assist Mr. Wiant in conducting his investigation."[280]

15-Year Anniversary Story

On Christmas Day 1960, another one of the traditional Sodder Christmas newspaper stories was written, this time in the *Beckley Post Herald and Register*. It was a re-hashing of the story but with some of the key players interviewed.

The current County Prosecuting Attorney, Zane Summerfield,

was interviewed and stated that the verdict of the coroner's inquest at the time was that the children had died by fire or suffocation. W. H. Level, the Fayette County Justice of the Peace, who presided over the three 1945 coroner inquests, was quoted as saying that nothing (human remains) was found in the fire.[281] Level added that the reason for the verdict at the inquest was only because "no one had seen the children leave the house." Former Fayette County Prosecuting Attorney, Carl Vickers, stated that he remembered that "a piece of a backbone and a human organ was found." However, Vickers added that he did not believe any medical investigation was made by authorities.[282]

The article went as far as to interview the current Kanawha County Coroner, Dr. Goff Lilly, asking if it was possible for all traces of a human body to be destroyed in an ordinary house fire. Dr. Goff stated that, "I wouldn't say it's impossible, but it's highly improbable." He continued, "I have seen about 120 burning deaths and there was always some remains left." Prosecutor Summerfield added that he would be glad to reopen the Sodder case if "some evidence of murder or kidnapping were shown."[283]

Site of the Sodder Billboard

The Former Sodder Property Present Day (photo by the author)

The Sodder house that burned stood at the high point of the asphalt road to the left, about where the basketball hoop stands. The house in the picture was built after the fire. A part of the six-foot chain link fence that George Sodder erected to protect his family can be seen behind the bushes in the foreground. This fence encircled the entire property at one time.

This photograph shows the backside of the existing house. (The basketball hoop can again be seen, this time from the rear). The chain-link fence has a plywood privacy fence added to it as well.

The Former Sodder Property Present Day (photo by the author)

At the time, the billboard was considered a unique idea to make the general public aware of the case. Today, billboards advertising criminal cases and asking for information is common.

For the Sodder billboard, it was more than just an advertisement for the missing children. The billboards were a way for the

Sodders to say what they thought of the officials who did not take their pleas for help seriously. The result of this strategy was more than likely an even more firm refusal by the officials to help. But there could be more here to consider about these various billboards than meets the eye.

It is impossible to know, but one possible explanation as to why the billboard was erected is that the Sodders later regretted not paying the extortion money. After the children were gone, they looked for any way to get them back. The billboards could have been to the people they thought may have been responsible for the crime saying, if our children are still alive, we will now give you the money you wanted if you will just give them back.

A more lurid speculative explanation could be that the extortionists had no intention of giving them back, even if they could, because this would have taken away from the original intent of why the fire was set. As described in a previous chapter, it was more to punish Mr. Sodder, not only for the nasty remarks he made about Mussolini, but also to make an example of him and his refusal to show the proper respect to the leadership of the local organized crime syndicate.

Although Mr. Sodder claimed that he had no enemies and could not explain why his home was burned; he and his wife stated in the very first police report that they believed the fire had been set.[284] In 1951, at a conference in Charleston he offered the theory that he was the victim of extortionists. Later, in another conference, he went further and expressed the names of the people he believed were involved.[285] While in earlier documents, Mr. Sodder had said he did not know of any enemies he might have, it was normal, especially in Italian culture, to not disclose everything they knew to the police.

The Doyle Fire

The February 19th, 1960 issue of the *Charleston Gazette* carried a letter-to-the-editor from Mary Ann Sodder who by his time was married to J. R. Crowder and living in Cleveland, Ohio. Mrs. Crowder brought to the attention of the editor a story the *Gazette* had carried 10 days before regarding a family of four who died in a house fire in Tophet, near the Mercer County border. Mrs. Crowder's reason for writing her letter was to compare the Doyle house fire to her family's house fire.[286]

The Doyle house was a two-story eight-room frame house with a basement. The *Gazette* story says the bodies of the three adults and one child of the Floyd family were found in the ruins of the basement and it was assumed the bodies had fallen through the two stories of the house as the floors burned away.[287] As was the case in the Sodder fire, there was no response by a fire department for several hours.

Apparently by the time the department arrived, the fire was out and the bodies had laid in smoldering ashes for more than five hours. But, when the authorities did arrive, the newspaper story stated that it was nearly dark so little could be done. The story also states that searchers had to wait for the ashes to cool in order to look for bodies. This makes it sound as if no water was applied to the fire. One official noted that, "All that's left is scrap. Not even a board."[288] Even still, the authorities found all four bodies with no problem and they were easily identified, including that of Doyle's two-year-old granddaughter.[289]

In her letter, Mrs. Crowder asked the question:

> *Is it possible for a farmhouse of eight rooms to burn completely to ashes and the bodies of four persons to be found almost intact, yet a smaller house burns and the law authorities say it is their belief that five bodies of five children, 6 to 14 years old, were completely destroyed, bones included?*
>
> *Now I ask you, don't you think they insult the intelligence of us and the rest of the people of West Virginia to expect us to believe such tommyrot? Or, maybe this is just the safest way to keep a horrible crime under cover.*[290]

Chapter 9

The West Virginia Mafia

When they come, they come at what you love.

Michael Corleone, Godfather III.

As it has been said throughout this book, there is no direct evidence that the children were kidnapped or that the Sodder house was intentionally set on fire. There is, however, considerable circumstantial evidence that this happened. If one chooses to interpret the circumstantial evidence, you could conclude that there was a possibility of kidnapping and an intentionally set fire.

The following chapters of this book will focus on trying to establish a theory of motive for why this crime was committed. This will be speculative use of circumstantial evidence, and care has been taken to try and remain within the bounds of reality and not go too far beyond the evidence.

For many years, talk of this mystery included talk about the possible involvement of the Mafia. In understanding the fact that there was a significant element of organized crime in Fayette County during the time of the incident, I felt it would be a mistake not to consider the possible involvement of organized crime. Therefore, I decided to learn everything I could about how the Italian Mafia started, how it came to America, and how it evolved in Fayette County.

I also began to research Italian historical tradition, forms of government, politics, and anything else that might seem significant. I even learned to speak the language, sort of. I felt that with this approach, I may find some element of the case, no matter how small, that matches up to my research and at least from a circumstantial level, could prove organized crime involvement, or at the least, the same techniques, at some level. Luckily, my approach and assumptions both paid off.

West Virginia Mafia

As part of trying to recognize a possible motive for the Sodder case, it is important to understand the presence of organized crime in West Virginia was a real thing:

- Many of the circumstances indicate a method to the crime typical of organized crime and old-world Italian culture.

- There was a low-grade organized crime presence in Fayette County, as well as the rest of West Virginia, at the time of the Sodder fire.

- There was a large Italian population in these same areas that were second generation immigrants.

- Attempts for extortion by the Black Hand or others, were typically made by Italians to other Italians.

- In southern West Virginia, there were several attempts at extortion using methods similar to the Sodder case in the earlier part of the 20th century.

- There is a documented source saying that before the fire, George Sodder did receive a Black Hand letter.[291]

I'm not saying the individuals who committed this crime were members of the Mafia or even leftovers from the Black Hand that terrorized West Virginia in the early 1900s. However, I believe they were familiar enough with the techniques used by these organizations to use them effectively and to instill fear into the Sodder family to extract revenge by stealing their children and then terrorizing them by not naming who did it.

Many books have been written about the Black Hand in places like New York, Chicago, and Pittsburgh in the early 1900s. But few people thought that organized crime could flourish in a small state like West Virginia. The truth is that where there is the potential for a lot of money to be spent, organized crime can be there. And for the type of Mafia that existed in West Virginia (or still does to some degree) it relied on the average Joe to support it. From coal miners, railroad and steel workers to John Q. Public, there were always many customers willing to accept the vice that was being offered.

My research has shown that the usual method of operation of extortion for the Black Hand was to send the potential victim a letter outlining their demands for money and threatening to kidnap a member of a family, if the money was not paid. After receiving a Black Hand Letter, some victims paid the money and were left alone. Others refused and sometimes fought back, but others who refused to pay were often the victims of murder, kidnapping or fire-bombing. For the most part, the potential victim was another Italian who may have found some financial success.

One widely accepted myth is that the Black Hand never touched the members of a man's family. The fact is that women and children were prime targets for their extortion demands.[292] What better way to get someone to give you what you want than to threaten to take away the thing they loved the most? And it nearly always worked.

The Black Hand was known in West Virginia for gambling operations that included large scale card games and sports betting. Their activities also included prostitution, bootlegging, and later, drug trafficking. All of these vices, and their consequences, were popular among the everyday working man and many a paycheck were lost with no explanation for a wife waiting at home.

Pittsburgh

While Pittsburgh is mostly known for the steel industry that thrived there, there was also considerable development and other manufacturing. It should be no stretch of the imagination to understand that organized crime followed closely behind the influx of the massive labor force required to produce these goods and services.

Organized crime in Pittsburgh began in the late 1800s as small independent groups that operated out of the local Italian and Sicilian communities. By the early 1900s, these independent organizations began to slowly consolidate their power, usually with a lot of bloodshed. The Pittsburgh Italian Mafia remained affiliated with organizations in Philadelphia and Northern Pennsylvania as well as the family in Cleveland, Ohio. They were also affiliated, or possibly controlled, by the Genovese Crime Family in New York City.

The Pittsburgh organization eventually became one central body, later expanding further, into other parts of Pennsylvania, Ohio, and Northern West Virginia. The rumor was that in the early 1900s, any organized crime in North Central West Virginia, and possibly even further south, was controlled by the extensive Mafia element in Pittsburgh, which ultimately reported to New York.

Some examples of figures in organized crime in Pittsburgh are Joseph "Jo Jo" Pecora who was a powerful gambling boss and labor racketeer. Pecora was a lieutenant of Sebastian LaRocca. Pecora controlled all gambling in the panhandle of West Virginia. When Pecora went to prison, this faction would later fall under the leadership of Pecora loyalists Paul "No Legs" Hankish and Charles "Chucky" Porter.

In 1979, both Pecora and a prosecutor of Hancock County, WV were convicted of illegal gambling and tampering with evidence. Both were fined $10,000 and sentenced to 5 years in prison. Soon after his release from prison, Pecora was made the underboss of the Pittsburgh family. It still exists to a degree but has gone further underground in its operations.

Clarksburg

National radio commentator Paul Harvey once stated, "If you ever want to commit multiple murders in broad daylight on your front lawn and be found unanimously not guilty by a jury of your peers, move to Clarksburg, WV."[293] In the early part of the 20th century, the Black Hand was very active in Clarksburg.

After receiving a Black Hand Letter, some victims paid the extortion money and were left alone, for a while at least. If the Black Hand found someone who could pay the extortion money, they would go back for more, even going so far as to re-kidnap victims' multiple times until their families were bled dry.

Over time, law enforcement began to successfully fight back by infiltrating the crime organizations. In 1923, after a series of seemingly related murders in the area, eight members of the Black Hand were arrested and prosecuted. Nicholas Salamante, Phillip Connizzaro and Richard Ferri were eventually executed. Approximately a month later, Samual Muratore was also executed.[294]

The downfall of the Black Hand, at least in Clarksburg, was due in large part to the efforts of Sheriff Laco L. Young, a huge man with no fear. Young brought a couple of the criminals to justice in 1923 and arranged for the court to go easy on them in exchange for information on others in the area.[295] The law-abiding Italian community in Harrison County were so appreciative of Young's efforts that they gave him a solid silver pocket watch as a token of their esteem.[296]

Later, there was Big John Gallo who supposedly controlled Clarksburg from the 1960s to the 80s, Steve Gallo who was wounded in the Towhead Adkins shootout, and Carl Lee Gallo who ran the "taxi cab" stand in Clarksburg that was eventually raided by the FBI in the late 70s and found to be a headquarters for organized crime. "Big Joe" Cenetti was also known to have been in charge of the Clarksburg group for a while.[297]

In the 70s, it was discovered that the Mayor of Clarksburg, S. James Shaffer, was directly involved in organized crime and was killed in a shootout by Calvin Adkins and Charles Moran. Shaffer's brother Joseph, who was president of the American Vending Machine Company, was later killed in another shootout with rival Towhead White over an unpaid debt.[298]

There were stories about an underground tunnel that ran from downtown Clarksburg to the Glen Elk section of town that was supposedly used for moving bootleg liquor and going to visit the local prostitutes. There were also stories about the Sanitary Restaurant as a place where, "children could be kidnapped by the Mafia and sold into white slavery." Remnants of the various crime families are said to still exist in Fairmont and Clarksburg as well as in parts of Jackson and Roane counties.

Wheeling

Infamous Chicago mobster Al Capone's bootlegging operation was popular in Wheeling in the 1930s. He transported his Canadian-made whiskey to Chicago and then out to other locations including Wheeling, Fairmont, and parts of Pennsylvania. Canada actually built extra distilleries to handle the demand for whiskey from the United States. The desire for Capone's liquor was enormous and bootlegging constituted a large portion of his wealth. Once the liquor reached Wheeling and Fairmont, it was distributed locally by members of the Black Hand.

William George Liakakos (or Big Bill Lias, as he was popularly known) ran a virtual crime empire for decades in the Wheeling area. His areas of expertise included gambling, bootlegging, and murder. Later in life he tried to go legit by owning and operating a racetrack in Wheeling. Despite a criminal career of more than half a century, Lias spent less than three years in prison. He spread his money around to as many local and state officials as possible. Unlike many of his competitors who died a bloody death, Lias died in 1970 of natural causes.[299]

Paul "No Legs" Hankish and his crime family assumed control of the Wheeling area in the mid-1960s. Hankish was called "No Legs" because he was caught in a car bombing by a supposed rival that caused him to lose both legs in 1965.[300] No arrests were ever made in that bombing.[301]

In April of 1990, Hankish was charged with 89 counts including extortion, drug trafficking, arson, and tax evasion. Associate Ron Asher testified that he committed multiple murders on Hankish's orders which included breaking a woman's neck as well as stabbing her to death. He also committed several arsons in Clarksburg. In addition, Asher testified that he shoplifted hundreds of record albums for Hankish using a special pair of pants, that ended up netting the mob several millions of dollars.

Fairmont

The Black Hand (*La Mano Nerva*) first appeared in Marion County around 1908. Marion County Prosecuting Attorney Tusca Morris was able to eventually shut down the organization, for a while at least. The Black Hand resurfaced in Marion County around 1921.

To become a Black Hand member, the applicant must have committed a murder at the order of the organization. A man named Dick Ferry was the official executioner of the group and at the time of his own execution, claimed to have killed 23 people. The group engaged in prostitution, liquor, and drug trafficking.[302] Although they also practiced extortion and kidnapping of children for ransom, their most profitable enterprise was illegal liquor distribution.

There are still stories of people who saw the sign of the Black Hand on a store entrance on Water Street at Fairmont as late as the early 1950s. Water Street was known to be crime ridden and most of the buildings there were condemned in the early 1960s. Locals in Fairmont can tell you that many former Mafia associates quietly retired there in the 60s.

Being fed up with the Black Hand presence in Fairmont, the local law enforcement began cracking down and many Black Handers were arrested, prosecuted and deported. Below is a photo of such a round-up from the early 20th Century:

Black Hand Members arrested in Fairmont around 1925.
Source: WVU Regional History Center

Typically, a Black Hand victim would receive a letter demanding money and would state the time and place for delivery. If the victim refused, a second letter was sent with an increase in the amount of money wanted. If this failed, the third letter would inform the victim that he and his family had been marked for death. Then, the Black Hand would take action by possibly kidnapping the victim's children or burning or dynamiting their house. During its peak, the Black Hand was known to be responsible for the burning or dynamiting of at least ten homes in the Fairmont area. If the victim survived this, and still did not pay, then the murder would be carried out.[303]

Southern West Virginia

In the early 1900s, the Black Hand was active in McDowell and Mingo counties. Italian immigrants had been hired as replacement workers during labor disputes in the coal mines. The Black Hand would prey on the weaknesses of these men and exploit their desires in an effort to take any and every dollar they earned. When gambling and prostitution did not bring in enough money, the Black Hand would resort to extortion, robbery, or murder.

In an interview with the *Bluefield Daily Telegraph* in May of 1914, Thomas Felts, co-founder of the Baldwin-Felts Detective Agency,[304] gave this description about the Black Hand:

Felts explained that there was a general organization of the Black Hand and in addition to this there were local sub organizations established in localities crowded with the lower elements of Italians which sometimes have large memberships.

He said experience had revealed the fact that where one of these organizations flourished the hundreds of other fellow countrymen of the Black Hand, though aloof from the organization, felt a mortal fear of it. Outsiders, he said, knew well enough the power of the organization and the daring which its members would risk, to know the significance of a threat from its members.

No organization on earth, he explained, required such

a pledge of an applicant for membership. A threat of death, he declared, was the seal which made so binding the oath of loyalty and, he asserted, it was his information that Black Handers need the cooperation of their fellow countrymen, though not one of their number, a threat was not even necessary to extort the service, with such horror was the organization held by the Italians as a people.

Murder, robbery, and revenge were the principal covenants to which the members were pledged and the failure to scrupulously conform to this pledge met absolute certain death or should one of their number turn informant, he was likewise somberly dealt with, he explained.

When a victim was selected to be killed, or scheme of revenge was to be executed, or some person, or concern, was to be robbed, he said the first mode of procedure was for the Black Handers to write their names on slips of paper which they shook up in a hat and the needed number of them necessary to carry out the plot were then drawn, and those names were drawn, the task fell to.[305]

White Slavery

Mostly forgotten is the kidnapping and white slavery that went on in the coal camps of southern West Virginia in the late 19th and 20th centuries. One of these stories is that of a young girl named Josephine Meo who grew up in the slums of New York City. In 1913, at the age of 19, she met a man named Antonio Romeo who convinced her to leave her less-than-ideal life and follow him to Keystone where Josephine later said she was held prisoner with other young girls and used for the profit of Romeo and his partner, Patsie Manguerica.[306]

Later the girl was taken to Maybeury in McDowell County for the same purposes. She later testified that if she resisted, she was severely beaten by Manguerica. Eventually, someone heard the cries of the girl while she was being assaulted, and this led to the arrest of both Romeo and Manguerica by a special representative of the Department of Justice.

Romeo and Manguerica were indicted by a federal grand jury for using the girl for immoral purposes under the newly created Mann White Slavery Act. Romeo was eventually arrested, tried and found guilty. He served only two years in the State Penitentiary at Moundsville. Manguerica was also later arrested and released on a $5,000 bond paid for by his cousin, Steve Romeo.

But while being taken by train to Charleston for trial Manguerica escaped out of a window while his train was stopped at Kenova.[307] His cousin eventually lost the house he had put up as collateral.[308] But not before the same house was firebombed by the Black Hand for Romeo's refusal to pay heed to several Black Hand letters telling him not to look for Manguerica.[309]

Six months later, the Black Hand struck again at the house of a man named Ed Lester for some of the same reasons. It was blown up the same way the Romeo house was in 1915.[310] Manguerica was not re-apprehended for this crime but was later identified as one of five men killed in a shoot-out with local authorities and Baldwin-Felts agents. The five men were attempting to rob a mine payroll at Glen Alum Coal Company.[311] Since there was no way to positively identify Manguerica, the Court did not release the bond paid by Steve Romeo.[312] Manguerica is believed to be the body on the far left in the picture shown below.

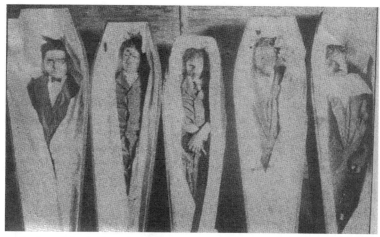

Italian Black Handers killed for robbing a payroll on display in front of McDowell County Court House, 1915.

There was also the case of two Pennsylvania men accused of luring young girls to southern West Virginia with the promise of lucrative employment as stenographers. But when the girls arrived, they were drugged and placed into crude houses surrounded by a stockade. Harry Culp, of Wilkinson, PA and Steve Stevens were charged with peonage and violating the Mann white slavery act in March of 1913.[313] While the girls were eventually taken to Switchback, WV for prostitution, it was decided their kidnappers would be tried in U. S. Federal Court in Pennsylvania where they had been recruiting the girls through ads in local newspapers, in Scranton, PA.[314]

During the trial, the government produced scores of girls who had also been the victims of these two men. They testified in horrid detail the effects their imprisonment had on them. Some of the girls had to be helped to the witness stand by physicians because of the abuse they had experienced.

The women, who were listed in the various newspaper stories (by name), said they were told that to earn their freedom, they had to associate with men who had been employed to take the place of striking coal miners and who had nothing else to do on their off hours. Many of the replacement workers had already left the area because of the monotony and the isolation and the women were brought in to "give them something to do."[315] Both Culp and Stevens were found guilty and served sentences between six months and two years in the federal penitentiary in Leavenworth, Kansas.[316]

This brief look at white slavery is very limited. I spent less than half a day doing the research for it and only cited a few of the many cases and specifically the ones that mentioned kidnapping and white slavery. No doubt that there are many more stories of young girls being kidnapped and thrown into human trafficking. For each victim who had the courage to come forward, there likely were numerous others who chose not to speak, and even more who may not have survived it.

The original point I wanted to make using this subject was that the theory that the Sodder children could have been kidnapped and sold into white slavery, which was first suggested by a private investigator in 1949. While there is no evidence this is what happened, it shows that it was within the realm of possibility. The children could have been kidnapped and used for profit.

Smithers/Montgomery

The idea that there was/is a Mafia in Smithers is not something new. There was a large influx of Italian immigrants to Smithers in the early 1900s. The man who was thought to be the most famous connected man in Smithers was "Big Al" Falbo who ran a very popular restaurant/ bar/ lounge where you could buy virtually anything you wanted or take advantage of the many other services that were offered there. At the time of his death in 1983, Falbo was under investigation by the FBI, who, with the aid of local law enforcement, videotaped Falbo's burial service using a surveillance van at the cemetery.[317]

The author was told by someone who was in the surveillance van at the time that at the end of the service, three men came forward and each placed a single rose on Al's coffin. The FBI told my friend that those roses represented the mob from New York, Chicago, and Kansas City. After Falbo's death, his wife, two sons, and 15 others were indicted and convicted of running gambling operations in five West Virginia towns and cities.

One defendant claimed that one of his regular duties was to deliver payoffs to local Fayette County officials.[318] While no specific people were named this was not an unusual occurrence. Falbo's bar/lounge was closed and eventually torn down. Today, Al Falbo's lasting legacy is the great sandwich that he created at his restaurant called "The Al Burger."

There were several bars and beer gardens located in Montgomery over the years. One noted example was The Top Hat, a social club and bar. It closed in the 1980s along with most everything else in Montgomery. Other organized gambling and bootlegging locations in Montgomery included the New Royal Hotel, The Owls Club, the Ritz, and Mammoth Cave, to name a few.[319] There is documentation of gambling and bootlegging arrests made at each of these locations in the 40s, 50s and 60s.

Fayetteville

During the same time, gambling raids were conducted at locations in and around Fayetteville such as The Smoke House Restaurant,[320] Mt. Hope Pool Room,[321] Clay Garden Beer Garden,[322] Skyline Drive-in,[323] and many others. Sometimes these raids were conducted because of public outcry to stop illegal gambling.

Other times, I was told the raids were performed because the police did not receive their share of the proceeds.[324] Sometimes the police would raid a questionable establishment after giving them plenty of notice just to make it appear to the public that they were enforcing the law.

A book could be written about the history of organized crime in West Virginia, but the point of this discussion is to show that it did exist and was very active.

Black Hand Methods

An understanding of the traditional methods used by the Black Hand can help in trying to piece together a motive and method for the Sodder case.

The following is an example of a typical Black Hand Letter:

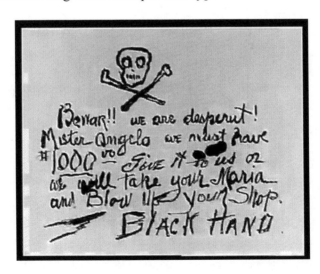

(The spelling errors of this particular letter are left in place, see below):

Beware, we are desperate! Mister Angelo we must have $1000 – give it to us or we will take your Maria and blow up your shop.
BLACK HAND

The following is another example Black Hand letter from 1903:

Nicola Cappiello, if you do not meet us tomorrow (with $10,000), your house will be dynamited and you and your family killed. The same fate awaits you in the event of your betraying our purposes to the police.

Mano Nerva (Black Hand)

This sounds very much like:

I see you refused to buy the insurance that was offered to you. Your house will go up in smoke and your children will be destroyed.

Most Black Hand threats went unreported. New York Italian-American police officers quoted in a June 1909 *Cosmopolitan* magazine article, estimated that for every extortion case reported there were probably ten times that many for which nothing was said. If this assessment is accurate, the Black Hand activity in the city must have been staggering.

Sometimes Black Hand gangs became the means by which businessmen reduced business rivals or eliminated them entirely.[325] Remember before opening his own business, Sodder worked for another local Italian businessman and they did not part on good terms.

The mobster is someone who thinks that if they have money and power, they have it all. He knows in his heart that he is a criminal, but he thinks that by having money and appearing to be a good person, then it makes up for any criminal activity. He cannot tolerate a lack of respect because he has such low self-esteem. The mobster only loves money and power and wants to control others by using his power to make them respect him out of fear. He wants everything for himself so he takes it with threats, force, and violence. This is a particular form of the God principle.[326]

The fact that no traces of human remains were found in the Sodder basement is yet another indicator of the involvement of the Mafia. The old-world thinking was that if you do not find a corpse, then there will always be a question as to if there actually was a crime. So, a Mafia signature is the fact that no corpses were found. So it is clearly a combination of revenge and terrorism. To the person who has done this, it feeds their low self-esteem to have other local citizens afraid of what could happen to them if they do not stay in line. It also helps feed the ego to have a symbol or marker at the site of the tragedy as a memento of what happened. Kind of like a serial killer who takes souvenirs of their victims to try and relive the thrill of what they have done.[327]

Omertà

In old world Italian culture, each person was expected to mind their own business.[328] The suspicion of being a stool pigeon, or *cascittuni*, constituted the blackest mark against a Silcian's manhood. Each individual had the obligation for proving his manliness by not appealing to authority (police) for personal grievances. A wronged person was expected to avenge himself or find a patron who would see that the job was done. This attitude showed clearly in the adage "blood washes blood," one of the sayings most commonly associated with the Mafia and *omertà*.[329]

The supreme accolade of a man's character is *Christu fa I fatti sui!* He looks after his own interests and doesn't intervene in the affairs of others.[330] An old Sicilian Proverb states:

Of that which does not concern you, say neither good nor evil.[331]

Radical Italians and Pro-Fascists

Organized crime in Fayette County was known to control gambling parlors, sports betting, amusement machines, prostitution, and bootlegging. However, in the 1940s, there was an even more radical element of Italian immigrant in Fayette County that today seems long forgotten.

In 1942, there were many newspaper articles describing a series of arrests of alien Italians in various towns in West Virginia including Smithers, Boomer, Cannelton, Beckley, Montgomery, and Weirton. In conjunction with these arrests was the confiscation of many different types of guns and ammunition. Also confiscated during the same raid were short-wave sending and receiving radios, 34 dynamite caps, various types of explosives, pro-fascist literature and other related documents, all in Italian. This was all considered contraband under the wartime enemy alien laws.[332]

What constituted an illegal alien in the 1940s? I found an interesting article written during the Second World War by a sportswriter for a Beckley newspaper. I found it significant enough in terms of understanding the mood of the American people at the time that I felt it should be reproduced here:

Speaking of Sports

By Roy Lee Harmon

I hope every citizen in this neck of the woods reads that story about a "covey" of enemy aliens being nabbed here yesterday. The FBI agents, state police and city police helped round up the dangerous and asinine foreigners. And I hope everybody took a look, a good long look, at that picture on the front page of the Register yesterday, that picture of rifles, ammunition, pistols and other destructive appurtenances which had been taken away from the aliens……

Furthermore, I know the aliens were convening once in a while. Each autumn during the past five years a big group met in the woods on a farm just outside the city limits. They have danced, made speeches and raised heck in general. Once I ventured near enough to witness a portion of the proceedings, probably taking my life in my hands. But I have been amazed because other good Americans refused to get excited about the enemies within our ranks. And I was naturally overjoyed yesterday when I learned that the enemies, claiming blessings

Uncle Sam bestows on all those who live in this great nation, have been rounded up. And I sincerely hope that the FBI and other law enforcement agencies won't stop now.....

The Raleigh and Fayette county areas proved to be a favorite hangout of the enemy aliens during the past few years. Most any foreigner with a strong back could make a good living in the mines... I'm sad to report that a few never forget the old country–and have no loyalty for America... One night, long before our nation entered the war, there was a boxing program under way at Beckley Arena on the new Raleigh road. Joe Dutton was the referee. After other announcements had been made from the ring, Dutton declared:

"If anybody doesn't like England I'll fight them right here in the ring."

Everybody laughed—everybody was in a kindly mood. Nationalism was not rampant here. Uncle Sam was just an innocent bystander in the war. But Joe Dutton was attacked by THREE men a few nights later, attacked by three men who did their best to beat him up. He lost a few teeth in the battle but he came out in good shape. Joe is an old time boxer, you know. I have never written about this incident before. But I have never forgotten it. Don't trust the enemy aliens.....

Remember that officers found 387 rounds of ammunition when they nabbed the aliens—and that one of the persons taken into custody owned a short-wave radio set which could pick up messages from Italy easily.[333]

The full article can be found in the *Beckley Post Herald* on October 7, 1942.

The point of all of this is to show that at the time, there was much conflict for immigrants. This also shows the extent of fascist leanings that existed in America at the time as well using violence to support their point of view.

George Sodder, while not a naturalized citizen, was still very patriotic and even more anti-Mussolini. Surprisingly, George Sodder's position concerning Mussolini put him in conflict with many local Italians who still considered Mussolini a great leader. Some of these pro-fascist Italians Mr. Sodder encountered were possibly part of the alien arrests discussed above.

From all of this and the documented threats about buying insurance on his children, and increasing his homeowner's insurance, it adds up to attempted extortion. Add to this that a threat was made that the Sodders had also refused to sign off on a property settlement for Mrs. Sodder's father after his death in 1944. And the most telling threat, that he would be paid back for his "dirty remarks" about Mussolini. This all sounds like the calling card of the enemy aliens and the methods of the Black Hand.

Many of these pro-Mussolini Italians were possibly members of the Sons of Italy in America (SOIA), a popular fraternal lodge. Before World War II, the SOIA was heavily involved in promoting Mussolini's fascist policies in the United States.[334] Interestingly enough, one of the guiding principles of the SOIA included the idea of purchasing insurance policies as a good means of helping to "develop the Italian presence in America." Could this have been why a Fayetteville businessman virtually demanded that the Sodders purchase life insurance on their family?

In an effort to thoroughly explain the methods of the early followers of the Black Hand and how they paralleled what happened to the Sodders and how it happened, I recommend reading Humbert Nelli's excellent book, *The Business of Crime, Italians and Syndicate Crime in the United States* and comparing this to what happened in the Sodder case.

George Sodder - Anarchist

It should first be noted that anarchy does not have the same connotation today as it did then, and that "anarchist" is a very subjective term. During this time in Italy, virtually anyone who opposed fascism could find themselves branded as an anarchist or communist. The term referred to a person or a group who opposed the policies and philosophies of the government in power at the time.

The record on file with the Italian government labeling a man named Giorgio Soddu as an anarchist was made between 1931 and 1933, some twenty years after George Sodder of Fayetteville left Italy. This could mean several things:

- This record is referring to a Giorgio Soddu, but not the one who settled in Fayette County.

- It could be referring to the Soddu family still remaining in Italy and there-by anyone else who was part of that family including the immigrated Giorgia Soddu.

- It could refer to George Sodder and someone from Fayetteville, who had the means to travel to Italy, and passed on information to the officials there and this document was created as a result.

George Sodder of Fayetteville, by the date of this document, was still living in Smithers, mining coal by day and driving a taxicab at night. He was married and five of his ten children had been born. He had not begun work for the Janutolo Company. Since it was F. Janutolo who told George that he would be paid back for his comments about Mussolini, it is doubtful that the split between Sodder and Janutolo came this early. He could have at this point expressed his opinion about Mussolini. If he was, and if the Janutolos had heard about this, it is likely that he would never have been hired in the first place.

While employed there, one of the Janutolos agreed to loan Mr. Sodder the money to finance the purchase of his house. I do not believe that the Janutolos would have done this for a man that they had such strong political disagreements with.

I believe it is safe to say that if George Sodder knew such a record existed that labeled him an anarchist he would feel honored to have been singled out to be against the government of Benito Mussolini.

Chapter 10

The Motive

Vendetta: An act or series of acts committed to cause harm to a disliked person or group.

Origin - Italian, revenge, from Latin, vindicta (vindictive).

There is no direct evidence known that shows what happened to the Sodder children. Sometimes, depending on the perspective one chooses to look from, circumstantial evidence can lead to possible answers. There are several possible scenarios that fit some of the circumstantial evidence associated with this case.

1. The first scenario is that the children all died on Christmas morning, 1945 so there is no further story to tell. All of the strange incidents that happened before, during, and after the fire are mere coincidence. The Sodders were probably victims of what is referred to today as "survivor guilt" meaning they simply refused to accept that their children died in the fire because they carried residual guilt for the accident.

2. A second possible scenario is the house was intentionally set on fire and the five children died. The house may have been burned as a warning or a vendetta.

3. A third possible scenario is one where the Sodders were the victims of an old-world style vendetta. Possibly the children were first taken out of the house and then their house was burned to cover up the crime, or it was the intent to kill the whole family in a fire. The younger children then were either murdered, sold, or possibly both.

This chapter will assume this third scenario is true and will try to explain how it may fit the evidence that exists and where it does not. In making this assumption, either as a whole or in part, a pattern quickly emerges that can explain much of the circumstantial evidence. This is what we will refer to in this chapter as a possible motive for this crime.

So far this book has been for the most part, just a telling of the Sodder story from newspaper stories, magazine articles and official reports and some family stories. Some of the chapters have some possible conclusions at hand but nothing that connects the whole case together.

However, I could not write this book and not try to offer some kind of possible conclusions. I have lived this case for years now, so I feel I am entitled to offer an educated guess as to the fate of the children.

Assuming the possible explanation described here is true, there were possibly two separate crimes–the kidnapping of the children and the burning of the house.

Motive: In any crime, there's always a motive. In the Sodder case, we can even draw a possible motive from the time-immortal seven deadly sins–pride (the need for respect), envy (wishing they had the success of Mr. Sodder), greed (obvious), and wrath (not getting the respect they felt was deserved).

Opportunity: Everyone who could have a motive was in Fayetteville the night it happened. Possibly even others, meaning the men who watched the Sodder children get off of their school bus.

Means: Virtually anyone could light a match to start the fire. But what else is included in means? Moving the ladder, taking the children in a car, cutting the phone lines, delaying the arrival of the fire department. Expanded further, who could have shut down the investigation, caused it to be limited and abbreviated–a coroner's inquest held ten hours after the fire, in the front yard. Who could have increased the amount of insurance the Sodders carried on their house, without telling the Sodders.

Means, opportunity and motive. In most court cases, that's what you have to have to get a conviction, assuming everybody is on the up and up and has no ulterior motives. Let's go further into the details to continue assembling this possible motive.

Evidence Primer

One of the first steps to provide an explanation as to what could have happened and why authorities chose not to investigate requires an explanation on some basic definitions of evidence.

The most commonly given reason why officials chose not to pursue the case was due to a lack of direct evidence.

There are many kinds of evidence. Just to name a few, there is physical evidence, direct, indirect, and circumstantial evidence. Physical evidence is also called real or material evidence. It can be eyewitness testimony, written statements, letters, diaries, confessions, physical material such as guns, fingerprints, DNA, etc. Basically, anything that can be used to directly prove an assertion to be a fact. Most prosecutors want physical evidence to pursue a criminal case because it gives the best odds of winning a case.

Circumstantial evidence requires an inference to connect it to a conclusion of fact. This inference can relate something or someone to a crime but it cannot independently prove someone committed the crime. This is usually because of another defining point of this type of evidence, the inference required may point to several other possible conclusions, not just the one you favor. This could mean that someone was at the scene of a crime but it does not directly prove when they were there or what they did while they were there. The ambiguity that defines this type of evidence is one reason why cases are not pursued. They are easily overturned on appeal. It is too easy for a good defense attorney to establish reasonable doubt and the case is lost.

An example is if you find someone's bloody fingerprints on a knife that is sticking out of a body, the odds are that you have the killer. But it is still circumstantial evidence. No one directly saw anyone stab the body. This means that reasonable doubt could still exist under the right circumstances or interpretation of the evidence. The knife alone allows for more than one explanation. The person with the fingerprint could have touched it before the body was stabbed and the person who stabbed the body might have worn gloves and left no prints.

A circumstantial evidence case that can be successfully prosecuted may require several pieces of that type of evidence, each pointing toward the same possible conclusion by using a common inference. However, as part of the assemblage of individual pieces of circumstantial evidence, the case can be made even stronger by providing explanations as to why other possible explanations can be dismissed or ruled out. In other words, peeling away what does not fit can be just as beneficial as knowing what does.

Circumstantial evidence also may require a trial to create, justify, or prove that required inference exists. Of course, the Sodder family never really cared about ending up in court, they just wanted their children back. This seemed to be, for many years, the disconnect. The Sodders felt there was enough justification for investigating the many odd occurrences that could be called circumstantial evidence. In order to actively pursue the case the officials needed direct evidence, which would have to amount to nothing less than a confession by one of the perpetrators or one of the missing children coming back and confirming they had been kidnapped. Of course, to achieve this, they would have had to first investigate.

One of the most famous trials where circumstantial evidence was used successfully was the Tate-Labianca murder trial in Los Angeles in 1970. Although defendant Charles Manson did not physically participate directly in the murders, the prosecutor used circumstantial evidence to show that Manson had orchestrated the murders by manipulating the minds of his followers with sex, drugs and various mind control techniques.

For the Sodder case, there are several pieces of circumstantial evidence that a possible conclusion, or an inference, can be drawn in regard to what may have happened and why.

Official Reports

Normally, it would have been the Fire Marshal's office who would have prepared a report regarding the fire but since the WV State Police arrived first the Fire Marshal deferred to them. And,

204

since it initially appeared the conclusion of the case was obvious, the Fire Marshal apparently saw no reason to begin his own investigation.

But, after the very publicized excavation and many newspaper stories after 1949, the Fire Marshal must have decided to produce a report, albeit late. Their office was being questioned by the media as well as various officials the Sodders had contacted asking for help, and there were a lot of unanswered questions.

There had been enough inconsistencies, questionable actions, and possible threats to the Sodders that would warrant further investigation of the case. Also keep in mind that acting Fayette County Coroner William Level stated that the only reason the coroner's jury reached the conclusion they did is because, "no one actually saw the children come out of the house during the fire." The logic of that statement escapes the author. Imagine if the validity of a crime was only based on visually witnessing it.

The Motive

Let's start with "why George Sodder?" Why did this happen to his family? The morning after the fire, when he was asked who would have it in for him, he said he had no enemies.[335] I believe Mr. Sodder was not truthful about this. He knew he had been threatened. I believe that Mr. Sodder was holding to the old Italian tradition of *omertà*, thinking that it was best to say nothing.[336] Following *omertà* was just a gut reaction or instinct for most Italian immigrants because they had had no trust for the government in Italy and that mistrust continued when they came to America. The basic principle of *omertà* is that it is not manly to seek aid from legally constituted authorities to settle personal grievances. The suspicion of being a *cascittuni* (informant) constitutes the blackest mark against manhood.[337]

Omertà is an extreme form of loyalty and solidarity in the face of authority. One of its absolute tenets is that it is deeply demeaning and shameful to betray even one's deadliest enemy to the authorities. For that reason, many Mafia-related crimes go unsolved. Many more times, not even reported.

George Sodder's first instinct was to follow the guiding principle with which he had been expressly instructed by everyone he had ever known from his home Sardinia. So, when he was asked on the morning after the fire, "do you have any enemies," his natural first response was to say "no." Perhaps thinking if he followed *omertà*, and if the children had been taken just for ransom, they might be returned. But as time passed he left the principles of the old world behind and appealed for help.

Why The Sodder Family

The 1950 State Fire Marshal report offers a number of reasons why the Sodder house was burned:

- Sodder was becoming a successful businessman in his chosen profession.
- He was very outspoken about his views on Italian politics.
- He would not take out life insurance policies on his children.
- Nor would he increase the amount of his homeowners insurance.
- He would not allow his wife to sign off on settling her father's estate.
- Mr. Sodder's refusal to be part of the extortion.
- Insulting the leader of the local Italians, also called a *sggaro*.

But you might be asking, extortion from whom? His next-door neighbor, a bunch of local thugs? What kind of hierarchy could exist that could cause this to happen? The Italians learned to ban together and create a new version of old-world Italian society in America. Whenever possible, they bought what they needed from each other. Groups of Italian families would live together in communities that many times became known as Little Italy. They did what they had to do to survive.

The Italians immigrants also came to realize that they could not depend on the police. They found they were resented for being brought to America to take jobs away from striking coal miners. So, just as in the old world, they learned to rely on themselves. The next section describes how this self-regulation was accomplished.

Local Leaders

In Italy, after the fall of the Roman Empire, a new form of local government developed that was similar to that of medieval England. The power of this feudal system was established by a form of stratified class based on one's position in the society. The traditional structure of this hierarchy was as follows:

Galaniuomini – benestanta	(gentleman or well-off)
Artigiani – mercanti	(artisans or merchants)
Contadini	(peasants)
Giornalieri	(day-laborers)

This traditional pattern of social stratification is typically shown in the form of a triangle with the *galaniuomini* at the top (few) and the *giornalieri* at the bottom (many).[338] Those at the top of the pyramid were usually large estate owners who had held wealth for centuries and employed the peasants or laborers to farm the crops and pay the land owners for the privilege.

The immigrants arriving in America were typically peasants and laborers but sometimes merchants, tradesmen, or craftsmen. Eventually someone drifts to the top of the group. A leadership developed which then could help control the uneducated peasants.

These leaders eventually carried a level of authority and responsibility for the people. As an Italian immigrant, you were not necessarily forced to participate but for the most part, since you were in a new country whose customs you may not understand, you were probably happy to have someone looking out for your interests.[339]

In return, this leadership could take care of virtually any problem you brought to them. Financial, marriage, death of a relative, social, finding a job, even trouble with the police. But in return for this protection, you gave your undying loyalty and respect, as well as a regular tribute or payment. It could extend to everyday things like where you bought your meat, if you carried insurance on your home, or if you even owned a home. The extent of help could include co-signing a note for you to buy a home. Arranging for a life insurance policy to help keep the family going in case of the death of the bread-winner.[340] Virtually anything to give Italian-Americans a leg-up in the new world.

As stated in the 1950 Fire Marshal report, neither George Sodder, nor any of his sons, belonged to any Italian organizations that were prevalent at that time. The report stated he did not participate in any lodge work.[341] This is a very significant statement. To the English, Italian lodge work could have created a perception of participation in subversive activities due to the fact that many Italians had been brought to America to take jobs from striking English workers.

There is every indication that George Sodder wanted nothing to do with the old-world way of life. He had found paradise in America, he wanted to be an entrepreneur, take care of his large family, and be in no one's debt. His family members tell the story that he worked just to survive as a young boy new to this country. Eventually, he began to see the fruit of his labor and how he could get ahead by being his own boss.

Being in someone's debt however, was often how leadership kept families in line. They would lend money, co-sign for loans, find them jobs, and then remind you of it when you stepped out of line. They wanted to control every aspect of your life. And there is no way that upon his arrival in the U.S. George Sodder survived as a 13-year-old boy without someone's help. Something may have happened to young George that caused him to see what it was like to owe a debt to these "leaders." As he got older, he became more determined to make his own way and follow his own convictions.

Man of Honor

The mafia were small self-governing organizations, independent of each other but aware of each other's actions and territories. They would support each other and if necessary, cross over each other's territory to help one another take care of business. It was more like a business with many franchises offering the same services but in different locations and each independently owned.

While the typical tiered structure was as described earlier, there were outlying members and associates also. One example of a man acting on the outside fringes of this organization, but still having ties, was called the *uomo d'onore*, or man of honor. In most organizations this fringe associate had the same rights and privileges as the capo or Don, but again, at a price which did not always involve money.

Local Italian leaders were men of dignity who earned respect without usually having to demand it and exerted a profound influence in the local economy and politics. To them, the people brought their problems and the leaders solved them in return for favors and pledges of support and respect. In the process, the leaders accumulated immense power and influence, and although they lived quietly, frugally, and inconspicuously, they also acquired great wealth. [342]

The comment about the amount of home insurance Mr. Sodder carried could be explained since Mr. Janutolo was the beneficiary of the policy. He may have been trying to protect his investment. The amount of the increase was just $250. The obvious question is what business is it of Janutolo what Mr. Sodder does? It almost sounds like he is in charge of Mr. Sodder, or at least he thinks he is and when Mr. Sodder refuses, it infuriates him like it was some sort of personal insult. And how would it be possible for Mr. Janutolo to have gotten the amount of the Sodder homeowner's insurance policy changed from $1,500 to $1,750 without telling the Sodders? The 1950 Fire Marshal report confirmed it. And the insurance was paid out after the fire.

F. Janutolo was personal friends with the insurance company president, Rosser Long, who first proposed the new insurance to Mr. Sodder at Janutolo's suggestion. No direct official business connection between the two could be found but there are dozens of newspaper articles connecting these two men through the Rotary Club, the Masonic Lodge, Fayetteville Businessmen's Association, The September Born Club, and others.

Regarding the comment about the settlement of Mr. Ciprinai's estate, it is alleged that during a conversation Mr. Sodder had with F. Janutolo about three months before the fire, one of the subjects brought up was that Mr. Sodder had told his wife not to sign the papers to settle her father's estate. Joseph Cipriani died in October of 1942. Previous investigators have always found it strange that Janutolo would make such a statement. Especially considering that there is no mention of Janutolo in Mr. Cipriani's will. Mr. Cipriani had many children and it is assumed that he left something for each child in his will. It is also reasonable to assume that in terms of typical heirship cases, that in order for everyone to get anything, that all the heirs had to sign off on the proposed settlement before it could be distributed.

It is also assumed that Mrs. Sodder had been included in her father's will, but that Mr. Sodder felt that something was not fair. Mr. Cipriani had owned a store, possibly in Smithers. It is possible that his assets were relatively significant.

In 2019, I had a conversation with one of George Sodder's great-grandsons who told me that the source of the controversy here was that one of Joe Cipriani's daughters was not mentioned in the will. The reason for this was unknown. By delaying the signing of the settlement papers, it was believed that this would somehow keep this sister from being able to participate in the financial distribution.

Since Mr. Janutolo made the statement in question to Mr. Sodder around September or October of 1945, that meant it had been two full years since Joseph Cipriani's death. So the conflict regarding the settlement of the estate had possibly been going on for a while. F. Janutolo was an Italian community leader, so it is reasonable that someone from the Cipriani family contacted him to convince George Sodder to let his wife sign off on the probate papers and, if Janutolo could solve this problem, he would likely get a cut of whatever inheritance was received. While all of this is speculation, it would fit the circumstances and answer some of the questions related to this strange part of the case.

If Janutolo was in fact a local Italian leader, he would think he could solve this issue and profit from it. A man who had the power to change the amount of another man's homeowners insurance (without his knowledge), would surely be able to resolve a simple question of heirship and collect his share. At least that is what the Cipriani's may have thought.

And perhaps the most curious part, the 1950 report states that 4 ½ years after the fire, Mr. Janutolo had never been questioned about any of the statements or threats he is alleged to have made. Again, what kind of power does this take? Not only power over Italian immigrants, but the ability to exert power over Fayette County prosecutors.

The *uomo d'onore* can operate close to the Mafia but stand on their own. And, by paying the *pizzo*, he accumulates credit in the local organized crime syndicate so that if something came up that he needed help with, like the initiation of a vendetta against someone who has committed a *sgarro*, he can call in a credit and get help from a capo-Mafia.

This can explain the unknown men who watched the Sodder children getting off the school bus weeks before the fire as well as the Italians who Mrs. Crutchfield said she saw with the four Sodder children at her hotel in Charleston days after the fire. They could have been outsiders who were brought in to handle a situation that could not be handled any other way.

It is a shame that no one tried to get a police artist drawing of the men at the school bus and the ones who were at the Alderson Hotel. If a comparison of the two men were a match, it could have been the spark of a renewed investigation. Another interesting fact about the school bus incident is that this fact never appeared in any official document or police correspondence that I discovered.

It was explained to me about the use of outsiders to accomplish Mafia business by an unnamed source (who chooses to remain unnamed) who was familiar with Italian organized crime:

This is done to confuse the police. If a mobster is import-
ant enough, or he has built up enough credit, then he can ask

211

another boss: you do a favor to me and I will do a favor for you. Otherwise, he will enter into an oral contract as would in a normal business situation. Then, if the boss accepts, he might ask for a payment for his services. Otherwise, he might want a discount for Mafia infiltration into the territory of the man asking for the favor. Either way, the man asking the favor will likely have his life and livelihood controlled forever. He would become a Mafia slave.[343] If the UD ever had dreams of climbing higher in the organization, this lack of respect, or sgarro between him and Sodder could have stopped his assent.

Sodder was very loud in his opposition to Mussolini, not only in volume but also to whom he voiced it. For someone to silence Sodder would show his power and ability to be the big boss in Fayette County. But eventually, it would be a man named Alfonse Falbo who became the big boss in that area. All other lower bosses paid tribute to him.

Whoever was using the role of the *uomo d'onore* could still ask for help from an out-of-town mobster to handle things like:

1. Watching the children when they got off the school bus.

2. Setting the fire.

3. Taking the children after the fire (the people who were seen with the four children at the Charleston hotel)

4. Taking them to either a baby farm where they were sold or taking them back to Italy and sold into slavery.

5. These contract workers could also have been responsible for murdering the children if that was their fate.

However, depending on the level of help that was needed, the payback that a local *uomo d'onore* would have to provide could be great. He may have to give up some of his territory or pay more *pizzo* money to the capo-Mafia. He may also lose the respect of the capo-Mafia because he could not handle his vendetta on his own.

212

Black Hand (La Mano Nerva)

I encountered many people who had the idea, no doubt from TV shows, that the Mafia never touched their intended victim's family. In reading about the Black Hand, I found that no member of a family was safe, especially those who were most vulnerable. But by the 1940s there was not much reported Black Hand activity and it is not implied that the kidnapping of the Sodder children was by a traditional Sicilian band of immigrants. But whoever did this followed many of the same patterns of a Black Hand. These tendencies and patterns are shown in the following table.

TYPICAL MAFIA / BLACK HAND METHODS	SODDER CASE OCCURRENCES
The Black Hand would watch their potential victims to learn their typical tendencies so they could be ready to kidnap a family member if it came to that.	Men who were unknown in the area, were noticed watching the Sodder children get off their school bus weeks before the fire.[344]
The whole insurance or protection money threat of extortion. The Black Hand was well known and successful at this.	The demand to buy life insurance for the children. Also pressured to settle Mr. Cipriani's estate, probably for a cut.
If someone does not want to pay the pizzo, or extortion money, then they are first given one or more warnings. Later, threatened with fire, and/ or kidnapping of a family member.	Mr. Sodder was told he would be sorry. Also, the man who came to the Sodder house and implied the electrical system was going to start a fire, gave a second warning. A few months later, it happened.

Black Hand was well known for learning about the children of a potential victim and threatening their lives.	"Your house will go up in smoke and your children are going to be destroyed."
After the vendetta is over, a way of telling someone to eat their heart out. They are beaten or defeated.	The symbolism of the liver placed in the ashes means I defeated you. And telling no one about it is a silent trophy for the one who ordered it to happen.
Just like Jimmy Hoffa case, there was a known connection to organized crime but there were no traces, no one talked. Stick to the *omerta* as a matter of honor.	The fact that no trace of the children have ever been found is a possible symbol of *omerta*. Mr. Sodder's initial denial of a known enemy as well.
The Black Hand would try to burn victims to a crisp to avoid identification by allowing a fire to burn out to completion.	The Fire Department did not respond for eight hours to allow the perception that the bodies burned completely. They were possibly told to wait before responding.

The *Sgarro*

An incident described in the 1950 Fire Marshal report could be the key to the entire case. If Mr. Janutolo held a position of leadership; he was not used to having someone go against his directions. The Sodder's made a sgarro–a disrespectful nature against a mobster.[345]

The bigger the sgarro, the bigger the punishment, especially if the sgarro is made in public. When Mr. Sodder had publicly denounced Mussolini and refused to pay the pizzo, this was a very big sgarro. To the eyes of a want-to-be capo, the refusal and disrespect were the main catalyst of the vendetta, the money was no longer that important.

This is what the investigators did not see. They thought the amount of money involved, meaning the homeowner's insurance policy, was not worth causing all this uproar over. They tried to investigate this case from the standpoint of English-based law and they did not understand the culture of the people involved. Or maybe they did not want to understand it. As my Italian culture expert told me:

The Mafia don't want just the money (pizzo) from Sodder, but also the respect and the control of all his life.[346]

This need for respect can be very important for a *uomo d'onore* to take the next step and join *La Cosa Nostra*. To do this, he needed to prove to the higher-ups that he had respect from the residents. But because of the perceived *sgarro* from the Sodder's, the refusal, the rebellion, implied disrespect, caused the *uomo d'onore* to be hurt in his quest for power. Sodder deserved an exemplary lesson, a punishment so great, that no one would have ever dared to rebel again. The refusal to follow the directions of the *uomo d'onore* (pay the pizzo) was rebellion, the rebellion was lack of respect; the lack of respect was the *sgarro*, the *sgarro* required a vendetta response.

Then a few weeks before the fire, Sodder received a visit from the man who wanted to talk about a hauling job, but was more interested in inspecting the back of the house and then told him that his electrical service to his house was going to start a fire. This could have been Sodder's first or second warning. His message was, "There could be a fire." This was someone who Sodder had never seen before, and he underestimated the danger.

Mr. and/or Mrs. Sodder may have made a *sgarro* to a local Italian leader (possibly unknowingly). An insult could justify the Sodder family disaster. And because the perceived insult was regarding life insurance on his children and insurance on his house, the *sgarro* and the subsequent vendetta had to be related to the children and the house.

Code of Pazienza

Revenge is a dish that is best served cold. When is the right time to enact revenge? Let your victim relax into a false sense of security thinking everything is fine, and nothing is going to happen, even though you offended this powerful Italian leader.

Late Night Phone Call

The late-night phone call from Mrs. Frank Harding was either a warning, or possibly a check to see if anyone was awake to alert them. That way, the planned vendetta would just be the burning of the house and no loss of life. It would have just been an accident that the children died because they may have suffered smoke inhalation. In other words, a vendetta that went too far? This would fit more as a possible accident.

Harding first admitted she made the call, then later she denied it. I think she was afraid to get involved, or someone got to her. But who could this woman be so afraid of? What could they do? The fact that Mrs. Harding first said she made the call, then later denied it shows that someone probably explained to Mrs. Harding to keep her mouth closed. This phenomenon was not uncommon. Several other key players reversed their stories at one time or another.

What Could Have Happened

So how did the whole thing start? The parents had gone to bed after 9 p.m. with baby Silva. The two older boys had gone upstairs about an hour later and Mary Ann was asleep on the couch near where the five younger children were playing. Mrs. Sodder got up to answer the phone at around 12:30 a.m. and saw that the usual chores assigned to the younger children had not been done. She assumed all five children had gone upstairs to bed.

Before entering the house, the person responsible first cut the phone line, for which they had to use a ladder. Then, they moved the ladder away so it could not be used in any kind of rescue attempt. From the variations surrounding his story and his disposition for lying, I believe this person was Lonnie Johnson and possibly his partner Dave Atkins. And Atkins was so scared, rather than pay a $25 fine, he chose to join the U. S. Army at a time when WWII was winding down in order to avoid telling his story.

Someone had to have previously arranged for transportation to take the children away. It is possible the children were taken out of the house sometime between when Mary Ann fell asleep and when Mrs. Sodder got up to answer the phone. It is possible that someone could have opened the front door and told the children something to lure them outside, like Santa is outside, come and see and be quiet so you don't scare the reindeer. This would explain why the same five children who were playing were the same five who disappeared. They never made it upstairs to bed.

Then once the children were gone, the house was set on fire, possibly by rolling flaming Molotov cocktails onto the roof. Since it was raining, or snowing, some sort of accelerant had to be used to start the fire. This would explain what the late-night bus driver saw when he passed the house.

This scenario would also explain why there were no bones of the children found in the ashes. They were already on their way out of Fayette County by the time the fire was started. And when it was extinguished, the children were either in Smithers or possibly at a trailer court outside of Charleston.

The oldest boy, Maurice (Mack), possibly resisted and was killed. That could be why Ida Crutchfield did not see him at her hotel in Charleston the next day. In her sworn statement, Mrs. Crutchfield also stated that the four children and their guardians left the following morning heading west. The remaining four children were probably told that if they talked about what had happened, the rest of their family would be killed or that their entire family had all died in the fire.

The fire department gave multiple excuses as to why it took over eight hours to get three firemen the two and a half miles from the station to the Sodder house. This was a typical Black Hand technique, as described in the last chapter. The fire was allowed to burn itself out to give the appearance that the children had burned up completely.

Mrs. Sodder told the police she believed the fire had been set,

217

but she did not say by whom. Mr. Sodder said he did not know of any enemies he might have, when asked by the authorities. I believe he thought that if the children had been taken, and he kept his mouth shut, the ones who had done this might return them. He later found out that this was not going to happen. Again, a methodology of the old Black Handers.

The coroner's inquest was held an hour after the smoldering ashes were extinguished on Christmas morning and all the children declared dead. For all intents and purposes, the official case was closed right there. The liver was planted later that evening by Morris (he admitted that much). Then he said nothing about it until nearly two years later, when he found out that Mr. Sodder intended to excavate. There is an explanation for this strange occurrence.

Eat Your Heart Out

As I researched the possible meaning of placing a piece of liver in the ashes, I was again struck by something that a friend in Italy, who was an expert on Italian history and culture, had said about this odd occurrence:

> *The liver is a precise Mafia trace that is about jealousy. It implies, "This has been done to you. Now, you can eat your liver, as I ate my own liver for jealousy about you and your family."*[347]

When Fire Chief Morris told Rev. James Frame that a body part had been found in the debris, Morris called the object a "heart." He admitted he placed the object in a wooden box and then in the ashes of the fire. However, a rough count gives nearly 15 people who searched the ashes throughout the day. But Morris claimed he came back in the evening and found the mass.[348] I believe the reason the mass was not found by searchers earlier in the day, is because it was not there. It was brought in by someone, who ordered Morris to plant it there.

Then, when questions were raised and no answers were forthcoming, the 1952 report was written later to document that the mass was found in the ruins on the day of the fire. This does not imply that the Fire Marshal's office was a conspirator in trying to cover up the missing children, but that they were trying to cover up the fact that they had not written a report themselves concerning the fire.

Being a chief of a volunteer fire department in Fayetteville in 1945 was not a full-time job. It probably did not pay at all. The following photograph is a copy of Forest Judson Morris's WWII draft card. Line 8 shows who his employer was in 1948.[349] More specifically, if you view the 1940 U. S. Census record Morris's occupation is listed as "Bookkeeper" for a lumber company, which was one of the holdings of the Janutolo's.[350]

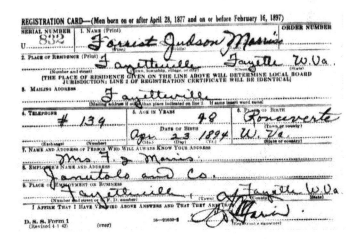

WWII draft registration card for Forest Morris, U. S. Census

Some writers have said that Morris possibly placed the mass to give the Sodders comfort in thinking the children did die in the fire. But does it not defeat that purpose to place the liver there and not tell the Sodders immediately? The secrecy surrounding the placement of the liver in the ruins did nothing to relieve the Sodder's suffering.

If it is true that the placing of the liver in the ashes is a symbolic message of revenge, then the message is not sent to Sodder if he does not know about it. The revenge is not complete. But again, the *pazienza*, or patience, calls for waiting until the right time. Was that the right time, a year and a half, after everything had died down, and Morris tells James Frame whom he knows will then tell the Sodders. So the message was sent through a back channel? The dish of revenge is therefore served cold.

It is also possible that the symbol was not meant to be known by Sodder, it was only for the benefit of the person who did it. Kind of like a serial killer who takes souvenirs of his victims in order to relive the experience. Maybe it gave them sadistic satisfaction to know they had beaten George Sodder. The insult, or *sgarro*, had been made right, in their mind. Unfortunately, the Sodder billboard probably performed the same function and acted as a device to give the instigator of this vendetta the same sadistic satisfaction every time they drove past it.

So it is my conclusion that the liver was placed by the person who instigated this vendetta as an old world Italian symbol saying, "You came to this country to enjoy the banquet of a new life. Now you are beaten, eat your liver, sit and suffer for the rest of your life as the pain and anguish slowly kills you."

For the people that Mr. Sodder suspected were involved in the disappearance of his children, he did nothing violent in retaliation. If Sodder did not kill those he suspected, for a back-vendetta, it was just because he did not want his other children killed.

The liver as a message of defeat or revenge was fulfilled, the damage done, the children gone. George's Sardinian heart was eaten out with grief. He lived another 25 years and his family said he hardly ever slept. He would walk around his house in the middle of the night, wondering where his children were. Even his own wife said that the stress probably caused him to develop cancer which was his eventual and official cause of death.

George and Jennie sometimes gave interviews around Christmas when the interest in the case is usually revived. As for Jennie Sodder, it was said that she always wore black clothing the rest of her life and rarely left her property. The Sodders built a giant fence with an electric gate around their property to protect them from any further attacks.

Some people have said to me, if George Sodder committed this insult to someone, why did they not come after him directly? Why take it out on his family? To kill someone is getting off easy. By doing what they did, they inflicted the maximum pain on George Sodder. They wanted him punished. They killed George Sodder many times over by taking what he loved. They enjoyed watching his pain, and probably enjoyed appearing to be playing the good Samaritan.

Why Christmas Day

One major question has always been that if this was an intentionally set fire and the children were taken out of the house, why wait until the clock was past midnight and it was officially Christmas Day? This is especially questionable considering the cold weather and icy conditions that existed at the time. Why would anyone make the trip to the Sodder house after midnight and instigate the *vendetta* on Christmas morning in that weather? My Italian culture expert tells me:

> *Because Christmas is a day of Feast, the greatest celebration. To receive pain on this day does much more harm to the entire family and so revenge is stronger, more satisfying to the one inflicting it. Also, nobody fears something on a day of Christian feast... and the surprise sharpens the pain... the intention was to cause the maximum pain possible... pure sadistic hatred against the Sodder family for a personal insult.*[351]

Que Bono

The term *que bono* is a Latin phrase meaning "to whom is it a benefit." It is usually used in the context of that when a crime is committed, the benefit goes to the one who commits it. The context usually means financial advantage, or profit, but it can mean other benefits such as power or revenge.

My Italian culture expert lists the following ways that the person or persons could have benefited:

- Financial – insurance on the Sodder house was increased just before the fire.

- Recognition / Respect – Teaches others that you go along, or this could happen to you. Showing proper respect to the upper bosses.

- Paying tributes (insurance). What happens when this is not done?

- Sadistic Pleasure – the desire to see someone hurting.

Co-Conspirators

Fire Chief: Forest Judson Morris, is one of the most controversial characters of this mystery. Many of his actions cannot be adequately explained or justified. But if you consider for a moment that he may have been acting as an agent for someone else, some answers start to fall into place.

Morris's documented actions included:

- When called about the fire, he told the caller that he knew about it. Then said nothing. He had to be told that there were children involved.

- Arriving at the scene of the fire eight hours after being called.

- Telling the Sodders that no trace of their children could be found but later claiming to have found a mass and somehow not informing them of his discovery.

- He placed the liver in the ashes of the fire that sent the old-world message "eat your heart out."

- Maintained his silence about finding remains through two inquests.

- Refuses to explain his mysterious actions regarding the liver.

Morris said that he did not mention finding what he claimed was a part of a child's dead body because no one asked him. I would suggest the reason he did not mention it was because it did not happen. He admitted placing a piece of a cow's liver in the ashes, or he had it done, as an Italian message to the Sodder's, saying, "the feast of life has been taken from you and all you have left is liver. Now, eat your heart out in grief for the rest of your life."

Non-Traditional Kidnapping

One persistent question is that if the children were kidnapped why did they not come back when they got older. In a traditional kidnapping, if money is paid, the subject of the kidnapping is released. The structure of the old-world vendetta was such that they either could not come back (murdered) or if they did survive and were sold, they were told that if they ever tried to come back, the rest of their family would be killed.

What is the difference between kidnapping and a vendetta? To the Black Hand, the kidnapping of children was not personal, it was business, a way to make money. In the case of the Sodder family, I believe the kidnapping was revenge. There was never any intent to return the children, or to let it be known if they were alive or dead. The thought of not knowing is ten times worse than outright murder. The purpose was to inflict pain, not financial gain. It was about control and showing respect.

Conclusions

In trying to determine a possible motive and method for this crime, I have chosen a possible conclusion that shows motive, method and opportunity. Using the logic of the State Police and State Fire Marshal's office, there is no evidence to show it did not happen this way.

I believe the Sodders may have tried to explain the idea of vendetta and the basic idea of *uomo d'onore* to the investigators, especially in the meeting at the WV State Attorney General's office in 1951 where names of possible suspects were brought up.

The investigators were either looking for a standard cookbook type of motive, or they were choosing to sweep the whole thing under the rug. I believe that this explanation of possible motive fits many of the facts of this case better than any other possible scenario and stands as a reasonable explanation.

223

Somewhere, either in this country or elsewhere, one or more of the missing Sodder children may still be alive and hopefully have lived reasonably good lives. But they may still be unwilling to attempt to make contact with their family in West Virginia for fear of a warning they were given to stay away. When I first considered this idea, it seemed far-fetched and unlikely. But if a warning is made like this, especially to a young child, I can see how it would resonate with them for the rest of their lives.

Some of the living family members who have contributed to the research of this book have done so under the condition of anonymity and in the agreement that their help would be limited to trying to locate the children. They would not, however, contribute anything about who may have done it. Not because they did not have their suspicions, but because "we still have family up there." Nearly 75 years later, there is still a lingering fear in the descendants of George and Jennie Sodder that something else could happen to their own family.

Chapter 11

The Tennessee Children's Home Society

We will not kill the boy…….. A childless family promised us by letter $2,000 if we send them the boy.

Black Hand letter to Vincenzo Mannino,
New York City 1904

The Children

In assuming the possible motive described in the last chapter is true, we have speculated about why, and how. The one remaining subject in this search for motive is what could have happened to the children. A few possibilities would include:

1. The children were murdered within hours or days of being taken.

2. The younger children were taken to a baby farm and sold but the older boy likely would not cooperate and was killed.

3. The children were taken to another state, or back to Italy, and sold there or placed with foster families. The female children could have been turned over to marriage brokers.

All these scenarios are pure speculation. To provide some possible answers, we can look at existing conditions, historical context, and cultural background.

The Sodder case is essentially the Jimmy Hoffa case of West Virginia. There are some rumors of what happened. But after all these years, there is still no verifiable hint of Hoffa. A perfect hit, no traces and no one talked. There have been some half-hearted deathbed confessions and a few rumors, but they have never even come close to turning up a body.

There were at least three suspected sightings of the Sodder children in the days following the fire:

- There was the questionable statement supposedly by Mrs. Mary Bree of Smithers that the children were in her house the morning after the fire, which she later denied.

- Another statement from an unnamed woman who owned a motor court between Fayetteville and Charleston who claimed she saw the children,

- Ida Crutchfield, owner of the Alderson Hotel in Charleston was emphatic that four of the five children were in her hotel a few days after Christmas.

If any one of these statements were true, then whoever took the children was heading West. What would be the purpose of taking them in that direction? If they were taking them back to Italy, they would have traveled east.

One of the private detectives Mr. Sodder hired was quoted in a 1948 article:

The general public is not aware there is a market for children. In the larger cities, they are sold for as much as $1,000 or more.

The detective said many people are willing to pay large sums of money for children in order to avoid the red tape of the adoption agencies.

Swain cited an article entitled, "Why You Can't Adopt A Baby" in the September, 1948 issue of *Reader's Digest*. The author Frederick G. Brownell states that persons have been known to pay from $500 to $3,000 "a head" and refers to black market operators—people who make a living by selling babies for cash. While the article was written primarily about adopting babies, it could apply to older children as well.[352]

What if Swain was right and at least some of them were sold to baby brokers? At the time, this theory was advanced by Swain but considered by state officials to be nonsense. It was not until several years later that stories would fill the national headlines about stolen children in Tennessee.[353]

The Tennessee Children's Home Society

The Tennessee Children's Home Society was first chartered in Memphis, TN in 1897.[354] It was a legitimate orphanage that took in children who were abandoned or orphaned and found parents for them, usually for a substantial fee. The agency's director was named Georgia Tann. Tann became self-aware of her sexual orientation at an early age and felt much more comfortable in a masculine persona. She desired to emulate the only male figure in her life, her father who was a federal judge known for his strict interpretation of the law. Tann passed the bar exam in Mississippi but her father would not allow her to practice law as it was considered unseemly for a woman. This disappointment caused Tann to harden and she became determined to get her own way in anything she tried to do.

Georgia Tann, Director of the Tennessee Children's

Tann's attention soon turned to "helping" less fortunate children in Mississippi, then in Tennessee. She found there was a big return on a minimal investment in semi-legal adoptions. Some writers said her extreme selfishness caused her to "depersonalize" the people she tried to help and see them as nothing more than assets to make money. Publicly, Tann had stated that, "Poor people were incapable of proper parenting." She believed children of the poor needed rescue.

Tann began her career of arranging illegal adoptions at the age of 15 in conjunction with her father, the judge. A few years later after more than a few cases where Tann just outright snatched children from their rightful parents, she and her family were more or less expelled from Mississippi. Tann's father, George, having contacts in Memphis, TN moved there.

Georgia followed her father and once again began arranging adoptions in the early 1920s. While most people did not trust adoption agencies, Tann worked to popularize advertising and marketing children for sale in nationally-syndicated newspapers, almost like used cars.

She turned the process into a machine that took homeless, poor, and stolen children and churned out shiny polished young candidates for adoption, with all new identities, and a spotless paper trail since all documents that identified the child's past were destroyed. The children were told to forget the old life where they had always been hungry and sick. Act as though it never happened. They were going to become blank slates. During the adoption process, as Tann was evaluating potential parents,[355] she would give them a story about the child designed to keep them from asking too many questions.

Method of Operation

The children Tann obtained were taken from parents who were too poor to protest. Many times, the child was taken right out of their parents' arms occasionally with the aid of the local police, who were said to get a share of the profits.

Tann operated within the law where the state welfare system allowed kids to be taken away from their parents if they lived in abject poverty. The parents were told that the child would be better off with parents who could afford to raise it.

When she received a child illegally, it was usually one of her spotters who alerted Tann. After the adoption was complete, the spotters would get a part of the adoption fees. Using these methods, Tann was able to operate all over the state of Tennessee and outside the state lines as well.

One case that was pointed out was when five children were on their way home from school and they were seized and sold to five separate families in Tennessee. But the oldest boy was returned because he was not considered intelligent enough to please his adoptive parents.[356]

Tann's spotters were also known to hang around playgrounds and grab a bunch of children playing who were not supervised by adults. Sometimes even if they were supervised. Tann was so insulated and protected by the police and the court system that she had no fear of reprisals.

Tann would also visit orphanages scouting for children she could legally steal and then resell. After she had the child, Tann would immediately change the name of the child and create a false birth certificate and paper trail to legitimize the adoption, thereby eliminating the child's past.

Although she kept no records of the adoptions, it is estimated between 1924 and 1950 she facilitated more than 5,000 adoptions to clients from all over the country and became wealthy in the process. Some estimates of Tann's net worth were nearly one million dollars. In today's dollars, that is around twenty million.

Many of the children acquired by Tann were eventually found to not be healthy enough, mentally or physically, to offer for adoption. These children, who were still healthy enough to survive, were placed in state or private institutions. These less fortunate children were not given any proper medical care and were eventually left to die.

Tann disposed of the bodies usually with the help of a local funeral home that had a crematorium. Some sources say to this day there were bodies of children buried on property that Tann had once owned.[357] In the 1930s, due in large part to the actions of Georgia Tann, Memphis had the highest infant mortality rate in the country. And the rate was actually much higher because many of the children's deaths went unreported. The children just disappeared.

As if this story could not get any worse, some of the people who worked for Tann reported that she regularly molested young girls and allowed adoptions to known or convicted pedophiles.[358]

They further described that Tann was the type of person that you never dared to say "no" to. She was a fanatic about her will being done without question and with the network of subordinates and public officials who were all taking money from her, no one dared cross her.

Baby Farm

Facilities that turn out babies for selling to potential parents seems like something you would hear about in China or other countries known for such practices. One would definitely not expect to find such customs in mid-19th century Tennessee. But it did happen on a regular basis.

In the 1940s, it was reported that Georgia Tann began showing up in a county courthouse outside Memphis with various pregnant women who she had found in a local home for unwed mothers. There to meet her, was a man who Tann had previously picked to be the pregnant woman's new husband. Tann arranged for the couple, who were meeting for the first time, to be married by a judge who would ask no questions.

Once the ceremony was complete, Tann would then keep the marriage certificate and use it later to prove to a prospective adoptive parent that the child had come from an "unsuitable" married couple and therefore had an untarnished good-Christian background. In reality, after the ceremony, Tann would pay off the official performing the ceremony and the so-called husband and send him on his way.

Once the pregnant woman gave birth at a local hospital, controlled by Tann, she was also sent away probably, with a fee of her own or promise of free medical care. The baby was then advertised in various media and adopted by parents who could pay Tann's huge fee. Later, when Tann's practices were exposed, an official at the courthouse told authorities how Tann arranged these marriages. It was a virtual baby mill with most of the money going in Tann's pocket.[359]

A partial list of well-known personalities who used, or were victimized by Tann and the Society included movie stars Joan Crawford, Smiley Burnette, June Allyson and Dick Powell. Professional wrestler Ric Flair even wrote in his biography about being illegally taken away from his mother by operatives of the Society and sold.[360]

Tann was once contacted by West Virginia native and Pulitzer Prize winning author Pearl Buck, who asked her to help write a book about adoption, and may have possibly used her services to acquire one of the several children Buck adopted. Tann died before the book could be published which probably saved Pearl Buck's reputation after the stories of Tann's true colors were discovered.[361]

It is well known that Tann insulated her high-end clients from ever knowing the methods of how she obtained her children. It was not until after Tann's death and the investigations made the national news that her clients began their own inquiries.

By the 1940s, questions had arisen. There had been so many attempts to sue Tann and the Home, but she used her team of contacts in the courts and police to hold them back. Eventually outside newspaper reporters and investigators began to make a dent in her armor of invincibility.

Soon after outside investigations began, Tann died in 1950 from complications of cancer. She really got off easy. Before she could be prosecuted, Judge Camille Kelley, who had aided Tann in her illegal adoptions, agreed to retire from public service in exchange for immunity from prosecution. Her death five years later in 1955 probably saved her from lawsuits that would eventually follow from the original parents. Kelley's death more than likely saved many other local officials from prosecution.

Georgia Tann's lesbian lover and business partner, Ann Atwood, died at the age of 92, in 1996. Although Atwood actively participated in the illegal adoptions, mainly by delivering children to their new parents and to collect Tann's fee, she was not prosecuted. She rarely spoke in public about Tann except to call her one of the most generous people she had even known.

State Investigation and Report

The Tennessee Children's Home Society was closed in the 1950s, but the lawsuits continued for decades. These lawsuits were later joined by those children, now grown, who were searching for their birth parents. There were countless officials involved with arranging the illegal adoptions and covering them up. This included attorneys, doctors, nurses, social workers, secretaries, judges, police officers and others. At the time, most managed to keep clear of prosecution by claiming the adoptions were for the benefit of the children and the names of the families they were relocated to was private.[362] The prevailing state adoption system of the time tended to agree with them.

In 1951, at the request of the governor of Tennessee, a comprehensive report was prepared of the entire incident. The state investigators confirmed virtually every rumor that was floating around about Tann and the Society. Secret bank account, bribes, embezzlement, stolen children, false identities, all true. Judge Camille Kelly had aided Tann in forcing through thousands of illegal adoptions and hiding the children's real identities.[363]

The Society reorganized after Tann's death but with huge bills and lawsuits they were not successful. The Home sued the administrators of Tann's estate in an attempt to recover money that Tann had pocketed. In 1953, the Society was awarded $100,000 but it was not enough to stay in operation.[364] And considering the sullied reputation of the Society, no one wanted to use their services anyway. After Tann's death, all of her business and private papers were confiscated by her attorney and for the most part destroyed in an attempt to head off any future lawsuits.[365]

While there is no evidence the missing Sodder children were victims of the Tennessee Children's Home, this chapter does prove what detective George Swain postulated. That there was a market for stolen children and there existed such an agency at the time of the Sodder fire. There is no doubt other such agencies with similar motivations existed in the United States at the time, but this facility was the largest operation of its kind and the most efficiently operated.

Memorial to the children who died at the Tennessee Children's Home Society, State of TN, Archives.

The Tennessee Children's Society was the one known to be located closest to West Virginia. While it is known that Georgia Tann's spotters traveled outside of Tennessee, there is no evidence that they ever reached West Virginia.

For the Sodder children to have been sold to the Tennessee Children's Home, someone in West Virginia, and involved in the plot to kidnap the children would have to know about the goings-on at the Home in advance and made arrangements for their transportation to Tennessee, some 650 miles from Fayetteville.

What we do know, if you chose to believe the statements given, is that the last time the Sodder children were seen alive was by Ida Crutchfield at her hotel in Charleston, a few days after the fire. And a train station is located in Charleston. The rest of the trip to Tennessee could have been relatively uneventful. The children would have been put out for adoption, told to forget their past, and never look back.

The adoptive parents would have been given all new birth certificates and identification papers. They would have been told a

233

false story about the children's past life. No record of an adoption would exist. Corrupt officials would put a stop to any inquiries if anyone ever got close to the truth.

Chapter 12

The End

I would love to know what happened. I know they could not have been in the fire. It's like you come to the end of a story, and there is no end.

Sylvia Sodder-Paxton

So what has been accomplished with this book? We have learned about a good man who believed in self-sufficiency, liberty, and family. Who wanted a better life by coming to America. Who wanted his family to understand what it meant to leave the old world behind and make your mark in the new. After Christmas of 1945, he also believed he was served a tragic injustice. On his headstone in High Lawn Memorial Park Cemetery, it is inscribed:

In memory of George Sodder, who believed in justice for everyone but was denied justice by the law when his five children were kidnapped Christmas Eve, 1945 at Fayetteville, W. Va.

The first Sodder billboard cried out, "What was their fate? Murdered, Kidnapped? Or are they still alive?" In writing this book, I didn't find any of the Sodder children, either dead or alive. While I do have my own conclusions as to what happened to the five Sodder children, I could not, in all good conscience, identify by name who may have been responsible for the fire and the deaths or kidnapping of the children. It is too late to prove anything conclusively and it is not worth naming someone who is not here now to defend themselves.

In a case such as this, the public is outraged, for a while. Then it just becomes another case that goes unsolved. A legend is born – meaning truth may take a small holiday. The public enjoys

235

believing the most bizarre, hard to explain aspects of the case. In this case, and with the use of the internet, the case is continually revived.

The investigation was conducted in such a way that satisfied virtually nobody. To this day, few people are satisfied, other than those who conducted the investigation. They closed the case in less than three weeks.

The National Fire Safety Board states that less than 15% of all arson cases are ever solved, even considering today's advanced investigation methods.

One Fayetteville official said in an interview that the only reason he believed the Sodder children died in the fire is because no one saw them come out of the house.

In reading the witness's statements, I cannot see the emotion or deception in their eyes. I can only read their words, now seventy-five years later. However, in some instances, I saw more than that. Sometimes it seemed the writer of some of these reports was trying to say something more than just what they were typing. It seemed in some instances they tried to remain neutral.

Other times it seemed they were trying to imply that there was more to it. For instance, after the section of the 1950 report that described what Fiorenzo Janutolo said to Mr. Sodder about how his house was going to burn to the ground, C. R. Cobb continued by adding that in the five years since the fire, Mr. Janutolo had not been questioned about his remarks.

With the lack of direct evidence, the absence of witnesses, no direct conclusions can reliably be made. Speculation of the available information causes or allows one to reach some conclusions. But what do the conclusions you reach say about you as a person? Are you dragging your own baggage into the case? Do you just want the children to be alive because they were so adorable? Or do you know they died simply because you see life so matter-of-factly or black and white. It is a Rorschach test. Your conclusions, many times, are based on what the sum of your life experiences and your particular frame of mind allows you to see.

In various discussions about this case, I have been asked to explain what I feel is the key fact that causes me to believe the children did not die in the fire. If I have to pick one, and I do not like to settle on just one, it would be the lack of remains. I simply do not think the fire burned hot enough to turn all five bodies to ashes. That is the fact of the case that caused me to look into it more.

I think a lot of information was lost by the authorities not conducting a proper investigation. It was only after the family complained vigorously that their concerns were addressed and for many, this lack of early interest is still perceived as a cover-up.

One Saturday night while I was writing this book, I was watching *Law and Order, Special Victims Unit* and there was an episode called "Lost Traveler." It was the story of an immigrant family of gypsies living in New York City. All the gypsies living in New York were under the protection or control of the regional leader and for that, they all paid him a healthy tribute. The father of a small gypsy family could no longer afford to pay the tribute to the leader any longer and as a result, the family was ostracized.

The family had a small boy who eventually turned up missing. Initially, it was thought that the regional leader had the boy taken and held until the family began to pay the tribute again. Then, the boy was murdered, and all eyes looked at the regional leader as the culprit. Sound familiar? I was struck at once by the irony. It appears this is not an uncommon story in many cultures who have a central authority figure and who subscribe to their own cultural laws.

In another movie called *Mickey Blue Eyes*, an Italian mob leader wanted revenge for the accidental death of his son. The man who he believed killed his son was getting married and he wanted the man killed on his wedding day, right after he and his bride took their wedding vows in order to take the happiest day of their life and make it the most terrible day. Sounds like the Sodder story and the Christmas day effect.

The Future

As time has passed and memories have faded, the telling and

re-telling of the Sodder story has caused some parts of the story to grow, some parts to wither away. Unfortunately, significant parts of the story have changed due to bad reporting, sensationalism, or embellishing the facts for the sake of selling papers and magazines. And unfortunately, the focus many times has turned to the more sensational, rather than the mundane details, where the solution may lay.

Investigation into true crime has shown, there are some crimes that will never be solved. Cases like Jack the Ripper where many records were destroyed during the WWII bombing of London that might have provided clues to the murderer's identity. Other infamous crimes such as the Jon Bonet Ramsey murder, The Black Dahlia, D. B. Cooper hijacking, kidnapping of Jimmy Hoffa, these all seem as if they will never be conclusively solved because of a lack of direct evidence, poor or ineffective investigation, etc. Unfortunately, the disappearance of the Sodder children falls into the same category.

In 1953, the owner of the *Charleston Daily Mail* was murdered. No arrest was made in part because of the notoriety of the victim, as well as the suspects. The Mayor decided to take the case out of the hands of the police and handle it himself (possibly to avoid investigating certain prominent citizens or police officers). Regardless, the killer was never identified. When the case was revisited in 2019 by local authors, it was discovered that the entire police file of several large boxes had disappeared.

With the Sodder investigation, many records and files are missing from the governing state agencies. They've either been taken home, intentionally removed, or someone assuming that the case was closed simply got rid of the files. I assume that very few people have seen many of the official documents and correspondence contained in this book. I also assume that the officials who wrote these documents never believed the public would someday see them.

Now, nearly all the witnesses to the fire are gone as well as possible perpetrators. There have been no known deathbed confessions, no new evidence, none of the children who were presumed to be missing instead of dead, have turned up alive.

DNA

A technique that is being used today to track a missing person is by the use of DNA. With the rise in popularity of genealogy companies, there now exists a greater opportunity to discover what may have happened to the Sodder children. With DNA testing kits and a small sample of saliva, your national origin can be determined with a reasonable degree of accuracy.

The DNA Doe Project is an exciting new method of investigation that uses genetic genealogy to identify John and Jane Does. The DDP Fund program allows access to this technology to virtually all law enforcement and investigative agencies, regardless of their size and resources. The Project has been able to achieve results with small quantities of DNA as well as some that has been degraded over years. The Project also offers training in forensic genealogy so that enforcement agencies can understand what the results they have obtained mean and how they can be used in crime investigation as well as criminal prosecution.

Now, law enforcement agencies are using the results of these companies to track serial killers and missing persons. Between 1976 and 1986, a man known as the Golden State Killer murdered 12 people and raped 45 women. He was never caught but he left trails of evidence. At the time, DNA was fully understood but was not being used to identify blood or semen left behind in a crime. Fortunately, in the case of the Golden State Killer, that evidence was kept in a climate-controlled evidence locker for several decades. When DNA usage in crime detection became commonly used, the FBI established their National DNA database which now contains the DNA of millions of offenders. But for those offenders who have never been arrested, their samples are not in the database, and they continue to elude justice.

That is until recently when someone in law enforcement saw the importance of the commercial genealogy databases, which have been growing much faster than the FBI database. A DNA profile from a relative of Joseph James DeAngelo was identified through a company called GEDmatch and with a little police investigative work, DeAngelo was eventually identified by his similar DNA matched against the samples left behind from his crimes and that was stored in the police storage locker. The 72-year-old United States Navy veteran and former police officer was charged with eight counts of first-degree murder based on DNA evidence obtained from a genealogical database.

Since law enforcement is no longer concerned with the Sodder case, it would be up to members of the Sodder family to submit their DNA and populate the overall DNA database. Hopefully, in a non-capitalistic gesture, the various companies that offer this service will eventually combine their databases so that no matter which company you use, you have an opportunity to find a missing relative.

If a member of the Sodder family has their DNA tested by one of these companies, and it becomes part of their database, it could eventually be used to compare to another customer who may have the DNA of one of the missing children, whether it be one of the five children, or their offspring. This would not be direct evidence of a kidnapping since the DNA of the missing children was never taken. But a positive hit on Sodder DNA in two different parts of the country, that cannot be explained any other way, could be a confirmation of one or more of the missing Sodder children being located.

Perpetrators

John Sodder, the oldest of the Sodder children, who was very quiet after the fire, spent his remaining years focused on the family business and for the most part, let his father look for the missing children. However, in a rare newspaper interview in the 1980s, John did say that the people he felt were involved had all passed away by that time.[366] This implies that he did have an idea of who may have taken the children. In speaking with a Sodder family member during the preparation of this book, it was implied to me that there was an idea of who may have been behind the fire and kidnapping but there was also a great concern about indiscriminately naming names for fear of reprisals or lawsuits because there was no direct proof.

Fayette County Organized Crime

It was common knowledge where I grew up that if you wanted to commit a major crime in West Virginia, go to Fayette County. Very few murders, robberies, etc. were ever solved there. More specifically, unsolved murders in the 1980s and 90s abounded in Fayette and nearby Raleigh Counties.

Today, the chief money makers for small-time organized crime like what has existed in Fayette County are no longer parlay cards and football betting, but it is now mainly drugs. Extortion, prostitution, and liquor bootlegging can't come close to the amount of money gleaned from drug trafficking.

The Italians who brought organized crime from the old country have now assimilated into West Virginia culture. Few probably have even heard of the Sodder case. If they have, no doubt their response would be, "it was a different time and different generation."

Obsolete Files

Obviously, official documents will disappear with time. The WV State Fire Marshal's file on the case was once called "voluminous." When I submitted a Freedom of Information Act Request, they said there were no files remaining. The WV State police were a little better. I received about six pages from their archives that were part of what I called the 1950 report. It is common practice to get rid of old records after a given number of years. I've done it myself at various places I have worked. There is honestly nothing sinister about it.

As mentioned before, a Sodder family member had shared with me a huge cache of files, reports, and letters related to the case. So ironically, I now have more records related to the case than any state agency. But at this point, I doubt that these state agencies would be interested or impressed.

On a day that I was researching in the Fayette County Courthouse, the person in charge of the records told me that they were making preparations to destroy their oldest records that were considered obsolete. It was not a matter of covering up anything, they had just run out of room. And, putting everything on microfiche was too expensive for a town with a limited budget.

Occam's Razor

Someone on Weblsueths.com once stated that the solution to the case should be based on the principle of Occam's Razor, which is defined as *entities must not be multiplied beyond necessity* and the conclusion thereof, that the simplest explanation or strategy tends to be the best one. The principle is attributed to 14th-century English logician, theologian and Franciscan friar, William of Ockham.

To apply this principle to the Sodder case, the simplest, or perhaps most logical explanation is that the fire was accidental, and the five children died that night. The fact that there was little, or no human remains, is simply a factor of the intensity of the fire. The eyewitnesses who claim to have seen the children in the days following the tragedy are mistaken. The man who claimed to see what were described as fireballs being thrown onto the roof actually saw the fire, which originated in the basement, streaking through the walls of the house. The questionable events that led up to the night of the fire are all mere coincidence. One could go on and on. And, yes, this could be the case.

What Occam's razor does not explain, is the unexplainable, or more specifically that, which has been deliberately made or designed to be unexplainable by human intervention. Another word for that, in one form or another, can be called "intentional manipulation of the truth."

Social Media

Social media is now playing a small part in the case. There have been some Fayette County citizens who have posted online that they have direct knowledge of the case and who did it. But these same people, for whatever reason, would not repeat to me what they know. Some offered to do so if I paid them, but I wouldn't.

Today, with the internet, the story of the Sodder children is revived on a more regular basis, with armchair detectives using criminal investigative chat sites to go over the details. The advantages of these websites are the networking and accumulation of experience and resources placed at the fingertips of anyone with even a mild interest in this case. The disadvantage is that many of these types of investigators are limited to their own ideas and experiences.

Finally

So there you have it. As promised, it was a look back at life and times of the last century. Some may call it a simpler time and in some ways it was. But in others, it was just as complicated as today. It was a time when Italians, even second or third generation, were still referred to as immigrants and not Americans. Today, these same Italians are not part of some isolated group that are held under control by a few leaders or organized crime. John Sodder said it best in 1984 when he was quoted as saying, "We've got more friends today and we're out more. If it happened today, we might get something done."[367]

Cast of Characters

SODDER FAMILY (By age)

George Sodder (1895–1969) Immigrated from Italy at age 13. Father to the Sodder family of ten children from Fayetteville. Responsible for erecting the famous billboard depicting the missing children. After the 1945 fire, he dedicated the remainder of his life to trying to locate the children.

Jennie Lauriessa Cipriani-Sodder (1903-1989) Immigrated from Italy with her family in 1905, eventually moving to West Virginia. She met George Sodder in Smithers and they married in 1922. After George's death, she continued efforts to find the missing children until her death.

John Fredrick Sodder (1923-2001) Born in Smithers, the oldest Sodder child who was 23 at the time of the fire. He was also one of the searchers of the debris after the fire. John was quoted in the earliest reports as saying that during the fire, he shook the younger male children to wake them but later claimed he was falsely quoted. Later, he was a driver for the Sodder Trucking Company.

Joseph Samuel Sodder (1924-2010) Born in Smithers, the second oldest Sodder child who was 21 at the time of the fire. Joe was still in the Army when the fire occurred.

Mary Ann Sodder-Crowder (1926-2005) Born in Smithers, Mary Ann was the oldest female child and was 18 at the time of the fire. She is sometimes referred to as Marion Sodder. She was known to have worked tirelessly to help her parents in getting the case reopened. She lived much of her later life in Ohio.

George "Ted" Sodder (1929-2012) Born in Smithers, the fourth oldest Sodder child and was 16 at the time of the fire. George was at home the night of the fire and barely escaped the flames with his brother John. He was also one of the searchers of the debris after the fire. He later became the president of Sodder Trucking Company.

Maurice (Mack) Antonio Sodder (1931-1945?) Born in Smithers, the fourth oldest Sodder child, and 14 years old at the time of the fire. Maurice was missing after the fire.

Martha Lee Sodder (1933 -1945?) Born in Fayetteville, and 12 years old at the time of the fire. One of the four missing children identified as being seen in a Charleston hotel days after the fire.

Louis Enrico Sodder (1935-1945?) Born in Fayetteville and nine years old at the time of the fire. Louis was one of the four missing children identified as being seen in a Charleston hotel days after the fire.

Jennie Irene Sodder (1937-1945?) Born in Fayetteville and eight years old at the time of the fire and one of the four missing children identified as being seen in a Charleston hotel days after the fire.

Betty "Sis" Dolly Sodder (1940-1945?) Born in Fayetteville and six years old at the time of the fire and one of the four missing children identified as being seen in a Charleston hotel days after the fire.

Sylvia Sodder-Paxton (1942-2021) The youngest Sodder child, Sylvia was born in Fayetteville and was three years old at the time of the fire. She and her husband worked for many years to help her parents determine what happened to the children.

SODDER CHILDREN SPOUSES

Margret Meadows-Sodder, married to John Sodder in 1947.

Clarice Buckland-Sodder, married Joe Sodder in 1947.

Elise Fish-Sodder, married George "Ted" Sodder in 1958.

John Crowder, married to Mary Ann Sodder in 1955.

Grover Paxton, married to Sylvia Sodder. Was known to have been very close to George Sodder, Sr. and helped him with his search until George's death.

SODDER RELATIVES

Giuseppe (Joseph) Cipriani (1872-1944) Jennie Sodder's Father, born in Italy and immigrated to the United States in 1904. Joe owned a store in Smithers where Jennie Cipriani first met George Sodder.

Martena (Martha) Cipriani (1877-1963) Jennie Sodder's Mother and wife to Joseph.

Francesco Paolo (Frank Paul) Cipriani (1898-1983) Brother to Jennie Cipriani Sodder, moved to Cortez, FL in the 1950s.

Alma Cipriani (1912-1948) Sister to Jennie Cipriani Sodder.

James (Jimmy) Cipriani (1913-1994) Brother to Jennie Cipriani Sodder. He was one of four people to have allegedly seen a mass of human remains at the sight of the fire. Later moved to Florida to work with his brother Frank in the fishing business.

Edna Cipriani (1915-1948) Sister to Jennie Cipriani Sodder.

OTHERS INVOLVED IN THE CASE

Fanny Ackers, witness to the fire according to Lonnie Johnson's statement to the State Police. Was also at Johnson's party at his apartment over the Moonlight Inn on the night of the fire.

Dave "Grover" Adkins, co-owner/operator of the Crass Place tavern located near the Sodder house. Avoided prosecution for stealing from Mr. Sodder on the night of the fire by joining the U.S. Army.

Garnett Arthur, one of the searchers of the debris after the fire. A neighbor of the Sodder family.

Jimmy Arthur, one of the searchers of the debris after the fire. A neighbor of the Sodder family.

M. M. Arthur, Assistant West Virginia State Fire Marshal involved in the preparation of the Supplemental Report of 1952 to State Fire Marshal, C. A. Raper which changed many of the details of the case from the original 1950 report.

Deputy Roy Baden, Bradenton County, Florida, involved in the investigation of the Sodder children.

Col. Raymond Boyles, head of the West Virginia State Police up to 1957.

Carl Bragg, one of the searchers of the debris after the fire. A neighbor of the Sodder family. Possibly an employee of the Sodder Trucking Company.

Thomas P. Brophy, former fire marshal of New York City, was contacted by private detective Swain to investigate the fire, but the $1,000 for expenses could not be raised by the Sodders.

Evert Buckland, a Fayetteville resident and witness to the fire. Also lived near the Sodders.

Virginia Beasley Buckland, Fayetteville resident and witness to the fire. Also lived near the Sodders.

Col. W. E. Burchett, Superintendent of the WV Department of Public Safety from 1945 to 1953. Burchett was present at several of the conferences and felt there was not enough evidence, direct or otherwise, to reopen the case.

Howard Carson, Assistant Fayette County Prosecuting Attorney in 1945, was present the morning of the fire. Carson called the state fire marshal's office asking for an investigation.

Joe Carter, owner of the Tampa Patrol and Detective System (Private Detectives). Former Chief of Detectives of the Tampa Police Department.

C.R. Cobb, Assistant State Fire Marshal, Arson Investigator. Prepared many of the reports including the 1950 report.

Lester Cook, Fayette County resident, was coming home on Christmas Eve night and drove past the Sodder house when it was burning.

Ida Crutchfield, owner of the Alderson Hotel in Charleston. She gave a sworn statement to the State Police that four of the five Sodder children had been in her hotel in the days following the fire. Her claims were not considered valid by the State Police.

Ernest Culbreath, Deputy Sheriff, Florida, possibly a relative of Sheriff Hugh Culbreath. Corresponded with C. R. Cobb of the West Virginia State Fire Marshal's Office concerning the case.

Hugh Culbreath, Sheriff, Hillsborough County, Florida. Corresponded with C. R. Cobb concerning the Florida aspect of the Sodder case.

Arnold Dempsey, listed as a Fayetteville fire fighter who was on the original dispatch to the Sodder fire. However, his name was not included in the 1950 report. In a mysterious twist, Jacobs was named in an anonymous note given to one of Mr. Sodder's private investigators in 1949.

Charles I. Dodd, Fayetteville mortician who came on Christmas morning to pick up the bodies of the children but was told there was nothing to collect. Later, the same day, Dodd also raked through the ashes for several hours and found no remains of the children. Dodd provided a sworn statement saying such.

O.D. (Dave) Fisher, Private investigator, believed to also work for the West Virginia Merchant Police.

Reverend James F. Frame, minister at the Fayetteville Baptist Church was at the Sodder house the morning after the fire consoling the family. He was also one of two clergymen who conducted the funeral. It is possible that Frame was one of several people who told the Sodders that the fire was "God's will". Several years later, Frame told the Sodders that Fire Chief Morris had told him he did find remains in the fire debris.

Dr. W. H. Fogalsong, conducted the funeral for the five children along with Reverend James Frame.

Harold Gaye, Director of the Gaye Funeral Home in Montgomery. In 1947, Gaye examined the "mass in the box" and told Mr. Sodder that it was beef liver.

Mrs. Frank Harding, (Lura or Laura), allegedly called the Sodder house on the night of the fire asking for someone who did not live there. Initially, Mrs. Harding admitted to making the call but later denied it.

Rush Dew Holt, Sr., U.S. Senator from West Virginia (1935-1941). Holt was asked in 1950 to aid in getting the case reopened, which after Holt conferred with the State Fire Marshal's Office, did not happen.

J. Edgar Hoover, Director of the Federal Bureau of Investigation. He was contacted several times by the Sodder family to intercede in the case but claimed it was out of his jurisdiction, unless requested by local authorities.

Oscar B. Hunter Jr., Pathologist, Smithsonian Institute. Present at second excavation. Hired by George Sodder to review the finding of the 1948 excavation. Hunter wrote the first pathologist report that stated the four human bones recovered had not been exposed to fire.

Arnold Jacobs, along with James Roles, Fayetteville fire fighter who was on the original dispatch to the Sodder fire.

Alan Janney, witness to the fire according to Lonnie Johnson's statement. Was at Johnson's party at his apartment over the Moonlight Inn on the night of the fire.

Cleante G. Janutolo, a prominent Fayetteville businessman who was the foreman of the coroner's jury. George Sodder worked for one of Janutolo's many companies up until about 1942. Janutolo signed the Sodder children death certificates.

Fiorenzo Janutolo, was a former employer of George Sodder, the co-signer to purchase their home in 1940, and he was the beneficiary of the policy on the Sodder house. Janutolo and his wife were estimated to have made over 20 trips to Italy.

Jackson Theodore Jennings, member of the coroner's jury, was a local coal miner who lived in Fayetteville in the 1940s. Possibly a Sodder neighbor.

Lonnie Johnson, co-owner/operator of the Crass Place tavern. Was present the night of the fire with his wife and others. Pled guilty to stealing a block and tackle from the Sodder barn during the fire. Admitted to cutting the phone lines.

Harley Kilgore, West Virginia Senator, referred the Sodders to the FBI when Detective Swain appealed for assistance. The FBI referred Swain to Washington, D.C. Fire Marshal and the District Coroner, who in turn referred him to the Smithsonian Institute, and Oscar B. Hunter.

Emanuel Kolea, one of the searchers of the debris after the fire. Possibly an employee of the Sodder Trucking Company.

William Harvey Level, Justice of the Peace, Fayette County, conducted the second coroner's inquest several days after the fire.

Rosser Long, Fayetteville insurance agent who informed the Sodders that Fiorenzo Janutolo wanted them to purchase life insurance on their children and to increase the amount of homeowner's insurance.

Arthur Moles, one of the searchers of the debris after the fire. A neighbor of the Sodder family.

Forrest Judson Morris, Fayetteville Fire Department Chief, notified of the fire at 2 a.m. but did not arrive until six hours later. Directed the search of the ashes. He informed the Sodder parents that no remains of the children had been found but he later admitted to burying a box containing what Morris described as a mass of human tissue.

William Morse, Charleston firefighter who in 1951 gave a signed affidavit to investigators saying that in all his years of experience, he had never seen a human body be completely destroyed by fire. There were always bones left.

T. A. Myles, Mayor of Fayetteville. Shortly after the fire, he presented a check to the Sodder family from the Fayetteville Catastrophe Committee.

Mathew. M. Neely, West Virginia Senator and former governor of West Virginia, along with Harley Kilgore, referred the Sodder's private investigator to the FBI.

Marshall T. Newman, Pathologist for the Smithsonian Institute, reviewed the findings of the excavation and wrote a second pathologist report, independent of Hunter's report, and found basically the same results. He also said the age of the bones did not match any of the Sodder children.

Lacy Neely, member of the coroner's jury, he was also the Fayette County Clerk at the time of the fire.

Bill Pickford, one of the searchers of the debris after the fire. Possibly an employee of the Sodder Trucking Company.

Peggy Price, was coming home in the same car as Lester Cook, as well as Evert and Virginia Buckland. A witness to the fire.

Carlyle Alonso (C.A.) Raper, Chief Assistant Fire Marshal, West Virginia State Fire Marshall's Office at the time of the fire. Later became the State Fire Marshal. Reported to have come to the site of the fire on Christmas morning. Raper was also present at the excavation in 1949.

N. C. Reger, Master Sergeant, Identification Bureau, West Virginia State Police. Reger was the author of several reports and letters from the WV State Police concerning the fire.

R.W. Rule, Department of Public Safety, (West Virginia State Police). Rule was the first official at the fire along with Trooper W. E. Springer. Rule wrote the first police report which essentially closed the case when the final version was issued on January 19, 1946.

Floyd C. Shuck, born in 1907 and was a bank bookkeeper. Member of the coroner's jury.

John Duvall Shultz, president of the Fayetteville Federal Savings and Loan, owned by the Janutolos. Also a member of the original Coroner's Jury. He was named in the Sodder pamphlet as someone who stated they would never change their mind about believing the children died in the fire no matter what evidence turned up.

Troy C. Simmons, Private investigator, President of the WV Merchant Police of Charleston. Simmons became involved after George Swain was dismissed in 1951. He worked on the case, on and off, for approximately two years.

Thomas E. Smith, was driving by the fire on Christmas night. Called the Fayetteville Fire Department around 2 a.m.

W. E. "Chick" Stull, Fayetteville Deputy Sheriff, was reported to have accompanied a private detective around 1949 to interview Lonnie Johnson. Stull later gave a statement saying Johnson had lied about Stull being present during that meeting.

George Swain, Private Investigator and president of the American Detective Agency. He worked on the case from approximately 1948 to 1951.

R. J. Thrift, Fayette County judge who sentenced Lonnie Johnson to a $25 fine and three years' probation for robbing George Sodder's barn during the fire.

C.C. Tinsley, Private Investigator, Gauley Bridge. He was the brother of O.C. Tinsley, and was known to have accompanied him in many of his cases.

O.C. (Oscar) Tinsley, private Investigator from Gauley Bridge.

Tinsley was believed to be the first investigator Mr. Sodder hired. He was present when the mass in the box was unearthed and took it to the Gaye Funeral Home for analysis.

Carl Vickers, Fayette County Prosecuting Attorney, was present the morning of the fire. Vickers convened a coroner's jury on the Sodder lawn to determine the cause of death of the five children.

Unidentified Bus Driver, witness to the fire according to a private investigator. This man was said to have either been driving or riding in a shuttle bus used for picking up employees of the Alloy Metals Plant. He was said to have seen fireballs being rolled onto the roof of the Sodder home on the night of the fire.

Unnamed Taxi Cab Driver, witness to the fire according to Lonnie Johnson's statement. Was at Johnson's party at his apartment over the Moonlight Inn on the night of the fire. The driver was stated to have been from Bluefield.

C. L. Walker, Captain, Company D, along with Sargent Callaghan, West Virginia State Police Investigated reports of the children being removed from the house and transported to Florida.

Howard M. Welcher, National Board of Fire Underwriters, Arson Department. Assisted in the case mainly to help satisfy Mr. Sodder that his claims were baseless.

Parker R. Wilson, Assistant Fire Marshal in the Beckley office of the State Fire Marshal's Office. Worked on the case with one of Mr. Sodder's private investigators.

SODDER CASE TIMELINE

November 24th, 1895 – Georgio Suddu (George Sodder) is born in Tula, Sardinia.

1903 - Jennie Cipriani-Sodder is born in Puglia, Italy.

March, 1919 – The Italian Fascist Party was founded by Benito Mussolini.

November 4, 1922 – George Sodder and Jennie Cipriani are married in Charleston.

1924 – The Tennessee Children's Home Society began illegally selling children. It is estimated that for nearly 25 years, more than 5,000 children were sold for up to $5,000 apiece.

1942 – George Sodder leaves the employment of the Janutolo Company and buys the Dempsey Transfer Company. The name was changed to The Sodder Trucking Company, which still exists today.

December 8th to 10th, 1942 – The FBI rounded up nearly 100 Italian aliens in West Virginia including in Smithers and Beckley. The aliens were arrested with guns, knives, maps, short wave radios, and pro-fascist literature.

August, 1945 – Fayetteville insurance agent Russel Long is told by Fiorenzo Janutolo to sell George Sodder life insurance policies on his ten children and increase his homeowners policy.

September, 1945 - George Sodder is warned by Janutolo that if he does not purchase insurance, that his "house will go up in smoke and his children will be destroyed."

November, 1945 - A man appears at the Sodder home and walks to the back of the house and makes the unsolicited remark, "That's going to cause a fire someday."

December 24th, 1945, approximately 6 p.m. - The Sodder children are given their Christmas gifts that were purchased by Mary Ann at the department store where she worked.

December 24th, 1945, approximately 10 p.m. - Mr. and Mrs. Sodder go to bed with the baby, Silva. The two oldest boys had already gone to bed and Mary Ann had fallen asleep on the living room couch, leaving Maurice, Louis, Betty, Jennie, and Martha to play with their new toys and listen to the radio.

December 25th, 1945, approximately midnight - Mrs. Frank Harding allegedly called the Sodder house asking for someone who did not live there.

December 25th, 1945, approximately midnight - An unidentified bus driver goes past the house and sees fireballs being rolled onto the roof.

December 25th, 1945, approximately 12:15 a.m. - Mrs. Sodder hears a noise like a rock being rolled onto the roof. Only hearing the sound once, she goes back to sleep.

December 25th, 1945, approximately 1:00 a.m. - Mrs. Sodder awakens to find the house on fire and alerts the family to get out.

December 25th, 1945, approximately 1:30 a.m. - Thomas E. Smith drives by the fire and calls the Fire Department. Smith is told by the fire chief that they know about the fire. When Smith tells Morris there are children in the house and asks if they are going to respond, he gets no response.

December 25th, 1945, approximately 8 a.m. - The Fayetteville Fire Department, led by Chief Morris, arrived at the scene of the fire. The West Virginia State Police arrive at around the same time.

December 25th, 1945, approximately 9 a.m. - Fayette County Prosecuting Attorney Carl Vickers arrives and almost immediately convenes a coroner's jury. A hearing is conducted in the yard that determines the fire was accidental and the children died as a result.

December 25th, 1945, approximately 9–10 a.m. – Fayette County

Assistant Prosecuting Attorney Howard Carson calls the State Fire Marshal's Office in Charleston requesting an investigation. Fire Chief Morris informs the Sodder parents that no remains of the missing children could be found. The State Police quickly concluded the fire was the result of faulty wiring.

December 25th, 1945, approximately noon – Chief Assistant State Fire Marshal Carlisle A. Raper and Howard Welcher of the National Board of Fire Underwriters Arson Department arrive together at the scene. Raper defers to the State Police for the report of the fire but cautions Mr. Sodder to not disturb the scene.

December 25th, 1945, approximately 4–6 p.m. – Charles I. Dodd, a mortician, returns to the scene and rakes through the ashes for several hours.

December 25th, 1945, approximately 3–5 p.m. – Fire Chief Morris claims he returned to the scene after everyone had left and found the mass of tissue in the ashes.

December 26th, 1945 – Fayette County Justice of the Peace, H. C. Level holds an inquest into the death of the Sodder children with Level serving as acting coroner. Cleante Janutolo acts as the foreman and reports that "no parts of missing the five children were found in the debris".

December 30th, 1945 – Death certificates are filed for the children based on the results of the inquest held four days before. Cleante Janutolo signs each certificate as the informant.

December 30th, 1945 - Mr. Sodder goes ahead with the family's original plans to turn the site into a burial place by commissioning Jimmy Cipriani to fill in the hole despite being told to leave the site alone.

December 31st, 1945 – A funeral is held for the children with hundreds of people attending. Mr. and Mrs. Sodder are too overwhelmed with grief to attend.

January 19th, 1946 – Lonnie Johnson is arrested for stealing a set of chain blocks on the night of the fire and charged with grand lar-

257

ceny. His partner in this crime, Dave Adkins, fled Fayette County and joined the Army.

January 21th, 1946 – The West Virginia State Police issued their final report stating the exact cause could not be determined but it was likely due to defective wiring. It further stated the children probably died from the effects of smoke inhalation and the heat of the fire.

July 10th, 1946 – Lonnie Johnson fails to appear for his hearing and Judge R. J. Thrift issues a warrant for his arrest.

September 23rd, 1946 – Judge Thrift sentences Lonnie Johnson to three years' probation and a fine of $25 for stealing a set of chain blocks from the Sodder barn during the fire.

July, 1947 – Nearly a year and a half after the fire, Fire Chief Morris informs Reverend James Frame that he did find something during the fire and that he buried it in the ashes of the fire.

Late, 1947 – Mr. and Mrs. Sodder appear in the office of the State Fire Marshal saying that due to several strange occurrences before, during, and after the fire, they now feel their children did not die.

September 9th, 1948 – C. A. Raper is appointed Acting State Fire Marshal.

November 1st, 1948 – An article appears in the *Charleston Gazette* claiming that several suspects are about to be arrested for possible murder of the missing children. However, no arrests are ever recorded.

November 14th, 1948 – *Charleston Gazette* reporter John Morgan writes a nearly full-page story summarizing the case. Morgan goes on to write eight more follow-up articles in as many years. The stories help motivate some state authorities to re-examine the case.

August 19th, 1949 – Mr. Sodder arranges to have the basement of his former home excavated to search for human remains.

August 25th, 1949 – Dr. Oscar Hunter, pathologist for the Smith-

258

sonian Institute states that the bones found at the second excavation belong to a male approximately 14 to 15 years old, but that they had never been exposed to fire.

September 8th, 1949 – Private detectives George Swain and Frank Hill formally withdraw from the case citing the fact that human bones were found during the site excavation. George Sodder and private detective Troy Simmons are quick to make it clear that Swain was dismissed from the case.

September 19th, 1949 – A letter appears in the office of the West Virginia Merchant Police in Charleston, claiming the bones came from a child buried at a cemetery in Mount Hope and were planted by a Fayetteville fireman named Arnold Jacobs.

September 22nd, 1949 – Dr. Marshall Newman, pathologist for the Smithsonian Institute, issues a second report, concurring with Hunter's conclusion regarding the lack of fire damage to the bones but believes the age of the child the bones belonged to could be anywhere between 14 and 22 years old.

July 18th, 1949, Assistant Fire Marshal C. A. Raper is appointed West Virginia State Fire Marshal.

March 5th, 1950 – A second article appears in the *Charleston Gazette* claiming that five people are going to be arrested in connection to the Sodder case for violating the West Virginia Red Man Act. However, no arrests are ever made.

March 30th, 1950 – The Sodders appeal to former U.S. Senator Rush Dew Holt, Sr. to get the case reopened. After consulting with the State Fire Marshal, Holt writes back a month later saying he cannot help.

June 30th, 1950 – C. R. Cobb, arson investigator with the State Fire Marshal's Office issues a 17 page report which reiterated the previous conclusions made by the State Police that there was no direct evidence showing that the children died by anything other than accidental means.

1950 – The Tennessee Children's Home Society in Memphis is closed after a report detailing the director's illegal child adoption procedures.

July 9th, 1951 – George Sodder writes to Governor Okey Patterson asking him to direct the State Police and the Fire Marshal to reopen the case based on the fact that the bones found during the 1949 excavation had never been exposed to fire. His request was declined.

July 24th through 30th, 1951 – Private Detectives in Florida issue several reports concerning the possibility that the missing children were sent to the Cipriani family living in Cortez, Florida.

September 19th, 1951 – C. R. Cobb issues a second report that summarizes the activity on the case since the 6/30/1950 report. The report specifically states that the death of the children cannot be determined at that time.

November 11th, 1951 – Fayetteville undertaker C. I. Dodd issues a notarized statement explaining his actions on the day of the fire. Dodd stated that since the fire lasted around a half hour and no remains were found, the children could not have perished in the fire.

November 27th, 1951 – Charleston fireman, William Morse, issues an affidavit stating that in his experience a human body cannot be completely consumed just from the heat of a residential house fire.

December 1st, 1951 – In response to a letter by one of Mr. Sodder's private investigators to the Cincinnati Cremation Company of Ohio, the company replies that it typically takes two hours in a cremation chamber, at 2,000 degrees to eradicate a human body with the exception of the bones which typically remain intact.

December 18th, 1951 – A meeting is held in the office of the Superintendent of the State Police, W. R. Burchett. The discussion was that Mrs. Tony Bree of Smithers claimed to have seen the Sodder children the day after Christmas in her house and that they were taken away in a car with Florida license plates. Upon further investigation by the state police, Mrs. Bree denied making the statement.

December 31st, 1951 – A second meeting was held regarding the case, this time in the office of the State Fire Marshal. It was determined that a list of people would be interviewed, and some re-interviewed. The results of these interviews would determine if any further investigation would be warranted.

January 3rd, 1952 – Lonnie Johnson gives a statement to the WV State Police saying he witnessed the Sodder fire and admitted he stole a set of chain blocks, but denied having anything to do with the fire or kidnapping the children.

January 4th, 1952 – State Police Corporal H. D. Gibbs writes a letter to the Commander of the Beckley office of the West Virginia State Police saying that Lonnie Johnson lied in his statement of January 3rd concerning the presence of a Fayette County Deputy Sheriff during the taking of his initial statement in 1949.

January 25th, 1952 – Assistant Fire Marshal C. R. Cobb issues a supplemental report. It contradicts key points of the June 1950 report, and leaves out many details contained previously. The tone of the report seems to discount the fact that the children did not die in the fire.

February 18th, 1952 – A report by the Florida office of the FBI states there was no validity to the claims that the children had been brought there.

February 26th, 1952 – Private investigator Troy Simmons notifies Fire Marshal Raper that he has withdrawn from the case due to Mr. Sodders use of "amateur investigators with whom he cannot work satisfactorily."

June 18th, 1952 – Ida Crutchfield, owner of the Alderson Hotel in Charleston gives a statement that four of the five missing children were in her hotel in the days following the fire in 1945. The State Police do not investigate.

September 10th, 1953 – The first Sodder billboard was erected along Route 16 and offers a $5,000 reward. Unfortunately, the offer initiates many unfounded leads.

February, 1954 – *Front Page Detective Magazine* publishes a story that George Sodder later calls about 75% inaccurate and states that he is planning to sue the New York publishing company.

August 4th, 1956 – Lonnie Johnson marries Freida Adkins, the sister of his business partner Grover "Dave" Adkins.

March to April, 1961 – Sylvia Sodder exchanges letters with Governor Wallace Barron asking him to reopen the case. Barron suggests the Sodder family would do well to accept that the children died in the fire, much to the outrage of the Sodder family.

1963 – Former Sodder private investigator Oscar Tinsley is convicted of conspiracy to defraud the Social Security Commission. His conviction was later overturned.

March, 1967 – *Inside Detective* and *Master Detective* Magazines both publish stories that renew interest and generate many new leads, mostly from people wanting to share in the reward.

June 9th, 1967 – George Sodder is sued by the United Mine Workers for a $42,000 underpayment to the Mine Workers Retirement Fund. The article states that Sodder Coal Company mined nearly 450,000 tons of coal over a seven year period.

1968 – Mary Ann Sodder publishes a statement regarding the night of the fire in which she and her father visited the Fayette County Prosecuting Attorney and asked him to investigate certain people that were believed to be involved with the case.

August 16th, 1969 – George Sodder dies in Fayetteville after a long illness.

December 22nd, 1970 – The Sodder case is featured on WCHS-TV on the Jackie Oblinger Show.

February 7th, 1974 - Lonnie Johnson is once again indicted for two counts of grand larceny relating to another case.

November 18th, 1984 – John Sodder, who had long maintained his silence, stated in a newspaper interview that the children had to have been taken out of the house. There was no evidence that they died in the fire.

1989 – Jennie Sodder dies while living with her daughter, Sylvia.

1990 – The last Sodder billboard is taken down.

2001 – John Sodder dies in Fayetteville, WV.

2005 – Mary Ann Sodder-Crowder dies in Alloy, WV.

2010 – Joseph Sodder dies in Oak Hill, WV.

2012 – George "Ted" Sodder dies in Falls View, WV.

December 23rd, 2013 – A *Charleston Gazette* story interviews the lone surviving Sodder child, Sylvia Sodder-Paxton. It is this article that inspires the author to write this book.

2021 – Sylvia Sodder-Paxton dies in St. Albans, WV.

Endnotes

1   1940 United States Federal Census, West Virginia, Fayette County, ҡ.. District 5, Page 8 of 39.

2   Personal Communication with Sodder Family Member, 2015

3   George Soddu WWI Draft Registration Card, 1917.

4   Tom D. Miller, West Virginia's Amazing Mystery, Master Detective Magazine, 3/1967, Pages 25

5   1920 United States Federal Census, West Virginia, Fayette County, Kanawha Falls, District 5, Page 38 of 41.

6   1940 United States Federal Census, West Virginia, Fayette County, Kanawha Falls, District 5, Page 8 of 39.

7   West Virginia Marriage Index, 1785 – 1971.

8   C.R. Cobb, op. cit., Page 8.

9   George Sodder Naturalization Application Record, Petitions for Naturalization, Book 5, Aug. "39 to Dec. '43, Fayette County Courthouse, Fayetteville, WV

10 Mark I. Choate, Emigrant Nation, The Making of Italy Abroad, Harvard University Press, Massachusetts, London 2008

11 Nicola Colella, Southern Italian Immigration, Italiamerica

12 Dennis Wepman, Immigration, 2002, page 171.

13 Alexandra Molnar, History of Italian Immigration, From Europe to America: Immigration Through Family Ties, 12/15/2010

14 This class of worker was generally known at the time as a peasant or serf.

15 Rita Kennedy, Why Did Italians Immigrate to the US Between 1880 and 1900?, The Classroom

16 Rita Kennedy, op. cit.

17 Translated into English meaning "boss" or "manager."

18 Alexandra Molnar, op. cit.

19 ibid.

20 Vesuvius Causes Terror; Loud Detonations and Frequent Earthquakes, The New York Times, April 6, 1906

21 Nicola Colella, Southern Italian Immigration, Italiamerica

22 Alexandra Molnar, op. cit.

23 Russell King & Allen Strachan, Patterns of Sardinian Migration, Tijdschrift voor Econ. En Soc. Geografie 71 (1980), Pages 209-211.

24 Francesco Floris, The Great Encyclopedia of Sardinia, Vol. 1, The Library of La Nuova Sardegna.

This estimate does not include slave labor from before the mid-19th Century.

John Cavalier, Panorama of Fayette County, Parsons, West Virginia, 1985, Page 115.

27   Ernest L. Biagi, The Purple Aster, A History of the Order Sons of Italy in America, Ventas Press, 1961, Pages 14-18.

28   The significance of Senator Robert K. Holiday to the Sodder case will be explained in later chapters.

29   C.R. Cobb, op. cit., Page 11.

30   Death Certificates for All Five Sodder Children, Fayetteville County Courthouse, 12/25/1945

31   C.R. Cobb, op. cit., Page 12.

32   Notice of Motor Carrier Hearing, Charleston Gazette, Charleston, WV, 6/9/1942, Page 14

33   Tom D. Miller, op. cit., Pages 25

34   Chuck Kinder, Last Mountain Dancer, Hard Learned Lessons in Love, Loss, and Honky-Tonk Outlaw Life, Carroll & Graff Publishers, New York, New York, 2004, Page 45.

35   Multiculturalism in the United States: A Comparative Guide to Acculturation and Ethnicity. Westport, CT: GREENWOOD PRESS, 2005

36   "Sons of Italy Fight Stigma', Charleston Gazette, Charleston, WV, October 9, 1942, Page 2

37   Italian Aliens Held Not Foes, Charleston Gazette, Charleston, WV, October 13, 1942, Page 1.

38   FBI Nabs 23 Aliens and Seizes Arsenal of Weapons, Radios, Raleigh Register, Beckley, WV, October 6, 1942, Pages 1 and 2.

39   FBI Raid Nabs 38 in Fayette, Charleston Gazette, Charleston, WV, 10/8/1942, Pages 1, 11, 24.

40   FBI Raids Aliens in Weirton Area, Raleigh Register, Beckley, WV, `0/9/1942, Page 1.

41   C.R. Cobb, W.V. Assistant WV Fire Marshal, Report on Sodder Fire, to C. A. Raper, State Fire Marshal, 6-30-1950, Page 11.

42   C.R. Cobb, W.V. Assistant WV Fire Marshal report on Sodder Fire, to C. A. Raper, State Fire Marshal, 6-30-1950, Pages 11-12.

43   Tom D. Miller, op. cit., Page 29.

44   C.R. Cobb, op. cit. Page 13.

45   In some accounts, there was more than one man in the car.

46   J. F. Scott, The Children Who Went Up In Smoke, Inside Detective Magazine, 11/9/1967, Pages 29.

47   John F. Sodder Obituary, Beckley Register Herald, Beckley WV, 11-13-2001, Page 6A

48   Other accounts have the two boys going to bed earlier.

49   5 Children Die in Early Christmas Fire, State Sentential, Fayetteville, WV, 12/26/1945, Page 1.

50   Ermel J. Wilson, Fayetteville Parents Renew Hunt for Five Children, Offer Reward, Raleigh Register, Beckley, WV, 9/11/1953, Page 2

51   5 Children Die in Early Christmas Fire, State Sentential, Fayetteville, WV, 12/26/1945, Page 5.

52   Conversation with Sodder Family member, 2017.

53   Trucks of that day were equipped with a standard transmission requiring the use of a clutch. Also, the cars and trucks of that time usually required the use of a "choke" which was used to limit the amount of air that went into the engine while trying to start it. The choke was usually activated by a handle on the dashboard and once the engine started and warmed up, the choke handle was deactivated. If the starting procedure was not followed correctly, it could lead to what was called a "flooded" engine.

54   1940 United States Federal Census, Fayetteville District, Page 35 of 52.

55   Lonnie Johnson of Gatewood, Statement to W.V. State Police, 1-3-1952

56   Marion Sodder, Marion Sodder Personal Statement, Fayetteville, WV, 1-1968

57   5 Children Die in Early Christmas Fire, State Sentential, Fayetteville, WV, 12/26/1945

58   C.R. Cobb, op. cit., Page 14.

59   Marion Sodder, Marion Sodder Personal Statement, Fayetteville, WV, 1-1968

60   J. F. Scott, op. cit., Pages 28-31.

61   Anonymous, Letter to West Virginia Merchant Police, 11-13-1951

62   F. J. Morris Made New Fire Chief, Raleigh Register, Beckley, WV, 11/10/1937, Page 1.

63   Also called "Mack" by his family.

64   Also called "Sis."

65   This photograph (of low quality) clearly shows the basement, the remains of two chimneys. Possibly one of the two truck motors kept in the basement. On the right side of the photo, several men dressed in suits can be seen overlooking the damage. A portion of another structure can be seen in the top left corner of the photograph, possibly the Sodder barn.

66   C.R. Cobb, op. cit., Page 4.

67   Marion Sodder, Marion Sodder Personal Statement, Fayetteville, WV, 1-1968

68   Tom D. Miller, op. cit., Page 29.

69   John G. Morgan, Fayette Family Seeks 5 Children Some Believe Dead, Charleston Gazette, Charleston, WV, 11/14/1948, Page 34.

70   Niles Jackson, What Really Happened to Children?, Charleston Gazette, Charleston, WV, 12/22/1968, Page 6A

71   F. J. Morris Made New Fire Chief, Raleigh Register, Beckely, WV, 11-10-1937, Page One.

72   J. F. Scott, op. cit.

73   John G. Morgan, op. cit.

74   5 Children Die as Fire Levels Fayette Home, Charleston Gazette, Charleston, WV, 12/26/1945

75   5 Children Die in Early Christmas Fire, State Sentential, Fayetteville, WV, 12/26/1945

76   John G. Morgan, op. cit.

77   C.R. Cobb, op. cit., Pages 14-15.

78   The significance of the fire chief's suggestion of burying something in a box would become more poignant later in the investigation of the case in the early 1950s.

79   Unnamed source, 2014

80   Troopers F. E. Springer and R. J. Rule, op. cit.

81   Home site Is Burial Place For Five Sodder Children; Portion of One Body Found, Montgomery News, Montgomery, WV, 12/26/1945, Page 1

82   Wreaths Placed Over Ashes of 5 Lost in Fire, Beckley Post-Herald, Beckley, WV, 12/29/1945, Page 2

83   C.R. Cobb, op. cit., Page 12.

84   Home site Is Burial Place For Five Sodder Children; Portion of One Body Found, Montgomery News, Montgomery, WV, 12/26/1945, Page 1

85   John G. Morgan, op. cit.

86   Ibid.

87   C.R. Cobb, op. cit.

88   Death Certificates for the Five Sodder Children.

89   C.R. Cobb, op. cit., Page 17.

90   J. F. Scott, op. cit., Page 29.

91   Troopers F. E. Springer and R. J. Rule, op. cit.

92   J. F. Scott, op. cit.

93   Five Children Die In Fayetteville Fire, Beckley Post-Herald, Beckley, WV, 12/26/1945, Page 1.

94   Other reports say the girls were taken to Mrs. Sodder's sister's house in Smithers, WV.

95   5 Children Die in Early Christmas Fire, State Sentential, Fayetteville, WV, 12/26/1945

96   Home site Is Burial Place For Five Sodder Children; Portion of One Body Found, Montgomery News, Montgomery, WV, 12/26/1945, Page 1.

97   C.R. Cobb, W.V. Assistant WV Fire Marshal, report on Sodder Fire, to C. A. Raper, State Fire Marshal, 6-30-1950, Page 12.

98   C.R. Cobb, W. V. Assistant Fire Marshal, Supplemental Report to C. E. Raper, W. V. Fire Marshal, 1-25-1952, Page 1.

99   *This is one of the first indication as to what the temperature was at the time of the fire)*

100 *Ibid.*

101 *C.R. Cobb, W.V. Assistant WV Fire Marshal, report on Sodder Fire, Op. Cit., Page 5.*

102 *Clente, rather than Forienzo Janutolo. It appears that the writer of the 1950 Fire Marshal report believed these two men to be the same man. They were in fact, cousins.*

103 *Keep in mind Morris was sitting right there in this inquest when all this was said and made no comments about what he supposedly found.*

104 *Ibid, Pages 14-15.*

105 *C.I. Dodd of Fayetteville, Statement to W.V. State Police, 11-11-1951*

106 *C.E. Dodd of Fayetteville, Statement to W.V. State Police, 11-18-1951*

107 *Inquest Set For Today In Deaths Of Five Children, Beckley Post-Herald, Beckley, WV, 12/28/1945, Page 5*

108 *Fayetteville Citizens Go To Aid Of Stricken Family, Beckley Post-Herald, Beckley, WV, 12/31/1945, Page 2*

109 *Fayetteville Mayor Blasts Magazine Unfair Report, The Charleston Gazette, Charleston, WV, 1/31/1954, Page 11*

110 *5 Children Die in Early Christmas Fire, State Sentential, Fayetteville, WV, 12/26/1945.*

111 *Mysterious Fate of Five Missing Children Pondered, Beckley Post-Herald Sunday Register, Beckley, WV, 11/14/1948, Page 8.*

112 *J. F. Scott, The Children Who Went Up In Smoke, Inside Detective Magazine, 11/9/1967, Pages 29.*

113 *C.R. Cobb, W.V. Assistant WV Fire Marshal, Report on Sodder Fire, Op. Cit., Page 4.*

114 *Dent, Luce, Where Are They?, Front Page Detective, Dell Publishing Co., Page 88.*

115 *Wreaths Placed Over Ashes of 5 Lost in Fire, Beckley Post-Herald, Beckley, WV, 12/29/1945, Page 2*

116 *Funeral Services are Held for Five Sodder Children, Fayette Tribune, Fayetteville, WV, 12/28/1945, Page 2.*

117 *Mysterious Fate of Five Missing Children Pondered, Op. Cit., Page 8.*

118 *Lonnie Johnson of Gatewood, Statement to W.V. State Police, 1-3-1952*

119 *C.R. Cobb, W.V. Assistant WV Fire Marshal, report on Sodder Fire, Op. Cit., Page 15.*

120 *Marion Sodder, Marion Sodder Personal Statement, Fayetteville, WV, 1-1968*

121 *Lonnie Johnson, Op. Cit.*

122 *H.D.Gibbs, W. V. State Police, Letter to State Police Beckley Commander, 1-4-1952*

269

123 C.R. Cobb, W.V. Assistant WV Fire Marshal report on Sodder Fire, Op. Cit.

124 J. F. Scott, Op. Cit., Page 56.

125 Ibid.

126 Tom D. Miller, West Virginia's Amazing Mystery, Master Detective Magazine, 3/1967, Pages 29.

127 Ibid.

128 West Virginia Marriage Records, Fayette County, WV, 1947.

129 Remember, at the time, there was no such thing as fiberglass insulation. Many people would stuff the inside of the walls of their houses with newspaper to act as a way to retain heat.

130 Resume of Investigation of Sodder Fire by State Fire Marshal, Author Unknown, circa 1951.

131 If this is true, the mystery stops here.

132 Like on the old Andy Griffith Show when they had to place a call, they would speak to "Sarah", the switchboard operator.

133 Officials for Blackout Named, Raleigh Register, Beckley, WV, 8/9/1942,Page-8

134 1940 United States Federal Census, Op. Cit., Page 35 of 42.

135 George Sodder, Letter to State Police W. E. Burchett, 8-9-51

136 Sodder Pamphlet, 1953.

137 Fiorenzo Janutolo Death Certificate, Fayette County Courthouse, Fayette County, WV, 1966.

138 No records can be found that would indicate that Oscar Tinsley had a brother named C. C. Tinsley. According to census records of the time, his brothers were named Ivan Charles, Orville Judson, and Burdette Ray Tinsley. The one and only reference to a C. C. Tinsley comes from the 1950 Fire Marshal Report and just as the writer of that report mistakenly called Rosser Long, Russel Long, he could have been mistaken about the name of the Tinsley brother also.

139 John G. Morgan, Fayette Family Seeks 5 Children Some Believe Dead, Charleston Gazette, Charleston, WV, 11/14/1948, Page 34

140 No call was made to Mr. Dodd, the local undertaker.

141 It is interesting that the writer of this report chose to use the term "missing children" at this point in the investigation when they were firm in their opinion that the children had died in the fire.

142 C.R. Cobb, W.V. Assistant WV Fire Marshal report on Sodder Fire, to C. A. Raper, State Fire Marshal, 6-30-1950, Pages 14-15.

143 Personal Communication with a Local Source.

144 Harold Gaye, Statement to W.V. State Police, 11-2-1949

145 J. F. Scott, The Children Who Went Up In Smoke, Inside Detective Magazine, 11/9/1967, Page 57.

270

146 C.R. Cobb, W. V. Assistant Fire Marshal, Supplemental Report to C. E. Raper, W. V. Fire Marshal, 1-25-1952, Pages 1-3.

147 John G. Morgan, Op. Cit.

148 Legion Installs Officers, Receives Special Awards, Beckley Post-Herald, Beckley, WV, 9/16/1955, Page 10

149 Fayetteville's Blackout was Grim Business, Raleigh Register, Beckley, WV, 8/16/1942, Page 9.

150 Blackout Plans Being Perfected, Raleigh Register, Beckley, WV, 7/30/1942, Page 2.

151   C.R. Cobb, W. V. Assistant Fire Marshal, Supplemental Report to C. E. Raper, Op. Cit., Page2.

152 This term is what inspired the title of this book.

153 This will be better illustrated in a later chapter.

154 C.I. Dodd of Fayetteville, Statement to W.V. State Police, 11-11-1951

155 Sodder Pamphlet, 1953.

156 C.E. Dodd, Mortician from Webster Springs, Statement to W. V. State Police, 11-28-1951

157 The 1950 report has many inferences that make the reader think the various private investigators are only working on the case to drum up business for themselves and basically extort money for the Sodders.

158 John G. Morgan, Op. Cit.

159 Interestingly, the writer of the report, himself (C. R. Cobb) calls the mass a liver.

160 C.R. Cobb, W. V. Assistant Fire Marshal, Supplemental Report to C. E. Raper,, Page 3.

161 Tom D. Miller, West Virginia's Amazing Mystery, Master Detective Magazine, 3/1967, Pages 29.

162 Dent, Luce, Where Are They? Front Page Detective, Dell Publishing Co., March, 1954,Pages 25, 87-91

163 Tom D. Miller, West Virginia's Amazing Mystery, Master Detective Magazine, 3/1967, Pages 29.

164 Dent, Luce, Where Are They?, Front Page Detective, Dell Publishing Co., March, 1954,Pages 25, 87-91

165 John G. Morgan, Fayette Family Seeks 5 Children Some Believe Dead, Charleston Gazette, Charleston, WV, 11/14/1948, Page 34

166 Charles Ray, W.V. State Police, Letter from Fire Marshal Raper, 2-2-1949

167 And because the conclusion seemed obvious at the time.

168 C.R. Cobb, W.V. Assistant WV Fire Marshal report on Sodder Fire, to C. A. Raper, State Fire Marshal, 6-30-1950, Page 3.

169 Nationwide Hunt for Clues Possible In Mystery of Five Children and Fire, Charleston Gazette, Charleston, WV, 1/31/1949, Page 5.

170 Ibid.

171 John G. Morgan, Ex-Marshal Brophy, Famous Investigator, May Probe Fire and Fate of Five Children, Charleston Gazette, Charleston, WV, 3/18/1949, Page 30.

172 Op cit, Charleston Gazette, 3/22/1949, Page 6

173 Op cit, Charleston Gazette ,5/10/1949, Page 6

174 Op cit, Charleston Gazette ,5/25/1949, Page 6

175 First Donations to Sodder Fund Make $51 Total, Charleston Gazette, Charleston, WV, 5/1/1949, Page 33

176 John G. Morgan, Six Bones Unearthed in Fire Ruins "Look Human" to Washington Expert, Charleston Gazette, Charleston, WV, 8/19/1949, Page 31

177 George Sodder, Letter to State Police W. E. Burchett, 8-9-51

178 John G. Morgan, Six Bones Unearthed in Fire Ruins "Look Human" to Washington Expert, Charleston Gazette, Charleston, WV, 8/19/1949, Page 31

179 Tom D. Miller, West Virginia's Amazing Mystery, Master Detective Magazine, 3/1967, Pages 29.

180 John G. Morgan, Six Bones Unearthed in Fire Ruins "Look Human" to Washington Expert, Charleston Gazette, Charleston, WV, 8/19/1949, Page 31.

181 C.R. Cobb, W.V. Assistant WV Fire Marshal report on Sodder Fire, to C. A. Raper, State Fire Marshal, 6-30-1950, Page 5.

182 Parents of Five Fayetteville Children Believed Burned to Death Not Convinced By Discovery of Bones in Ashes, Beckley Post-Herald, Beckley, WV, 8/19/1949, Page 1

183 John G. Morgan, Six Bones Unearthed in Fire Ruins "Look Human" to Washington Expert, Charleston Gazette, Charleston, WV, 8/19/1949, Page 31

184 Parents of Five Fayetteville Children Believed Burned to Death Not Convinced By Discovery of Bones in Ashes, Beckley Post-Herald, Beckley, WV, 8/19/1949, Page 1

185 Oscar B. Hunter, Pathologist Report of Examination of Bones from Sodder Fire, Smithsonian Institute, 9-19-1949

186 C.R. Cobb, W.V. Assistant WV Fire Marshal report on Sodder Fire, to C. A. Raper, State Fire Marshal, 6-30-1950, Page 6.

187 Detectives Drop Probing of Case of Sodder Blaze, Charleston Gazette, Charleston, WV, 9/8/1949, Page 6

188 John G. Morgan, Bone Analysis Again Spurs Search for 5 Sodder Tots, Charleston Gazette, Charleston, WV, 10/18/1949, Page 1.

189 West Virginia Merchant Police Ad, Charleston Gazette, Charleston WV, 1/22/1953, Page 19

190 Probers May Make Arrests In Case of 5 Missing Tots, Charleston Gazette, Charleston, WV, 11/1/1949, Pages 1, 10

191 Marshall Newman, Pathologist Report on Bones from Sodder Fire, Smithsonian Institute, 9-20-1949

192 John G. Morgan, Bone Analysis Again Spurs Search for 5 Sodder Tots, Charleston Gazette, Charleston, WV, 10/18/1949, Pages 1, 10

193 Parents of Five Fayetteville Children Believed Burned to Death Not Convinced By

272

   Discovery of Bones in Ashes, Beckley Post-Herald, Beckley, WV, 8/19/1949, Page 1

194 *Anonymous, Letter to West Virginia Merchant Police, 11-13-1951*

195 *Susan Williams, Mystery Still Surrounds Family's Deadly Fire, Charleston Gazette, Charleston, WV, 12/25/1995*

196 *Anonymous, Letter to West Virginia Merchant Police, 11-13-1951*

197 *C.R. Cobb, W.V. Assistant WV Fire Marshal report on Sodder Fire, to C. A. Raper, State Fire Marshal, 6-30-1950, Page 11.*

198 *Edward A. Scohott, Cincinnati Cremation Co., Letter to O. D. Fisher, WV Merchant Police, 12-1-1951*

199 *Linda Geddes, Body Burners: The Forensics of Fire, New Scientist, May, 2009.*

200 *Elayne J. Pope, O.C. Smith, Timothy G. Huff, Op. Cit., Page 25.*

201 *Journal of Forensic Sciences, Volume 49, Page 431.*

202 *Also keep in mind that the air temperature was below freezing which causes heat transfer between the bricks and the air to happen quickly.*

203 *Anonymous, Letter to West Virginia Merchant Police from "A Miner Who Needs Money", 9-1949*

204 *Harold Gay, Sworn Statement, 11-2-1949*

205 *Raper Appointed as Fire Marshal, Charleston Gazette, Charleston, WV, 7/19/1949, Pages 1,5*

206 *Probers May Make Arrests In Case of 5 Missing Tots, Charleston Gazette, Charleston, WV, 11/1/1949, Pages 1, 10*

207 *Police Suspect Five of Conspiracy In Sodder Case, Charleston Gazette, Charleston, WV, 3/5/1950, Page 5*

208 *Rush D. Holt, U. S. Senator Letter to C. A. Raper, State Fire Marshal, 3/30/1950*

209 *C. A. Raper, State Fire Marshal, Letter to Rush D. Holt, U. Senator, 4/4/1959*

210 *Rush D. Holt, U. S. Senator Letter to C. A. Raper, State Fire Marshal, 4/8/1950*

211 *C.R. Cobb, Ibid, Page 11*

212 *Incorrectly referred to in the 1950 report as Russel Long.*

213 *C.R. Cobb, Ibid, Page 13*

214 *Death Certificates for all five Sodder children*

215 *C.R. Cobb, Op. Cit., Page 18.*

216 *Ibid.*

217 *In researching this aspect of the case. I located someone who had known the name of this man but since the fireball man has since passed away, he thought it best not to name him. This person did reaffirm that the man did claim to have seen "fireballs" being rolled onto the Sodder house.*

218 *George Sodder, Letter to W. V. Gov. Patterson, 7-9-1951*

219 *W. V. Gov. Okey Patterson, Letter from to George Sodder, 7-18-1951*

220 *W. E. Burchett, W. V. State Police, Letter to George Sodder, 7-19-1951*

221 *I hope these gentlemen were good detectives because they were not great at spelling and syntax. All of their mistakes are reprinted as they were reported.*

222 *All errors contained in these reports here and in subsequent pages are left in place.*

223 *Ibid.*

224 *Agents Wyly & Carter, Tampa Patrol & Detective System Agent Report to T.C. Simmons, WV Merchant Police, 7-24-1951*

225 *Ibid, 7-25-1951*

226 *Ibid, 7-27-1951*

227 *Ibid, 7-30-1951*

228 *George Sodder, Letter to State Police W. E. Burchett, 8-9-51*

229 *John G. Morgan, Fayette Family Seeks 5 Children Some Believe Dead, Charleston Gazette, Charleston, WV, 11/14/1948, Page 34*

230 *Mary Ann Sodder, Mary Ann Sodder Personal Statement, Fayetteville, WV, 1-1968*

231 *A Miner who Needs Money Letter to WV Merchant Police given to WV State Police on 51-11-13*

232 *John G. Morgan, Fayette Family Seeks 5 Children Some Believe Dead, Charleston Gazette, Charleston, WV, 11/14/1948, Page. 34*

233 *George Sodder, Letter to State Police superintendent, W. E. Burchett, 8-23-51.*

234 *State Police Superintendent, W. E. Burchett, Letter to G. Sodder, 10-4-51*

235 *C.R. Cobb, W.V. Assistant WV Fire Marshal, Report on Sodder Fire, to C. A. Raper, 9-17-1951*

236 *Before joining the West Virginia Fire Marshal's Office, Mr. Cobb was employed by the State Police.*

237 *C. R. Cobb, WV Asst Fire Marshal Letter to Dep. Sheriff Ernest "Rookie" Culbreath Tampa FL, 12-27-1951*

238 *But it was probably assumed at the time that these letters would never be seen by anyone other than the writer and receiver and maybe some of their superiors. They had no way of knowing about the Freedom of Information Act of 1967 which made public documents accessible.*

239 *N.C. Reger, W. V. State Police, Report, 12-20-1951*

240 *C. R. Cobb, Asst. W. V. State, Fire Marshal, Letter to C. E. Raper, concerning Raymond Wise, 12-28-1951*

241 *Letter from State Police Callaghan to Burchett concerning Brees*

242 *The names of everyone on this list has been lost to time.*

243 *Note: in the document, Mr. Sodder's name is frequently mis-spelled as "Soddard". State Trooper Reger cannot seem to decide if he wants to refer to Mr. Sodder or Mr. Soddard.*

244 *State Police Report from N.C. Reger concerning meeting of 12-31-51*

245 *Letter from State Police Reger to State Police C.L. Walker concerning Lonnie Johnson*

274

246 Letter from State Police H.D.Gibbs to State Police Beckley Cmder. Contradicting Lonnie Johnson

247 C.R. Cobb, W. V. Assistant Fire Marshal, Supplemental Report to C. E. Raper, W. V. Fire Marshal, 1-25-1952

248 Letter from Bradenton FL Dpty D.G. Swann to Raper

249 Report from John Woodruff of FBI to WV State Police Reger

250 T. C. Simmons, W. V. Merchant Police, Letter to C. A. Raper, 2-26-1952

251 Statement of Ida Crutchfield, 6-1952

252 The Alderson Hotel was torn down in a Charleston urban renewal program of the 1970s.

253 Unless they were flying, which is very unlikely.

254 Letter from W. V. Governor. W. C. Marland to Jennie Sodder

255 Sodder Pamphlet, George Sodder, 1953

256 Mary Ann Sodder, Mary Ann Sodder Personal Statement, Fayetteville, WV, 1-1968

257 George Sodder, Letter to State Police W. E. Burchett, 8-9-51

258 Ermel J. Wilson, Search For Sodder Children Renewed; Billboard erected at Scene of Fire, Beckley Post-Herald, Beckley, WV, 9/11/1953, Page 11.

259 Fayetteville Man Renews Search for Children, Charleston Daily Mail, Charleston, WV, 9/13/1953, Page 37

260 Sodder Offers $5,000 Reward For 5 Children, Charleston Gazette, Charleston, WV, 9/13/1953, Page 3

261 Ermel J. Wilson, Op. Cit.

262 Famous Billboard Riddled with Bullet Holes, Beckley Raleigh Register, Beckley, WV, 8/19/76, Page 9.

263 George and Melody Bragg, West Virginia Unsolved Murders, GEM Publications, Beaver, WV, 2012, Page 100.

264 Niles Jackson, What Really Happened to Children? Charleston Gazette, Charleston, WV, 12/22/1968, Page 6A

265 Sodder Pamphlet, 1953.

266 C.R. Cobb, W.V. Assistant WV Fire Marshal, Report on Sodder Fire, to C. A. Raper, State Fire Marshal, 6-30-1950

267 U. S. WWII Draft Cards, Young Men, 1940-1947, Lehi, UT, USA: Ancestry.com Operations, Inc., 2011.

268 Joseph Dempsey Death Certificate, 1940.

269 Dent, Luce, Where Are They? Front Page Detective, Dell Publishing Co., March 1954, Pages 25, 87-91

270 Sodder Story in Magazine Resented in Fayetteville, Beckley Post Herald, Beckley, WV, 1/12/1954, Page 2

271 *George Sodder Says Magazine Story On Children Wrong, Beckley Post Herald, Beckley, WV, 1/16/1954, Page 4*

272 *Which in today's dollars would be approximately $20,000.*

273 *Fayetteville Mayor Blasts Magazine's Unfair Report, Charleston Gazette, Charleston, WV, 1/31/1954, Page 11.*

274 *For this part of the investigation of the case, a pseudonym is being used to protect this person's identity and that of her family due to mental illness. Several existing sources and references used during the preparation of this particular part of the story will not be citied to preserve confidentiality. After a thorough review of this part of the case, the author determined that nothing significant can be gained by identifying her but this part of the story must still be told if for no other reason but the eliminate "Sally's" claims as having no place in fact.*

275 *N. G. Reger Letter from WV State Police to State Police Superintendent Fare, 5-3-1957*

276 *Whether or not this was actually Mr. Raper in Florida or one of his investigators is unknown.*

277 *Sodder Pamphlet, 1953.*

278 *Man Saved in Big Rain Dies at Age 60, Charleston Gazette, Charleston, WV, July 19, 1957, Page 8.*

279 *Letter from Troy Simmons to C. A. Raper withdrawing from the case, 2/26/1952.*

280 *Memo from State Police Jack to State Police Superintendent Fair, November 2, 1959*

281 *Fayetteville Fire Tragedy Remains a Mystery After Fifteen Years, Beckley Post Herald and Register, Beckley, WV, December 25, 1960, Page 4.*

282 *Ibid.*

283 *Ibid.*

284 *Troopers F. E. Springer and R. J. Rule, West Virginia State Police, Report of George Sodder Fire from December 25, 1945, Fayetteville, West Virginia, 1-21-1946*

285 *Resume of the Investigation of Sodders Fire, State Fire Marshal, Circa 1951.*

286 *Mrs. J. R. Crowder Letter to the Editor, Charleston Gazette, Charleston, WV, February 29, 1960, Page 18.*

287 *Family of Four in Hinton Burned to Death, Charleston Gazette, Charleston, WV, February 19, 1960, Pages 1 and 10.*

288 *Four Die as Fire Levels Residence of Summers Pair, Beckley Post Herald, Beckley, WV, February 18, 1960, Page 1.*

289 *Bodies of Four Recovered from Summers Ashes, Raleigh Register, Beckley, WV, February 18, 1960, Page One.*

290 *Mrs. J. R. Crowder Letter to the Editor, Charleston Gazette, Charleston, WV, February 29, 1960, Page 18.*

291 *Kinder, Chuck, Last Mountain Dancer, Hard Learned Lessons in Love, Loss, and Honky-Tonk Outlaw Life, Carroll & Graff Publishers, New York City, New York, 2004, Page 45.*

292 Stephan Talty, *The Black Hand, The Epic War Between A Brilliant Detective and the Deadliest Secret Society in American History*, Houghton Mifflin Harcourt Publishing Company, New York, New York, 2017, Page 29.

293 Almost the exact same statement has been made more recently about Fayette Co., WV (where the Sodder family was located) due to the number of unsolved homicides in the County.

294 Comstock, Jim, ed. *West Virginia Heritage Encyclopedia, Volume 3*, Richwood, 1976.

295 Shirley Donnelly, *Yesterday and Today, Early Matt Dillion Cleaned up Harrison County*, Beckley Post-Herald, Beckley, WV, May 2, 1974, Page 4

296 Ibid.

297 *Two Dead, one injured in Bridgeport shooting*, Bluefield Daily Telegraph, Jan. 12, 1986, Page B-8.

298 *Man Charged in Clarksburg Shooting Event*, Charleston Daily Mail, Feb. 5, 1977, Page 2A.

299 *Big Bill Lias of Bootlegging Fame Dead at Age 69*, Charleston Gazette, June 2, 1970, page 1,8.

300 Bluefield Daily Telegraph, Bluefield, WV, July 18, 1990, Page B-4.

301 The Dominion News, Morgantown, WV, December 22, 1964, Page 4.

302 Ibid.

303 Hoffman, Joseph E., *Marion County Centennial Yearbook, 1863-1963: Official Program and Souvenir of the Centennial Year*, Marion County Centennial Committee, Marion County, WV, 1963.

304 The Baldwin-Felts agency was employed by various coal mines owners to look after their interests in West Virginia.

305 Bluefield Daily Telegraph, Op. Cit., August 21, 1914, Pages 1 and 4

306 In all of my research into this man, I found that there were as many different spellings of his name as there were syllables in it as well. So it was difficult to locate information about him.

307 Charleston Daily Mail, Charleston, WV, November 25, 1914, page 1

308 Bluefield Daily Telegraph, Op. Cit., July 29, 1916, Page 2

309 Ibid., January 6, 1915, Page 5

310 Ibid., July 23, 1915, Page 1

311 Ibid., August 20, 1914, Page 1

312 This is possibly why there are no records documenting Manguerica's death.

313 meaning unfree labor in which a laborer (peon) has little control over their own employment conditions.

314 Ibid.

315 Or scabs as they were commonly called.

316 Ibid., March 23, 1913, Page 1

317 *The Beckley Register Herald, Beckley, WV, Oct-31-1986, Page 17*

318 *Ibid. August 27, 1986, Page 3.*

319 *Ibid, February 10, 1950, Page 2.*

320 *Ibid, November 10, 1942, Page 2.*

321 *Ibid, February 16, 1961, Page 6.*

322 *Ibid, November 21, 1957, Page 1.*

323 *Ibid. February 16, 1961, Page 6.*

324 *Unnamed source, 2017.*

325 *Ibid, Pages 81-82.*

326 *Personal Communication with an unnamed source, 2016.*

327 *Ibid*

328 *Boissevain, Poverty and Politics in a Sicilian Agro-Town, 1971, Page 202.*

329 *Antonio Cutrera, La Mafia e I Mafiosi, Kessinger Publishing, 2008, Page 27.*

330 *Boissevain, Poverty and Politics in a Sicilian Agro-Town, 1971, Page 204.*

331 *Boissevain, The Mafia in Sicily, Poverty and Politics in a Sicilian Agro-Town, 1971, Page 222.*

332 *FBI Nabs 23 Aliens, Seizes Arsenal of Weapons, Radios, Raleigh Register, Beckley, WV, 10/6/1942, Page 1,2*

333 *Roy Lee Harman, Speaking of Sports, Beckley Post Herald, Beckley, WV, October 7, 1942, Page 8.*

334 *Multiculturalism in the United States: A Comparative Guide to Acculturation and Ethnicity. Westport, CT: GREENWOOD PRESS, 2005*

335 *Homesite is Burial Place for Five Sodder Children, Montgomery News, Montgomery, WV, 12/26/1945, Page one.*

336 *Mrs. Sodder was not so withholding. The morning after the fire, she made the statement that she thought the fire had been "set."*

337 *Antonio Cutrera, La Mafia e i mafiosi, Reber, Palermo: 1900.*

338 *Leonard W. Moss and Stephan C. Cappanari, Estate and Class in a South Italian Hill Village, Central States Anthropological Association, 1959.*

339 *Just as coal miners were not forced to buy their goods from the local "Company Store", but if they wanted to eat, there was no other choice.*

340 *This was a major organizing tenant of the SOIA.*

341 *C.R. Cobb, W.V. Assistant WV Fire Marshal, Report on Sodder Fire, to C. A. Raper, State Fire Marshal, 6-30-1950, Page 14.*

342 *Eric Hobsbawm, Primitive Rebels, Studies in Archaic Forms of Social Movement in the 19th and 20th Centuries, W. W. Norton & Company , 1965, Pages 49-52*

343 *Personal Communication with an expert in Italian organized crime. 2016. This source requested that their name not be used.*

344 *Ironically, this incident was never mentioned in any police or fire marshal report concerning this case (that I was able to locate.) It was however, covered in many newspaper and magazine articles about the case. Almost like the authorities were making a conscious decision to ignore this part of the case.*

345 *Also called getting -out-of-line.*

346 *Personal Communication with an expert in Italian organized crime. 2016.*

347 *Ibid, 2017.*

348 *Which we have already identified evening to be after 6 p.m., and at this time of year, it would have been after dark.*

349 *U. S., World War II Draft Registration Cards, 1942.*

350 *1940 Federal Census, West Virginia, Fayette County, Fayetteville District, Page 18 of 37.*

351 *Ibid.*

352 *Fayette Family Seeks Five Children Some Believe Dead, Charleston Gazette, Charleston, WV, November 11, 1948, Page 34.*

353 *The Baby Thief, The Untold Story of Georgia Tann, the Baby Seller Who Corrupted Adoption, Barbara Bisantz Raymond, Carroll & Graff Publishers, New York, New York, 1997,Page viii.*

354 *Georgia Tann/Tennessee Children's Home Society Investigation Scrapbooks, 1950" (PDF). State of Tennessee Department of State Tennessee State Library and Archives.*

355 *Which mostly involved researching their ability to pay for the child.*

356 *Ibid, Page 10.*

357 *Raymond, Op Cit, Page 55.*

358 *Ibid, 168-169.*

359 *Ibid, Pages 134-135*

360 *Ric Flair with Keith Elliot Greenberg, Ric Flair, To Be the Man, Pocket Books, A Division of Simon and Schuster, In., New York, NY, Page 5.*

361 *Raymond, Op Cit, Page 137.*

362 *Ibid, Page 5.*

363 *Report to Governor Gordon Browning on Shelby County Branch, Tennessee Children's Home Society 1951, [Nashville]: State of Tennessee, Dept. of Public Welfare*

364 *Kingsport News, Kingsport, TN, 1/23/1954, Page 3.*

365 *Ibid, Page 6.*

366 *84-11-18 Missing or Dead Families Crusade to Determine Fate if Five Children Continues, Greensboro News and Record, Joe Kennedy, Landmark New Service, Greensboro, NC, 11-18-1984, Pages F1 and F8.*

367 *Ibid.*

About the Author

Bob Bragg was raised in Handley, WV, a small town near Montgomery. He graduated from East Bank High School in 1977, and then attended college at West Virginia Tech. He holds degrees in Electrical Engineering Technology, Electronic Engineering Technology and a BS in Civil Engineering. Bob is a registered professional engineer in West Virginia, Virginia and Kentucky. He is a member of the American Water Works Association and the Project Management Institute.

Bob has worked for almost 40 years in consulting engineering in the design, management, and construction of municipal water and wastewater projects, as well as storm water control and site development. He also worked in the natural gas transmission industry for 10 years and for five years as an electrical engineer in the design and construction of nuclear reactors for U. S. Navel aircraft carriers for Newport News Shipbuilding in Virginia.

Bob has always had an interest in true-crime and cold cases. His interest in the Sodder case began when he was a young boy and first saw the Sodder billboard outside of Fayetteville around 1967. He began researching this case in 2015 and has spent almost seven years delving into every possible angle in the case.

Made in the USA
Columbia, SC
30 July 2023

21024889R00163